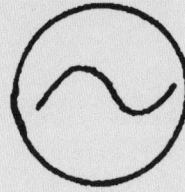

1001101011
1000110110
0110001101
1001000111

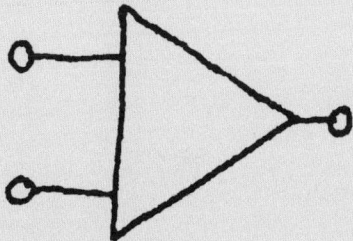
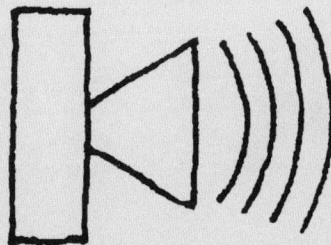

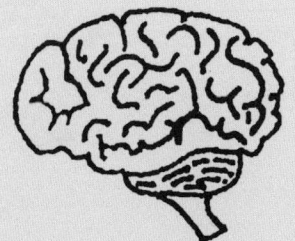

LIKE TRYING TO CATCH LIGHTNING IN A BOTTLE

40 YEARS
OF MAKING MUSIC
AT EASTCOTE STUDIOS

Martin Terefe

West Ten Publishing

This book is dedicated to Philip Bagenal

This second edition published in 2021
by West Ten Publishing Ltd.
14 Conlan Street
London W10 5AR

Endpapers: Based on illustrations by Philip Bagenal

ISBN 978-1-8383408-1-0

Designed by Damian Jaques
Book production by Mark Fletcher, Fletcher Books
Printed in the China

CONTENTS

FOREWORD

Summer 2009 saw the closure of Olympic, the once-great studio which oversaw recordings by The Stones, Hendrix, Led Zep and The Beatles; in its place, a members' club, dining room and cinema.

The recession, residential development and technology had already seen the departure of many of London's world-class recording studios. Gone, amongst others, were The Townhouse, Sarm, Eden, Mayfair, Battery, Brittania Row and Maison Rouge. And with them, a generation of pioneering engineers who had helped to shape the history of recorded music.

That same summer, Eastcote was home to Mumford and Sons who, with their producer Markus Dravs and under the watchful eye of Philip Bagenal, were recording *Sigh No More*. This album would go on to reach No 2 on both the Billboard 200 and the UK album chart and win Album of the Year at the Brit Awards.

This is the story of how Eastcote, in 2020, comes to celebrate 40 years of independence – years of creativity, ingenuity and brilliance.

Charlie Seaward – Man Jumping

Philip called and said: *'If you don't move your piano now, I'll take it out in the courtyard and bash it with a sledgehammer'*. I didn't want it, so out and in bits it went. I wrote 'Hit Me With Your Rhythm Stick' on it.
– Chaz Jankel

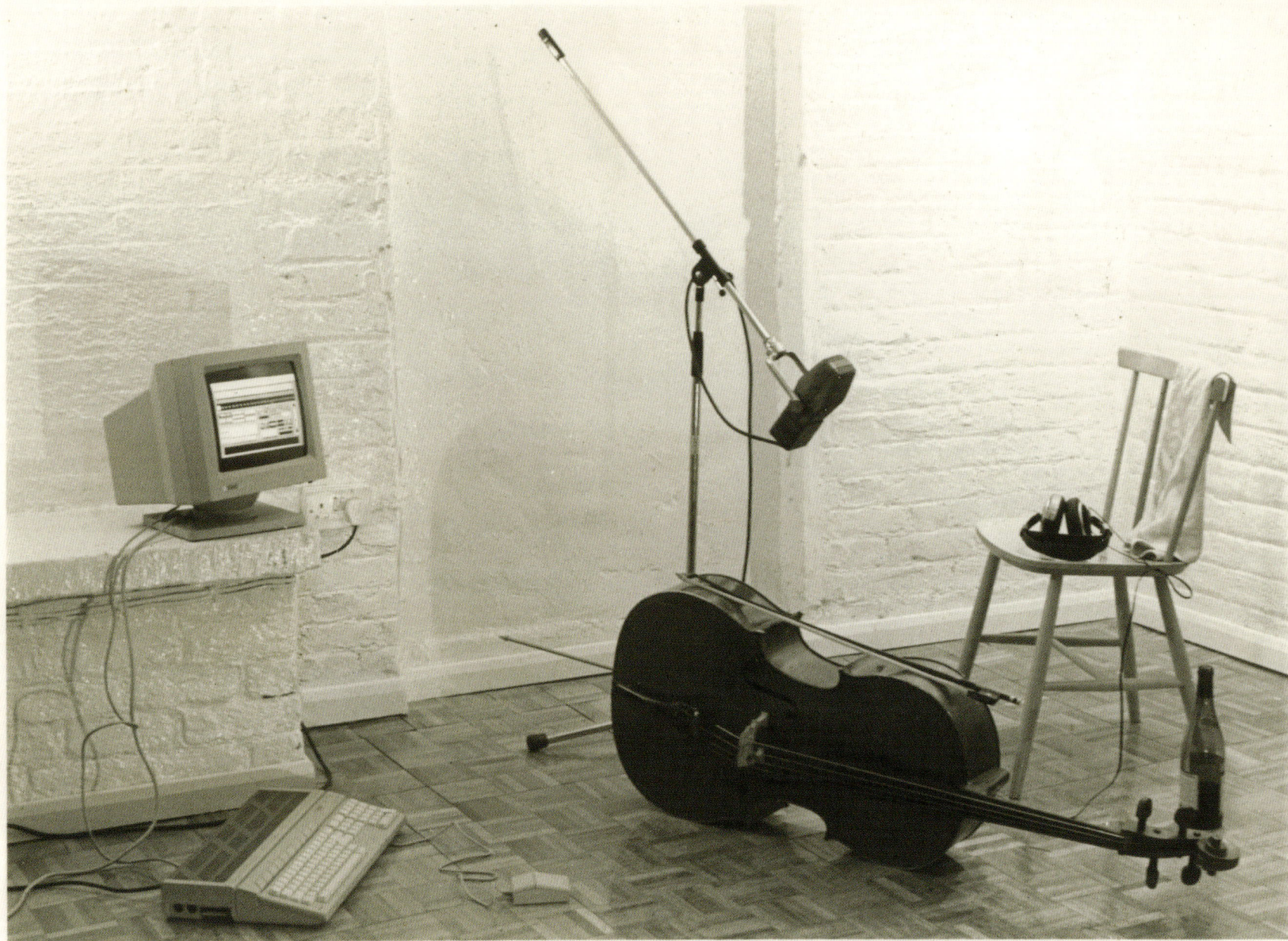

8

Eastcote (Photo: Franki Raffles).

INTRODUCTION

The first time I recorded at Eastcote was in 1995. I was travelling regularly to London to work with a songwriter I had met a few years earlier. Ladbroke Grove felt like an adventure back then. It was one of the great melting-pots of culture and creativity and I still remember the cab ride to the studio on a cold but sunny winter's morning. When we arrived there we were met by Philip Bagenal, the man whose studio legacy, ideas and sonic pioneering this book is really about. The songwriter was Nick Whitecross from the band Kissing The Pink and he had spent a lot of time at Eastcote and knew Philip well.

It immediately felt like I'd been invited to a music world unlike any I'd experienced before.

The place was like an eccentric's living-room and as Philip showed us around Studio 2 I realised that's exactly what it was. It was a recording studio yes, but more importantly it was one of those magical spaces that instantly make you want to be creative and leave your preconceived ideas behind. I loved it. I loved it so much that it changed the way I thought of recording forever and it would come to shape my career as a record producer. It was the quirks, the DIY feel, the daylight, the worn but comfy sofas, the instruments... keyboards everywhere, samplers, guitars, drums all lying around as if someone had left them there with a note saying 'Please pick us up'. In every string and on each floppy disc a story of a record made and a promise of one to be.

It was the absolute antiserum to the sterile studios designed for and by sound engineers that I'd worked in before and thought were standard throughout the industry. This was a studio made for musicians and artists, built by a young man with an architecture degree from Cambridge University who had been on a life-changing trip to a post-Warhol New York City and become enamoured by music, sound and technology. The place resonated with me. It was reminiscent of the garage in my parents' house where I built my first 4-track recording setup to make demos with my band. And the ADAT studio I set up in a summerhouse in the Stockholm archipelago with my friend Sven Lindvall when I produced my first major-label album. It felt like it was permanently temporary. A studio that would constantly change according to what any artist or musician desired or imagined. And unpretentious as fuck.

It was, of course, London too, and a magical music, art and fashion scene with no rules and I felt liberated. Back in Stockholm a few weeks later, I made plans to sell my studio there and eventually found someone offering 4,000 pounds for my share and I took it. I had just got married to Tia and with the money from the sale in hand we packed up her dad's Renault Traffic van with stuff and moved to a small flat a few blocks from Ladbroke Grove Underground station. It was just a 10-minute walk from Eastcote, but as things turned out it would be 15 years before I recorded there again. ∎

Philip Bagenal and his cello.

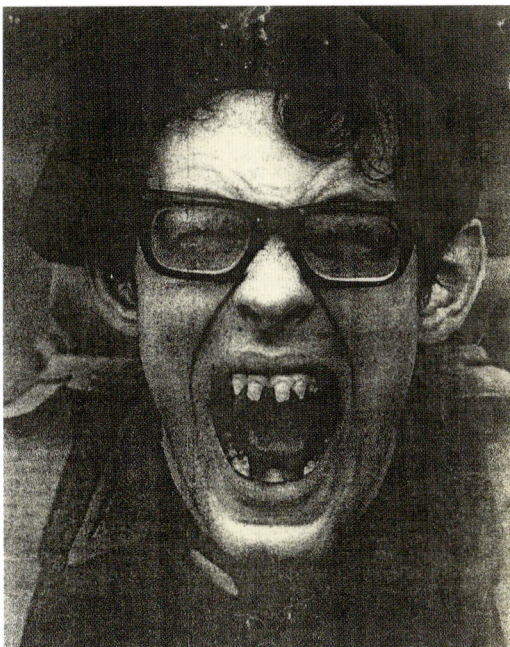

BEGINNINGS

You got to lean over the edge to make a great record. You got to take risks, and it's no good churning out the same old stuff again and again and again. Things change, people grow up, their taste in music changes and fans come and go. So, you've got to be able to respond to that, but at the same time recording as an activity hasn't changed at all really. It's still a matter of performance.

Philip Bagenal

It's a sunny day during the weirdest summer of my life. June 2020, and the UK is slowly waking up from several months of nationwide lockdown. I'm in the car on the way out of London and I'm thinking about Philip who I met such a long time ago but only really know from studio sessions and barbeques in the courtyard at Walters Workshops, and because three years ago I took over Eastcote when he decided to retire. Philip built the studio and ran it for almost four decades. I'd been there many times, but only occasionally to record as I had my own studio complex, Kensaltown, across the courtyard. We were studio neighbours.

Philip used to come down on the bus with his pushbike and cycle the last bit to Kensal Road. He was frequently in the studio late, quite often all night and sometimes for days in a row. I was so used to seeing him at the studio that I had a hard time imagining him anywhere else. We had been talking for years about me coming up to visit him and his family where they lived in Oxfordshire, but it never happened. I guess we were both always working.

There was hardly any traffic this morning as schools and most businesses were still closed but for some reason I managed to run late. George Murphy, who is the head engineer at Eastcote, and Dyre Gormsen, my long-time friend and collaborator, were both going to meet me at Philip's house, and we were all struggling a bit to find it. A beautiful old white house hidden on a rare hillside just outside Oxford. A calm and quiet oasis with blooming gardens and a front room filled to the brim with his grandkids' toys.

Was this really where Philip lived?

Charlie Seaward, who recorded at Eastcote with his band Man Jumping in the early '80s, lives next-door and was already there. Philip's wife Esther had made us a fresh pot of coffee and we all sat down on the front patio. It seemed a thousand miles from Ladbroke Grove.

Philip: *I actually found the building towards the end of '79. What had happened was, I met somebody called Johnny Carroll who had a house in Deptford which belonged to his parents and that had a basement. And there was nothing*

Philip as Peanuts in Lindsay Anderson's movie *if....* from 1968.

in the basement. We got talking, and I said, I want to build a studio (this would've been about 1974–75). He said, well why don't you come and build a studio in my basement? He got very excited about it and so did I. At the time, I was working for a rather defunct magazine called *The Architect* as a journalist, but I spent all my spare time soldiering to make a recording desk because in those days you couldn't just walk in and buy a small one for 200 pounds. A mixing desk cost about a quarter of a million dollars but there were magazines around, hobby magazines, that gave you the circuits, so I was making my own printed circuits in the kitchen with all kinds of now-banned chemicals, which is why I think I got Parkinson's disease. I made a desk, which I put into the basement studio, and I found a company up in Camden who had a BTR1 for sale, and that was the two-track stereo machine that was designed and made by EMI for the BBC and Abbey Road. A huge big thing. Made out of a wonky flywheel which was slightly out of true, a great big brass thing which meant it vibrated. So it would move across the room as the mixing progressed, slightly frightening but it was a huge heavy thing with great big drawers full of valves and it used to smell.

Charlie: *How did you get that into the basement?*

Philip: *It was quite difficult, but we got it down there and sadly I wished I kept it, because when we founded Eastcote we didn't need it, so I put it in the skip. It would've been nice to have kept it. So, I built the studio and I didn't really think that was going to add up to anything more than just a hobby really. Just something to while away the hours. But I then at some point met Chaz [Jankel] and Ian [Dury] at the pub in Deptford. I think it was a mutual friend that put us together. What had happened was, their record company boss, Dave Robinson at Stiff Records, had the idea of putting together Ian and Chaz with Norman Watt-Roy and Charley Charles who were a recognized rhythm section playing for all sorts of bands. He put them all together in the studio and I ended up doing a couple of*

Philip Bagenal and Chaz Jankel installing a brand new Teac 4-Track tape recorder at Chaz's house in Eastcote, Northwest London, late 1970s.

demos for them: 'Sex and Drugs' and 'Hit me'. They came to the studio and recorded it very roughly live and it went straight to the stereo. It was amazingly primitive, God knows how I managed to do it, but I managed. Of course, it was obvious that they had potential and they charged off to the Workhouse Studio on the Old Kent Road which belonged to Manfred Mann, another home studio which was quite difficult to work in because the recording space was in the basement and the control room was upstairs, neither could see each other.

That's how it started. Chaz and I got on very well, he then wanted to be able to do some recording at home, so I set up one of his bedrooms into a studio and bought some very primitive equipment and wired it up for him. He used that to write a few songs – one of which was 'Ai No Corrida' – or actually no, 'Ai No Corrida' I think he wrote in the hotel in LA while he was waiting for the other members of the tour to turn up. I think he had a spare evening and he sat down with a guitar and wrote that song.

Anyway, I built him the bedroom studio and he did write quite a few songs there, like one of them was called 'Am I Honest With Myself Really?', which had Pete Van Hooke playing the drums. Sort of a mad track.

Charlie: *That was on the first album, wasn't it?*

Philip: *Yes, it was on Chaz's first album. Pete Townshend really liked it. Bits of it were recorded at the home studio, and bits at The Townhouse, and it was self-financed. Andy Heath then got him a deal with A&M Records and David Green. So it was obvious that he would need somewhere that was bit more sophisticated, but he wanted to have his own place, he wanted control, he didn't want to go and record it at another (established) studio.*

Now I lived at the time in Maida Vale, in a flat on Randolph Avenue on the third floor. On the second floor, the guitarist of quite a well-known band at the time came back off tour with two girls he was having it off with and his wife came back and found him, and she chucked all three out stark-naked. I had just come back

from the local shop and there were these three naked people, and I wasn't quite sure what was happening, so I had to lend them something to wear and off they went. Anyway: things young people get up to.

There was a famous Radio 1 DJ who lived up at the top, and we used to walk down the canal on a Sunday. I remember walking past the old Victorian industrial buildings in North Kensington, and thinking to myself... Wow, wouldn't it be brilliant to build a studio in one of those places. They looked absolutely amazing... what a place to do it.

And lo and behold, Chaz has a discussion with his accountant who said yes, spend some money because if you don't spend it, the tax man will spend it. So, he was being encouraged by all sides to do it. He asked me whether I would look into it, and I immediately said I know where to look first. Let's go look in North Kensington, the top end of Ladbroke Grove.

From a young age Philip Bagenal was being torn in two directions. He had two uncles deep into the science of the world. Archer J.P. Martin won the Nobel Prize in Chemistry in 1952 for inventing paper partition chromatography together with Richard Synge. His other uncle, Hope Bagenal, was a famous acoustic engineer, remembered mainly for his work building the Royal Festival Hall and the refurbishment of the Royal Albert Hall, but who had also consulted on the acoustics for buildings as diverse as Abbey Road Studios and Newry Town Hall.

Philip's paternal lineage tended towards the bohemian, more eccentric side. His grandmother was a member of the Bloomsbury group and whilst showing me a bookshelf full of the amazing books she kept he tells me:

She had an interesting life, was friends with Picasso and spent a lot of time with him in France and Spain. It wasn't their art so much as their way of life. The way they were so contemptuous of the Etonians who ran the country, and still do.

I was trying to make out what direction I wanted to go, and the thing is I saw making

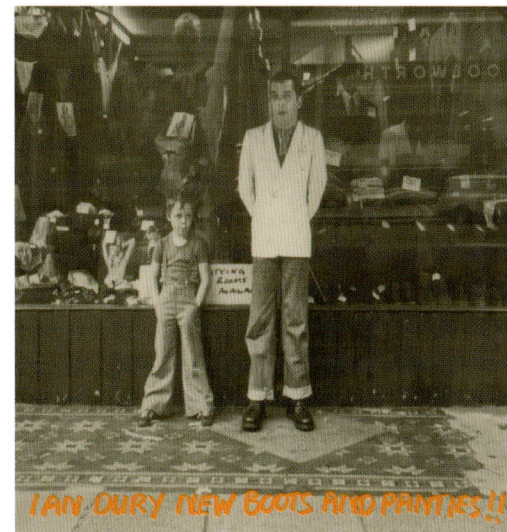

Ian Dury, *New Boots and Panties*, Stiff Records, 1977.

music has this sort of architectural part, the way you had the foundations and structures, and then you had the decoration applied and there was repetition and the repetition was a key part of music. In fact, when I was at Cambridge, Karl Heinz Stockhausen came and gave a lecture about repetition. He was really dramatic, he was in the main lecture room in the Music Faculty with this kind of blond hair and he was talking about how if you make a noise and then make another noise, you don't really connect them but if you make a rhythm, the brain has this amazing capacity that can interpret this in terms of movement. And if you speed that up enough, you get a tone, and again you recognize that form of repetition. If you then write a tune and you repeat it enough times, it becomes a whole, and so on. So, in the structure of music, repetition is an integral part and he was describing it in this sort of detailed and interesting way, and I remember being fascinated by that. There were a few amateur recording machines that arrived, we're talking now about the mid-'60s where you could buy Revox tape recorders and record stuff, and I bought one of the first tape machines made by Sony, I suppose it would've been about 1960, and it was a stereo machine but you could bounce from track to track and add things as you went along.

Philip's interest in recording equipment continued and the next machine became the classic Teak 4-track and now he could mimic the way The Beatles recorded on 4-track at Abbey Road with more options to mix down several tracks to one. He was reading articles in *Electronics Today International* about how to make pre-amps and circuit boards. 'I still have some of the sketches and diagrams of the gear I built somewhere here', says Philip as our conversation turns to across the Atlantic.

After graduating from Cambridge with a degree in Architecture, Philip's interest was shifting away from academia and towards music. He was really interested in the Warhol movement that was starting to phase out. In 1971 he went

Philip and John McLaughlin at Eastcote Studios in March 2017.

Jerry Goodman (violin), John McLaughlin (guitar), Billy Cobham (drums), Rick Laird (bass) and Jan Hammer (keyboard) performing with the Mahavishnu Orchestra in the early 1970s.

to New York. He managed to rent a loft – 'big enough to drive a motorcycle in', with a water bed on a kind of podium – and got his first gig as a sound engineer at the Gaslight at the Au Go Go. At the club he got to mix the live sound for blues artists and experimental funk outfits alike. John Lee Hooker, Sunny Boy Williamson and Buddy Guy played there as well as Miles Davis and Parliament Funkadelic.

One especially great story is about one of Philip's first times engineering at the club. It was for John McLaughlin's Mahavishnu Orchestra. Philip was intrigued by their experimental style and describes them as 'a kind of fallout group from Miles's early electronic work'. He recalls:

The percussionist turned up with an old bag that had a pair of Birkenstocks that he used to flap together. None of it was percussion, he just made noises while the drummer just kept the steady groove going and the awful thing was that at the end of the week we didn't get enough people through the doors to pay them the full amount that was due. I was the one that had to go in and announce it, and almost got beaten up by the drummer who was very cross.

Subsequently McLaughlin and Philip got to know each other well during the times they recorded together at Eastcote, and Philip's last sound engineering session was with John only a couple of years ago in Studio 1. Nearly 50 years of sound engineering started and finished working with one of the most ground-breaking guitarists of all time. Of course, given that Philip never stopped coming up with new and sometimes quite eccentric ways of recording sound, it is clear that that was the way it was meant to be.

As we keep talking it becomes increasingly obvious that one of the things that have made Eastcote what it is are the sessions that happened between the 'big' sessions. Philip never considered one artist more important than another, and learnt early on that the most exciting session could well be the one with a budding singer who had just about scraped together the fee for a half day in the studio.

He taught recording assistants with great care, aware that some of them could well go on to become award-winning mixers and producers a few years later. The biggest superstars in his view were the bravest and most creative clients, those who wanted to accompany him on his quest to throw out the rule books and make unique recordings. Whether it was punk, jazz, rock'n'roll or synth pop, the mission was always to push the limits just a little bit further.

Of course, sometimes the budding singer became a world-famous star, and the experimenting band a part of modern music history. I'm conscious that, to paint the full picture of what Eastcote is, I need to dig as deep into the quirky sessions that never went anywhere as into the stand-out moments that put the Studios on the world map, those sessions that kept the bailiffs away during times when so many other famous studios went out of business.

Before we went back to London that afternoon Philip showed us around his gardens. A sort of mystical place surrounded by woods, parts of it perfectly kept with immaculate lawns, growing gardens for the vegetables, a small playground for the grandchildren and blooming flowers everywhere. Other parts more eccentric. Drums hidden in the trees. An outdoor theatre and, of course, Philip's workshop. As we walk into it, I feel like I am back at the studio again. Speakers, electronic components and various odd music gear and microphones.

A self-built pump organ that used to be in the Eastcote lobby that uses a vacuum cleaner to propel air through the valves. And boxes of photos. Notes. Booking calendars. Full of Eastcote's history.

Later that evening, after slowly beginning to digest two hours of remarkable stories, I put on an album with Glen Scott, an amazing musician and artist I met during my first year in London. I remember my own home studio in the flat Tia and I rented on St Charles Square. It was small and there were 2-inch-tall pale-looking mushrooms growing in the blue carpet by the stairs, but we were young and it felt like a palace. We lived in the front room so I could have a recording studio set up in the bedroom. Glen and I wrote some really good songs in that room, but in the end we needed a place where we could record drums too and make some more noise. We scrambled together every single penny we had to rent a space in an industrial building on Kensal Road. That was pretty primitive, too. We had to prioritize electricity over paying the gas heating bill and after a winter of recording 40 songs in the cold through a 16-channel Mackie console we somehow ended up in a New York boardroom to sign a record deal with Epic Records. Back home I bought an old Trident B-range console. It was the summer of 1997. *OK Computer* had just been released, Tony Blair had demolished the Tories in the general election, and everything seemed possible. Those days were my beginnings as a record producer in London.

Earlier that year, a few blocks down the road, Depeche Mode had just finished their ninth album, *Ultra*, at Eastcote Studios. We were close by, but not quite neighbours yet. ∎

16

Walters Workshops seen from Conlan Street and the
Kensaltown Telegraph Works entrance ca 1930.

WALTERS WORKSHOPS

It's impossible to write about Eastcote Studios without a bit of background on the building where it is located. It deserves a book of its own, and after comparing memories with Philip a few common threads stand out. The Colonel. Whiskey. Mahogany. Wires. An ever-changing and eclectic community of tenants during different periods of their careers. And a big plane tree.

I became a studio neighbour proper with Philip and Eastcote in 2000.

Having always seen myself as primarily a songwriter, I'd become increasingly busy producing records after moving to London, and I had started a small imprint label with my then manager Michael Dixon. I was too excited about all the amazing artists I got to work with to say no to anything, and had just been to LA to work on a song for a film with David Foster and came back full of confidence and inspiration. After years of working on a project at a time, often whole albums with indie bands or other singer songwriters, I got a glimpse into a different way of making records. I decided I needed more space so I could work on more than one project at once.

I often thought about my early experience meeting Philip at Eastcote and had been made aware of quite a large space that was opening up in the same building. Walters Workshops.

It was just across the road from the Saga Centre where I had my studio and I went to have a look. All the memories of the place came back. The courtyard and greenery. All the loose old wires, all on top of each other, hanging on the walls or attached to wooden beams running across the main walkway leading from Kensal Road to Conlan Street.

The room itself was run-down but perfect. It was a proper studio control room with a huge window into a big room next door. It wasn't soundproofed at all but had been used as a 'live room' anyway. The previous tenant was an early Internet company that built technology which enabled musicians to work via midi together in different locations, so it was wired up with multiple ISDN lines and the latest Internet technology.

Back then the most common way to connect to the Internet was by dialling up through a modem from your landline phone. I didn't need that much space or the technology either really, but I loved the room and had just gotten my first substantial publishing advance so decided I wanted to take it. But it wasn't that easy.

Walters had a queue of prospective tenants wanting space and also you had to get a meeting with the Colonel. Tom Lacey, a retired military man, owned the building with his family, and I had heard stories about how particular he was about who he let space to.

I got a meeting set up and came prepared with my best arguments and a rehearsed speech. Before I really had a chance to say much more than my name, he turned to a mahogany cupboard behind his desk and took out a bottle

Walters Electrical Manufacturing Co. Originally called
Kensaltown Telegraph Works, the company changed the
name to Walters in 1908.

of Scotch and two glasses. He poured the whiskey, and even though I'm Swedish I thought those are some serious drinks. He raised his glass for a toast, and I knew then I was going to move into the building. We both drank up in one go, had a brief conversation about the rent and shook hands.

I moved in at Walters and built my second London studio during a transition period for the Lacey family that owned the building. Tom's two daughters now managed the building, and as the years went by I saw less and less of the Colonel himself. I opened a transcript from a conversation Charlie Seaward recorded between him and Philip at the start of the summer and was struck by the similarities of our respective first impressions of Walters.

Philip: *There was this company called Walters Workshops who occupied one of the buildings by the canal, a beautiful old industrial building, built in the 1880s, and Walters Manufacturing Co were an electrical company that made the parts for… Morse code, telegraph systems, all in sort of beautiful mahogany boxes, and everything was mahogany, brass and ebony. What happened was, that sort of very labour-intensive work disappeared, so by the time I arrived half the place was empty and the few people that were left were making spare parts for old aircraft… Fokker Friendships, you know… small passenger planes which had been bought by African states. These were dodgy old planes, and they made spare parts like air hostess call buttons and things, which had to be made individually by hand. So, they still had a few people doing that… and a bit of metal-bashing.*

Charlie: *Except for you then, was anyone else renting parts of that building, or was it all being used?*

Philip: *It was all being used. His daughter Alex was using one room as an artist studio and in other rooms there was just piles of stuff, I mean… it was a dusty old place and it was clear it was on the way out. In order to sort of keep going, they decided to let some space out and*

the first space made available was the ground floor of the building in the middle of the site, which is now Eastcote Studio 1.

Charlie: *So it was just by just a chance that you happened to come across this? And did you see the Colonel?*

Philip: *The Colonel was there, I used to have a whiskey with him every evening, we got on very well. And he made that famous remark when I met him, 'You'll have to speak up, dear, I have gunner-ear'. But he was an air-force pilot, and in the Second World War he flew aircraft in Africa. Basically reconnaissance.*

Charlie: *It was a link between what he was, and the things that they were making?*

Philip:*There must've been a connection, maybe he got that work from contacts and people he knew.*

Charlie: *He was a part of the family, was he?*

Philip: *He was the head of the family, he was the man, the patriarch. He founded the company originally and as far as I can see, I don't know a lot about the history of it, but by the time I got there he must've been in his late seventies.*

Charlie: *He went on for a long time, then?*

Philip: *He had someone there, a man that did the day-to-day management for him, but he was still around.*

Charlie: *So he encouraged you?*

Philip: *He encouraged me, we got on very well and he was very helpful.*

Charlie: *To begin with, you just had the unit on the ground floor for Studio 1?*

Philip: *Yes, one of the first tenants that arrived after us was a designer, Peter Saville. He made many album covers there for bands like Joy Division and New Order. On the first floor, where there had been a machine shop, they soon let to Knockabout Comics, who were a publishing firm that were selling American content. They also let out space to Levi's who had a repair shop there for repairing jeans. This was the single building in the middle and we were the only tenants for the first few years.*

Charlie: *So all the other parts of the building on the right when you came into the courtyard,*

Walter's truck from Kensal Road out on a London delivery.

they were still being used by Walters Workshops?

Philip: *Yes, they were still being used and there was still some metal-bashing. I think there were a couple of companies that took over one of the workshops and kept the equipment and carried on doing a similar thing. Separate company but in the same business. One of the things we were worried about was the noise coming into the studio, but in fact that didn't turn out to be a problem because it was a Victorian factory building, it was built with 18-inch brick walls.*

Charlie: *So in a way it was ideal?*

Philip: *Of course, it was ideal, because the floor loadings were 200 pounds per square foot, and just to give you an idea, the normal domestic load is 30 per square foot, so you'd expect a domestic floor to be enough and these were industrials floors. It's an iron-frame building basically made from cast-iron columns and connecting beams and within that was a built timber structure.*

Charlie: *Ideal for a potential recording studio?*

Philip: *I mean there were some things, like the iron frame would transfer sound from one space to another, but there were ways around that. The ground floor that I had used was in fact originally the stable, and the company used to have a couple of horse-drawn carts and they would collect stuff on the barges on the canal. You know, a lot of the metal itself came down from up north, from Sheffield and so on, by water.*

Charlie: *So the materials that the Walters Workshops were using for their business came down by canal, got picked up by horse and brought to Walters Workshops?*

Philip: *And we knew about this because of the famous crane just outside the studio, which if you saw the pictures it was fairly obvious. A big crane that was used to unload everything and the horses would come in under the arch and they'd go into the stable to be mucked out and looked after. And in the far tiny room, which is now a part of our live room, there was a forge so that the farrier could come and attend to their horses' shoes.*

The original iron staircase in the courtyard at Walters is still there today.

Charlie: *So when you took on Eastcote, the previous use had been as a stable and forge?*
Philip: *Yes, that's right. And then as a store. I don't think they ever made anything in there. I mean I didn't enquire too much about it because to be frank I was so focused on the studio and the future, the way one is, that I didn't keep much of a record of precisely what was going on.*
Charlie: *What was the blueprint for the actual construction of Eastcote, given that you hadn't worked as a recording engineer?*
Philip: *Well, I visited studios and I'd gone with Chaz to The Workhouse and to The Townhouse. I remember there was a studio in Kingsway and what was interesting about it was that they had a control room in the middle of the place and then a number of spaces around it. I remember it was Pete Van Hooke who was particularly keen on that arrangement because he said it was wonderful that you could see people in the control room, you could see the other musicians, it was very good communication. He said I should go look and I went, and on the day that I*

went they had a disaster because they had just finished mixing something for someone who was quite well-known, I can't remember who it was. They had a stereo mix which was put together on a quarter-inch machine and the tape op was rewinding it onto the reel so that it could be taken off to be mastered, and something went wrong with the motor and it span out of control and the reel came flying off. And the tape flew round the control room in bits, with all the edits coming to pieces. It was a nightmare, so they had to spend a whole day trying to recreate it. But that illustrates what we were doing in those days. It wasn't a digital thing that could be endlessly safety copied.*
Charlie: *Did you and Chaz have an idea of how you wanted the structure of Eastcote to appear?*
Philip: *Well, the basic concept came from there, I think. Pete Van Hooke was quite helpful in that respect. We were also constrained by the cast-iron columns, so I had to work around that… the location of the walls generally enclosed the columns, so you don't see them. Only a few of the columns are left in the bigger spaces. I had to put a lot of sand deadening in the roof, and I'm amazed that we didn't have a fire there because my electrics back then were extremely dodgy. My brother helped, he studied furniture-making at Goldsmiths. And I had various people come and do things for me. We ordered an Otari 24-track, we were actually the second studio in the country to have one. There was a company in Camden that imported them, and they were called Industrial Tape Applications, and the reason for that was they were selling 'amateur' machines, but they were selling them to professionals. They didn't have to pay some tax that the Chancellor was levying because it was an industrial application.*

In 1979, we went to the annual APRS show which is usually in Wembley, where people show off their equipment. Trident had a new mixing desk that they were trying to flog, but what they had produced was a desk that looked very impressive but was actually a cheapskate version of their famous earlier mixing consoles.

22

The first picture of Chaz Jankel recording at his new studio Eastcote in 1980. With a brand new Oberheim OBX on top of the Hammond organ.

The patch bay was done with PCB soldered contacts which came loose every time you put in a patch bay. We got one but it was a nightmare and I just about managed to keep it going for about a year or so.

Then for Chaz's second album we went and did some work in a studio in the Bahamas called Compass Point, which was built by Island Records. We ended up doing two weeks there, Chaz and me. There was this amazing young Jamaican engineer who would dance around the desk. The desk to him was a musical instrument. And he would do this sort of ballet as he'd twiddle one knob... twiddle another. And there was I going... should it be 2db at 16khz with a Q of what, or should it be 3dB or 2.5? He knew none of that shit. He'd go whack, whack and it would either sound amazing or it would sound terrible. He was extraordinary, he wouldn't take any instructions from anybody and when he finished a mix he would just walk out the room and go play pool.

Eventually of course Philip and Chaz got a desk that was worth dancing around: an MCI JH500 console, custom-built in 1971 for Island Records' studio on Basing Street, that has now been in Eastcote Studio 1 for nearly four decades. After a five-month renovation of the studio, during a sweltering London summer we will all remember mainly as the coronavirus lockdown, I'm standing on the new-laid oak floor in the control room watching the engineers take knobs and buttons out of a sock that has been through several hot cycles in the washing machine. As they are carefully put back on the console to be pushed and twiddled again, shining like they are brand new, I look out into the live room and try to imagine the horses being mucked out and the farrier by the forge.

I imagine the months and years Philip has been building, soldering, painting, tweaking, improving, engineering, making now-classic records and cooking amazing meals for some of the most influential music artists of their generation. I think of the dancing engineer who inspired Philip to stop worrying about how many dB to add to the top end and I look at the MCI console and wonder whether we should really have cleaned all the muck off those knobs. After all, they had been twiddled by Aston 'Family Man' Barrett, Jack Nuber and Chris Blackwell when they mixed Bob Marley's *Exodus*, one of the greatest records of all time. I am assured they have been washed many times before and brilliant music has been recorded and mixed consistently after each spin in the washing machine. I feel calm again.

I haven't built this studio. It doesn't really feel like I actually own it either. I am the new caretaker. The temporary guardian of a space with 18-inch brick walls filled with history, music, creativity and aspiration. After 40 years the studio is still promising to keep the old stable doors open for more musicians, producers and engineers to come and experiment with new sounds, play with new and ancient machines and most likely find ways of making music we haven't thought of yet.

Now, let's go back to 1980. Eastcote Studio 1 has just opened for business. ∎

In the office with Colonel Tom Lacey, ca 2005. Left to right: Martin Terefe, Ron Handley, Kelly Pribble (studio designer at Kensaltown), Philip Bagenal, Colonel Tom and Emma Feather.

1980

Eastcote Studio 1 control room at opening in 1980.

WHERE IS IT? WELL IT'S NOT IN EASTCOTE

It's not where I'm from, but I had bought a house there. It's near Harrow, you know? So the name had nothing to do with where the studio actually was. It was just the first thing that came to mind. In fact, I do remember there was a musician who didn't look up the details when he was told to go to Eastcote Studios. So, he called me and said, I'm in Eastcote, where is it? And I said, 'Well it's not in Eastcote'.

I'm on a video call with Chaz Jankel. A technology only fantasized about in science fiction films in the mid-'70s when he and Ian Dury wrote the songs for *New Boots and Panties*. In our brave new world, though, screens that we connect through are in plentiful supply. With the coronavirus pandemic keeping the world in a stranglehold, it's the new normal way of meeting someone. Chaz and his screen are walking around the back garden of his house

and I'm sitting in front of my computer in the office above Eastcote Studio 2. It would be an understatement to say that the album they went on to make would change both of their lives, as well as those of a generation of British artists and songwriters since. They needed to demo the songs and Chaz tells me:

Ian Dury had a friend called Johnny Carroll, an Irish guy who either owned or rented a house in Bermondsey. Which is near Deptford, but I remember it as being in Bermondsey. And in the basement of that house Philip had a tape recorder and a few instruments. And it was really damp in there, it wasn't pleasant. And so, when I wrote the album New Boots and Panties *with Ian, we demoed it in this studio with Philip. And that was when I met him, and that was when I first worked with him. So then we went on, Ian and I, and we recorded the album for real*

Chaz Jankel, original owner of Eastcote and Ian Dury's songwriting partner with The Blockheads. At the studio in September 1980.

198

at The Workhouse in the Old Kent Road, which was Manfred Mann's studio. But a few months later I had some other material that wasn't really suitable for what I was doing with Ian, it was kind of a bit Latin-inspired and I somehow met these two guys, Charlie Spiteri and his brother. Do you know about the Spiteri Brothers? Does it ring any bells?

It does ring a bell, but I have no idea why. Looking into it, it's another crazy coincidence.

This would have been in the late '70s, I was 8 or 9 years old and living with my parents in Caracas, Venezuela. Our neighbour's kids had a teacher who came around their house to show them how to play the cuatro and I asked if he could come and teach me too. There were no musicians in my family, but I immediately got lost in the magic of it. He taught me to play the guitar and he'd write down the lyrics of Spanish and Latin American folk-songs. He would show me how to play and sing them and, as he didn't know that many chords, I quickly figured out that the same 4 or 5 chords he was using worked on most songs I heard. It could be kids' songs from school or funky stuff like Curtis Mayfield that I heard on the soundtracks to the cop shows on TV. And on the radio Elvis, Julio Iglesias and more American soul music. I understood the chord patterns and by the time I moved back to Sweden a couple of years later it was enough for my guitar teacher to sing me almost any melody and I could figure out the chords. Caracas is where my music journey started.

The Spiteri brothers were Venezuelan and came to the UK in the '70s. Young pioneers of Latin funk, they mixed their roots music with psychedelic rock and were soon hanging out in West London with Jimi Hendrix, Stevie Wonder and Bob Marley, and playing at clubs around town. Chaz continues:

They were Venezuelan brothers and somehow I hooked up with them. I must have had a mutual friend that knew them. And I needed somewhere to record some demos and I did it with Philip. Yeah, I think I must have gone back to Bermondsey to do it. And we then re-established our friendship. And in that session, I remember I also recorded the first instrumental demo for what was to become 'Inbetweenies', that was the opening track on our second album. We recorded four songs in that session, me, Philip and the Venezuelan musicians.

In the following couple of years Chaz and Ian would write and record a series of hit singles, sign to Stiff Records and become Ian Dury and The Blockheads. Together they went on the legendary Live Stiff Tour together with Elvis Costello and The Attractions, Wreckless Eric, Nick Lowe and Larry Wallis, an early member of the band Motörhead who had become an in-house producer at Stiff.

But Chaz and Ian had a fiery relationship and several times between album recordings Chaz would leave the band and go the United States to keep working on his own music. He had also bought a house in Eastcote, a sleepy suburb in Northwest London, and when he decided to get a Teac 4-track and build a home studio, Philip came to help him. They recorded several demos there and one of them was for a song Chaz had written called 'Ai No Corrida'. Chaz says:

1980

Eastcote Studio 1 in 1980.

19

I carried on with my life with Ian and gradually we became more successful, and I started making more money. Along the way Philip said that he was buying a flat, part of a housing cooperative in Notting Hill on Penzance Place. He asked did I want to buy in, and I said yeah, I would. So I bought the flat above him, literally above Philip. A&M Records had at that time heard my demo of 'Ai No Corrida' and one other song and signed me to a record deal. Between the royalties I got from the successful songs I was writing with Ian and the advance from A&M, I now had sufficient money to buy the equipment to build a real studio. A Trident mixing board and an Otari 24-track tape machine. Philip and I first saw another location, by the river on Lots Road. Another warehouse space. It was on the top floor of a building, but it was facing the City, not towards the Thames and I thought that being by the river but not seeing it defeats the purpose. We saw the space in Walters Workshops in North Kensington and decided that was the place to go.

While Chaz was recording the master for 'Ai No Corrida' at Townhouse Studios, Philip was now the architect of the building, drawing up the layout, putting up partition walls and wiring up the new gear. When it was ready, Chaz moved his piano and musicians in to continue working on the album for A&M. Peter Van Hooke was playing drums, Kuma Harada bass, Mark Isham and Chris Hunter saxophones and Chris Warwick doing various programming and synthesizer work. Philip Bagenal was engineering. It was 1980 and the first year that records were made at the brand-new Eastcote Studios.

Later that year, Chaz's first solo album *Chas Jankel* was released. So was *Laughter*, Ian Dury and The Blockheads' only album without him. 'Ai No Corrida' would become a big hit in the UK and around the world. But with neither of them. ∎

Philip installing some new equipment in Studio 1.

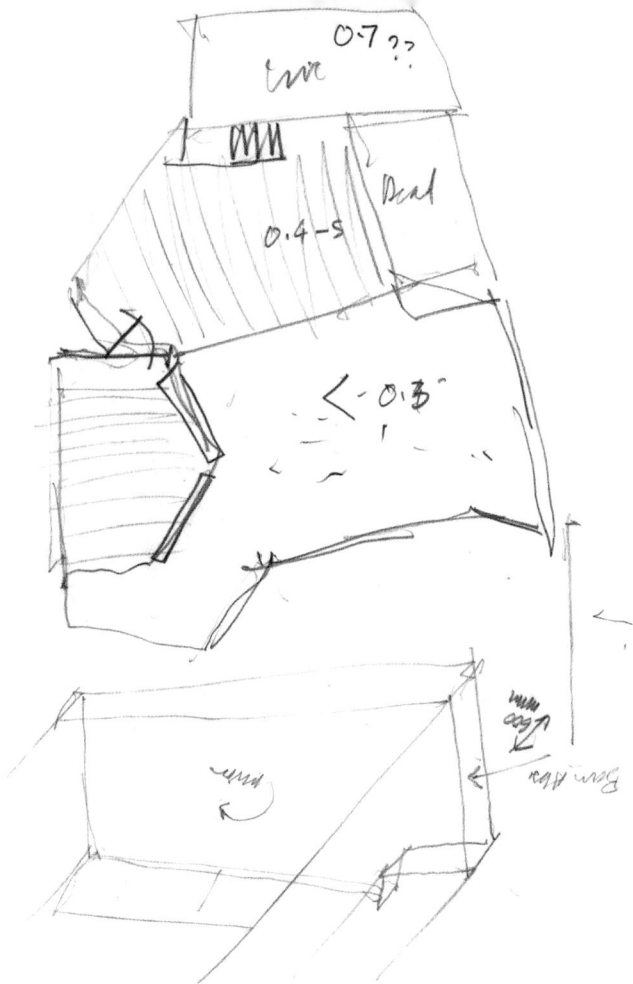

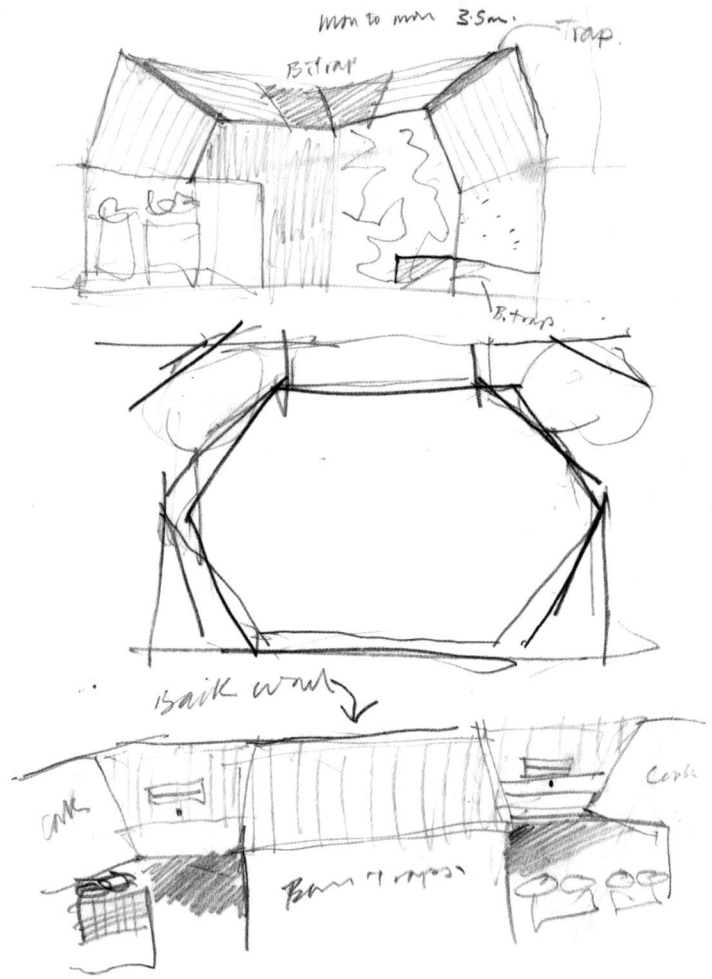

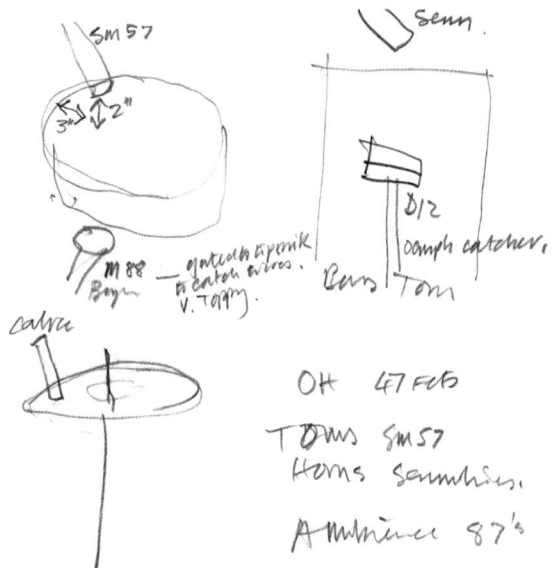

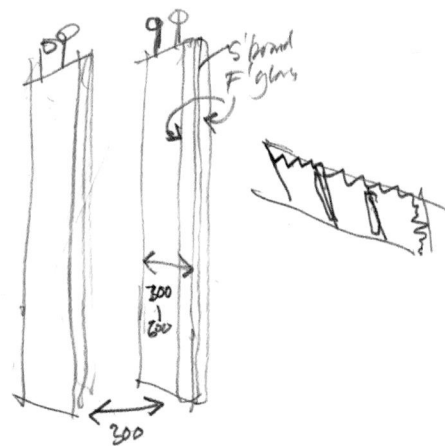

Philip's original drawings for the studio.

1980

EASTCOTE PRODUCTIONS

PRODUCER'S AND ENGINEER'S COOKBOOK

Pitch Ratios

Semitones	Up	Down
1	1.059	0944
2	1.122	.891
3	1.189	.841
4	1.260	.794
5	1.335	.749
6	1.414	.707
7	1.498	.667
8	1.587	.630
9	1.682	.595
10	1.782	.561
11	1.888	.530

Pitch/Tape Speed

30 IPS

Semitones	Up	Down
1	31.77	28.32
2	33.66	26.73
3	35.67	25.23
4	37.80	23.82
5	40.05	22.47

15 IPS

Semitones	Up	Down
1	15.89	14.16
2	16.83	13.37
3	17.84	12.615
4	18.90	11.91
5	20.03	11.24

Frequency	Wavelength
20 Hz	17.03m
50	6.81
100	3.41
125	2.72
250	1.36
500	680mm
1KHz	340
10KHz	34
20KHz	1.7

1 milli = 10^{-3}
1 micro = 10^{-3}
1 nano = 10^{-9}
1 pico = 10^{-12}

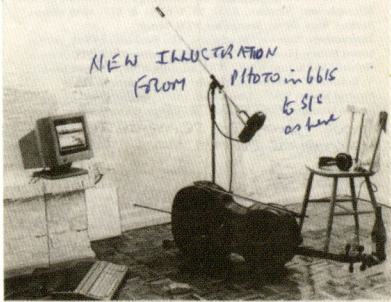

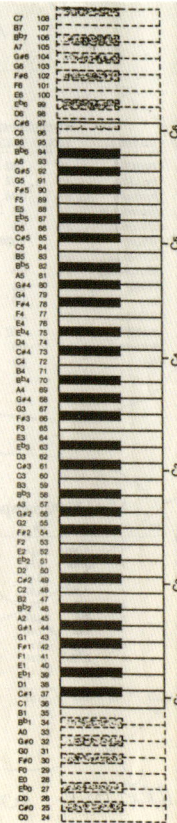

EASTCOTE PRODUCTIONS LTD
249 KENSAL ROAD, LONDON W10
01 969 3739
Two 24 track recording studios
just off Ladbroke Grove

BPM	1/16	3/32	1/8	5/32	3/16	7/32	1/4	5/8	3/4	MS PER 1/4 BAR	FRAMES PER BEAT (EBU)
110	136	204	272	340	408	476	545	681	817	2180	13.635
111	135	202	270	337	405	472	540	675	810	2160	13.5
112	133	200	267	334	401	468	535	668	802	2140	13.375
113	132	298	265	331	397	463	530	662	795	2129	13.25
114	131	197	263	328	394	460	526	657	789	2104	13.15
115	130	195	260	325	290	455	521	651	781	2084	13.025
116	129	193	258	323	287	452	517	646	775	2068	12.975
117	128	192	256	320	284	448	512	640	768	2048	12.8
118	127	190	254	317	381	444	508	635	762	2032	12.7
119	126	189	252	315	378	441	504	630	756	2016	12.6
120	125	187	250	312	375	437	500	625	750	2000	12.5
121	123	185	247	308	371	433	495	618	742	1980	12.375
122	122	184	245	306	368	429	491	613	736	1964	12.275
123	121	182	243	304	365	426	487	608	730	1948	12.175
124	120	181	241	301	362	422	483	603	724	1932	12.075
125	120	180	240	300	360	420	480	600	720	1920	12
126	119	178	238	297	357	416	476	595	714	1904	11.9
127	118	177	236	295	354	413	472	590	708	1888	11.8
128	117	175	234	292	351	409	468	585	702	1872	11.7
129	116	174	232	290	348	406	465	581	697	1860	11.625
130	115	172	230	288	345	403	461	576	691	1844	11.525
131	115	171	229	286	343	400	458	572	687	1832	11.45
132	113	170	227	283	340	397	454	567	681	1816	11.35
133	112	169	225	281	338	394	451	563	676	1804	11.275
134	111	167	223	279	335	391	447	558	670	1788	11.175
135	111	166	222	277	333	388	444	555	666	1776	11.1
136	110	165	220	275	330	385	441	551	661	1764	11.025
137	109	163	218	273	327	382	437	546	655	1748	10.925
138	108	162	217	271	325	379	434	542	651	1736	10.85
139	107	161	215	269	323	377	431	538	646	1724	10.775
140	107	160	214	267	321	374	428	535	642	1712	10.7
141	106	159	212	265	318	371	425	531	637	1700	10.625
142	105	158	211	263	316	369	422	527	633	1688	10.55
143	104	157	209	261	314	366	419	523	628	1676	10.475
144	104	156	208	260	312	364	416	520	624	1664	10.4
145	103	154	206	258	309	361	413	516	619	1652	10.325
146	102	153	205	256	308	358	410	512	615	1640	10.25
147	102	153	204	255	306	357	408	510	612	1632	10.2
148	101	151	202	253	303	354	405	506	607	1720	10.125
149	100	150	201	251	301	351	402	502	603	1608	10.05
150	100	150	200	250	300	350	400	500	600	1600	10
151	99	148	198	248	297	347	397	496	595	1588	9.925
152	98	147	197	246	295	344	394	492	591	1576	9.85
153	98	147	196	245	294	343	392	490	588	1568	9.8
154	97	145	194	243	291	340	389	486	583	1556	9.725
155	96	145	193	241	290	338	387	483	580	1548	9.675
156	96	144	192	240	288	336	384	480	576	1538	9.6
157	95	143	191	238	286	334	382	477	573	1528	9.55
158	94	142	189	236	284	331	379	473	568	1516	9.475
159	94	141	188	235	282	329	377	471	565	1508	9.425
160	93	140	187	234	281	328	375	468	562	1500	9.375

THE DUDES ON KENSAL ROAD

Eastcote was a busy place from the beginning, but at first all the action revolved around Chaz Jankel. It was built as his personal studio and he was now at work on album number 2, *Chasanova*. The album was released in 1981 and Philip was involved as producer, engineer and mixer alongside Chaz and Peter Van Hooke. Philip was spending most of his time in the studio and when there was no recording going on, Chaz explains, he had other ways to keep busy:

Philip was always busy doing something: soldering, fixing an amp, building a new room, a new monitoring system for the musicians. I think at one point he designed algorithms for delays. Do you remember that handbook... you put them in one of those diaries? A Filofax, they were made to fit in a Filofax. To work out delay times. All the producers would have them. Philip invented that.

It was a busy time for Jankel, who was now back writing with Ian Dury. They teamed up with reggae production duo Sly and Robbie to record *Lord Upminster* and were touring in the UK and Europe with The Blockheads. Ian had some issues with coming to Eastcote, partly because the awkward high step through the old stable doors made it difficult for him to get in. Philip remembers that 'Chaz never wanted to fix that', but Dury nevertheless spent a lot of time at the studio.

Through the ups and downs of everything that was going on, Philip was the rock-solid patience in the room. Chaz continues:

He's a genius in lots of respects, and I remember his patience was incredible. One time, for a song called '109', we'd been working on a remix the whole day and we had lots of bits of half-inch tape of different parts of the mix

1981

Philip's Filofax insert with calculations of delay times in various tempos was used by many producers.

Questionnaire: original sheet of music by Ian Dury and Chaz Jankel.

QUESTIONNAIRE

Words and Music by
(W) IAN DURY,
(M) CHAS. JANKEL.

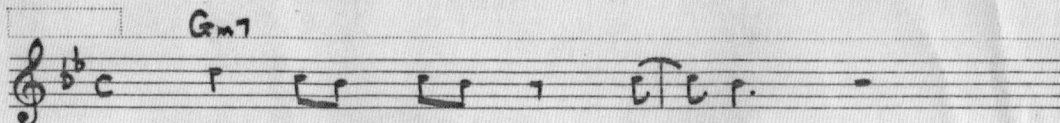

Gm7

WHAT SORT OF PERSON ARE_ YOU,
WHICH SIDE DO YOU SLEEP_ ON.

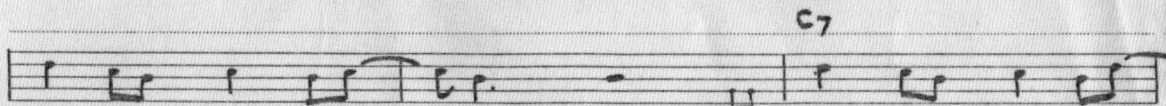

C7

WHAT SIDE OF LIFE COMES YOUR_ WAY   WHAT KIND OF THINGS DO YOU_
ARE YOU FORMAL OR RELAXED____   ARE YOU IN OR OUT OF BUSI-

E   Gm7

_ DO,   TRY TO DE-SCRIBE A NORM-AL DAY.
-NESS,   BE-FORE OR_ AFT-ER TAX.____

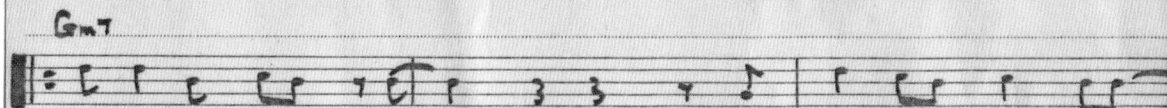

Gm7

ARE YOU THE QUIET TYPE____   OR MORE OF AN EXTROVERT__
WHAT DO YOU DO IN THE EVE-NINGS   WHAT SORT OF THING MAKES YOU
PLEASE GIVE YOUR NAME AND ADDRESS._   AND THE NUMBER OF YOUR
WILL YOU ANSWER ALL THESE QUESTIONS   ON A POSTCARD IF YOU PLEASE._

C7   E

_   IS YOUR JOURN-EY QUITE IM-PORTANT
LAUGH.   DO YOU HAVE ANY HOBBIES _ OR _ INTERESTS   PLEASE
PHONE.   WHAT ARE YOU DOING NEXT FRIDAY
____   TO THE MINISTRY OF_ THE FUTURE

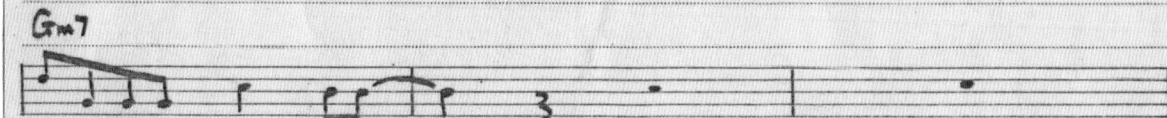

Gm7

DO YOU WEAR A WORK-ING SHIRT.__
ANSWER ON YOUR OWN BE-HALF.__
ARE YOU SURE YOU'LL BE A LONE.__
IN THE LAND OF BIRDS AND BEES.__

leadsheet:
Roger Day

lying all over the studio. He was going to splice and edit them together later. I'm sitting around listening as it's coming together, and now it's about two in the morning and I suddenly thought, oh my God, and I came up with a new piano motif and thought it would sound great. I went into the studio where Philip had been patiently splicing the tape back together, and he thought the job was now pretty much done. I say to Philip: 'Look, you're not going to like this, but I have this great new idea for a piano chop', and he went really quiet. He went very, very quiet and there was a long silence and I didn't know if he was going to shout at me or whatever. And there's the longest pause, about two and a half minutes of silence, and then he says: 'All right then. Okay'.

And we had to get the 2-inch machine out again and put the mics back up on the piano. And in the middle of the night there I am, adding a new piano on a remix of '109'. And at that moment I thought, my God. I don't know another human being that would do that.

For the past five years The Blockheads had been so successful they were already putting out a greatest hits album, and Chaz remembers another occasion when Ian came down to the studio to listen to a vocal he had recorded with Philip for a new song they'd written.

We were in the control room and Ian felt that Philip wasn't giving him the attention that he would have liked, so Ian got angry and said 'Chaz, do you mind leaving the room?' And I was about to leave, but I kept just standing there,

thinking, what's going to happen next? And Philip lies down on the floor. Full length, you know how tall he is! He lies down on the floor and says 'Ian, would you like just to walk over me right here?'

Would you like to walk all over me? I'll never forget that!

It really was a big year for Chaz, and as an unlikely cherry on the cake he ended up with another big chart success that year. 'Ai No Corrida' was covered by Quincy Jones and became a hit both in the UK and Stateside, and to this day the track is an R&B classic. Taking its cue heavily from Chaz's original production, Quincy's version with Dune (Charles May) on lead vocals is a slick affair and reads like a Who's Who of the early 1980s' LA recording scene:

32

Philip in the control room, early '80s.

1983

Herbie Hancock on piano, Greg Phillinganes on synths, Jerry Hey arranging the horns and Patti Austin the backing vocals, just to name a quarter of the personnel!

It's odd to think about the connection between these LA heavies and a small recording studio in an old stable in North Kensington, but the exercise feels like a poetic tribute to Chaz Jankel and his deep musicianship and songcraft.

How extraordinarily unlikely a journey for a song. It started after a gig with Ian Dury at the Paraiso in Amsterdam. Chaz had just come back to his room at the Americain with romantic company – he once described the moment as 'euphoric and the atmosphere erotic'. He hears a melody in his head and picks up the guitar. Then calls The Blockheads' bass player Norman Watt-Roy and asks him to come by the room to listen. He realizes the melody is not right for Ian Dury and decides to use it for his own project. Then threads and acquaintances. Another member of The Blockheads, Johnny Turnbull, has a friend who is a publisher called Dick Leahy who suggests Kenny Young to write the lyric. From an event in Cannes, Kenny calls Chaz and says he's got a lyric. It's now called 'Ai No Corrida' and the title is taken from a Japanese erotic art film he explains over the phone. Chaz records the song for his solo album. Now, Johnny's girlfriend works at Chaz's new label A&M in LA. Rod Temperton is looking for songs for an album with Quincy Jones and… Confused? Well, in the end let's sum it up like this: the melody became the song; the song became the classic track 'Ai No Corrida' from Quincy Jones's seminal R&B album *The Dude*.

I think it's fair to say that in 1981 Chaz Jankel and Philip Bagenal were The Dudes. ∎

Left to right: Philip Bagenal, Charlie Charles, Norman Watt-Roy and Robbie Shakespeare. Early '80s.

Synth-loving new wave band Kissing The Pink were one
of the first outside clients at Eastcote when they came
to work with Philip in 1982.

On the fourth floor above the Peter Robinson department store on Oxford Street were George Martin's famous AIR Studios. They were built in the late 1960s and when they opened their doors in 1970 they were one of the first world-class recording studios in London that was not owned by one of the big record labels. In the decades following, dozens of great independent studios would open up in AIR's wake. These studios were owned by producers, engineers, musicians and managers and ten years later one of them would of course be Eastcote.

There were two large studios at AIR and in 1982, while George Martin was recording with Paul McCartney in one of them, Nick Whitecross and Kissing The Pink were in the other studio working on their debut album *Naked* with producer Colin Thurston. Colin had previously engineered Iggy Pop's *Lust for Life* and Bowie's *Heroes* and produced Duran Duran's *Rio*.

The original band had met at the Royal College of Music. Their first single, 'Don't Hide in the Shadows', was recorded at Strawberry Studios in Manchester with Martin Hannett, whose work with Joy Division was much admired by the band. Having signed to Magnet Records with Heath Levy as publishers, the band really wanted to work with Brian Eno, but the label thought Thurston would be a more commercial choice, having had a big hit with Duran Duran's debut album and the single 'Girls On Film'.

Nick Whitecross is one of my long-time friends and collaborators and when we're walking through Hyde Park early one morning, he tells me:

I remember the sessions at AIR. There was a lot of pressure from the label, but we were wanting to experiment and make it sound better than our demos. At one time I remember our producer actually breaking down in tears. Our manager Liam Teeling worked for Heath Levy, a publishing company only a few blocks down from AIR on Regent Street. They had an actual writing studio, which was really rare. We used to be there a lot, packed into a tiny space with Rudy Pascal, the house engineer. I remember unknowingly ingesting something lysergic with Nick Nicely in that place and ended up playing the piano and recording a strange speech on his track '49 Cigars'. Nick's approach to recording, typified by his classic piece of psychedelia, 'Hilly Fields', helped us to deconstruct some of the more procedural aspects of the recording process.

The publishing company was owned by Eddie Levy and Geoffrey Heath whose brother, Andy Heath, managed Chaz Jankel. Philip and Eastcote were still mainly busy with Chaz's projects but, through Andy, Kissing The Pink arrived one day to do some initial recording for their sophomore album, *Naked*.

Nick continues:

When we arrived at Eastcote it felt like coming home. AIR had a 60-channel SSL desk, Paul McCartney was recording next door. It was George Martin's centre of operations, whereas Eastcote was more like a converted garage. It was such a relief. We immediately connected with Philip, he was un-rock-'n'-roll and unaffected... the benevolent father figure you never had, with an enormous interest in the experimental. At one point we spent hours moving speakers around in the courtyard, recording ambient sound. Other times, we'd all

IT WAS THE LAST FILM I EVER SAW

82!

sit at the desk and be hands-on with the mixing, rather than exiled to the back of the room while the 'producer' did it all. We ended up recording at Eastcote a lot and Philip produced most of our second album, What Noise, with Neil Richmond assisting. We remixed 'The Last Film' from the first album at Eastcote as well as 'In Awe of Industry'. I used to sit and talk with Philip for hours. He was about connecting the musicians with their music. A vital service in an industry that can quickly disable that connection in the rush to monetize a product. Subjecting art to cost-benefit analysis was not Philip's concern. I can't remember any other tenants in the building. Once you had walked in through the green door, there was no reason to leave. In Philip's hands, exploring the abstract was normal practice and we loved it.

'The Last Film I Ever Saw' became a top 20 hit in the UK, but Kissing The Pink remained largely an underground band until they released their third album, *Certain Things Are Likely*, and had a number 1 hit on the US dance chart and the European hit, 'One Step'. Much of this album was also recorded at Eastcote and on the track 'I Won't Wait' Chaz Jankel is playing the bass.

It brings back a lot of memories talking to Nick. I think about the deciding moments in life and the thread that binds them together. I was only twelve when Kissing The Pink started recording with Philip at Eastcote. At fifteen I met a publisher in Stockholm called Roffe Persson who I ended up working with for many years and who eventually signed me to a sub-publishing deal with Nick Phillips at MCA publishing in London. They had offices and a small studio in Hammersmith on the Fulham Palace Road, and

that's where I was introduced to Nick Whitecross who was also signed to MCA in the early '90s. We became good friends and worked on so many projects together, and the first studio that we hired for one of them was Eastcote Studio 2.

1982 was the year that the slow transition from a personal to a commercial studio started for Chaz and Philip and their self-built, self-financed set-up by the canal. Chaz was continuing to have solo hits, a lot of them now on the dance charts around Europe, including a number 1 Hot Dance hit in the UK with triple A-side 'Glad To Know You/3,000,000 Synths/Ai No Corrida'. When working with Philip on his third album, *Chazablanca*, they went back to Compass Point in the Bahamas for some of the recording. It made sense that others could rent the studio when it wasn't busy, and the word was spreading about the little gem of a recording space that Philip had built. It was only a few outside projects in those days. Some Chaz would bring in and also his drummer Peter Van Hook, who had got very interested in the production side of things. But it was Chaz's manager Andy Heath who would help spread the word about Eastcote and what was happening there further afield. Andy is now the Chairman of Beggars Music and his experience as a publisher and of the music business as a whole goes deeper than most. In 2008 he founded UK Music, the world's first public affairs organization for the music industry and in 2019 he received a CBE in acknowledgement of his more than 50 years of service to British music. I get on a call with Andy and he explains;

To be honest, I wasn't that involved with Eastcote apart from being the only one around

with a business mind. And to be frank, at that time I didn't have much of one either, because if I did I would probably have stopped them. I mean Philip was so eccentric and Chaz's problem was that he had a hard time finishing anything because he was never fully satisfied. Which I think is a testament to his immense talent. As a musician and songwriter I rank him right up there with the very best. It really is remarkable what they started and the music that was made there. I'm so pleased the studio is still going and I guess my main contribution really was connecting Chaz and Philip to others in the business.

Kissing The Pink was one of the connections made by Andy. It wasn't the last one and soon the road to Eastcote studios as we know it now, was being paved. ∎

1982!

Chaz Jankel and Ian Dury at Compass Point Studios
in the Bahamas in 1981. They recorded *Lord Upminster*
there with legendary rhythm section Sly Dunbar and
Robbie Shakespeare and co-producer Steven Stanley.

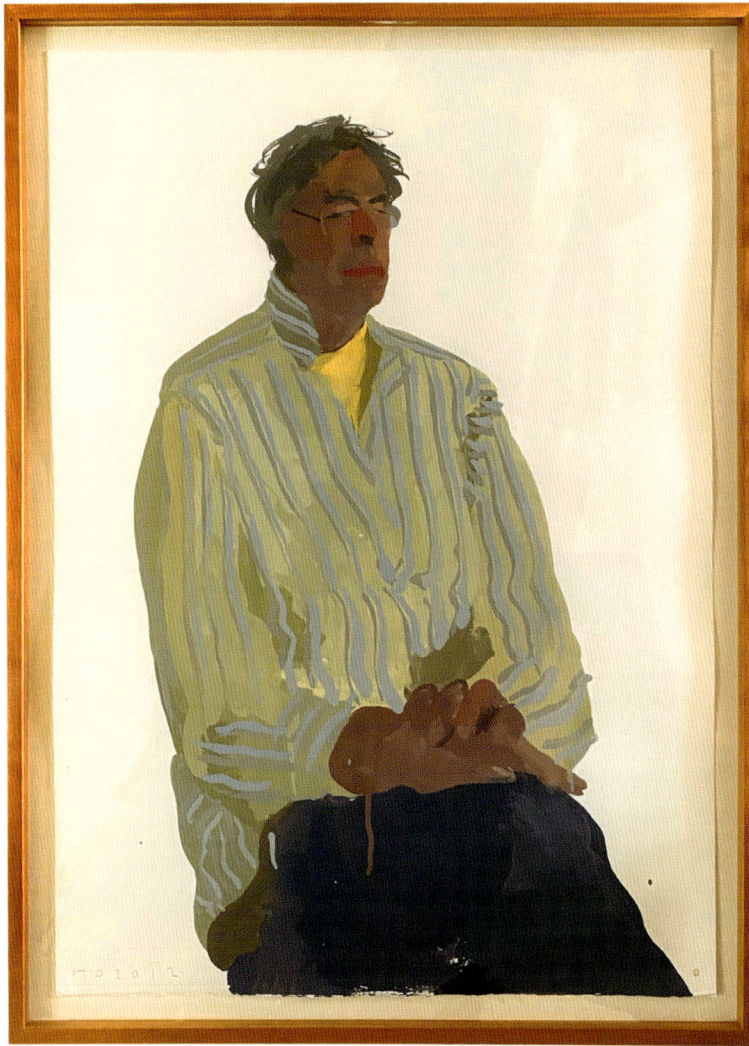

OVER MY DEAD BODY

As with so many other recording studios, the success of Eastcote Studios is about the people that were (and are) there. Philip and Chaz came with their own community of musicians, academics and visual artists. This was the early '80s in Notting Hill, where they both lived. The whole neighbourhood was a hotpot of culture, and a really important part of this story is how their world came to interact both with the surrounding area, the building they were in and those they shared it with.

The first tenant to move into Walters Workshops after Eastcote had opened was a young designer called Peter Saville. Together with Tony Wilson, Alan Erasmus and Martin Hannett, he was a partner in Factory Records. The record sleeves he designed for Joy Division, New Order and the many other influential artists signed to the label were the beginning of a remarkable design career. It would have been the early '80s when Peter moved in, shortly after Chaz and Philip. By coincidence, a friend of mine, Paul Stolper, is Peter Saville's gallerist. I decide to give him a call and a few days later we're having a cup of tea in the top floor art studio above Eastcote Studio 2 that used to be Peter Saville's design studio. I tell him a bit about the book and show him some sketches. On one of the pages there is a portrait of Philip, a painting that has been used on the Eastcote website for as long as I can recall and according to Philip is by 'a friend. It was at the National Portrait Gallery for a while'. Paul looks at it and says: 'That's by Humphrey Ocean, I'm sure it is. He's a friend of mine'.

Humphrey used to be the bass player in Kilburn and The Highroads, the band Ian Dury fronted before he met Chaz and formed The Blockheads. I send a message to Philip to try and figure out the connections here, and get this back:

Peter Blake was Ian Dury's art teacher at Waltham Forest College and subsequently at The Royal College of Art. He did the artwork for New Boots and Panties. Ian Dury was Humphrey Ocean's teacher at Canterbury College of Art.

It all becomes clearer. Paul Stolper is also Peter Blake's gallerist, and Brian Eno's, whose name appears in the Eastcote booking calendar on and off for decades. Later that evening when everything is quiet, I'm trying to finish a new song in Studio 2, where I've recently moved all

1983

Portait of Philip Bagenal by Humphrey Ocean. Displayed at the National Portrait Gallery. Now in private ownership.

Mr Love Pants, silkscreen and diamond dust, Peter Blake, 2005 (Courtesy Paul Stolper Gallery, London).

A/P   'Mr Love Pants'   Peter Blake

of my instruments. There's a message from Paul and he has found some great photos of Peter Saville and Tony Wilson in his design studio at Walters and in one of them I see the big plane tree in the courtyard, and I turn around and look at it. Same angle, same tree, standing tall now for a few hundred years I would imagine. I remember a story of when someone had suggested to the old colonel Tom Lacey that he should cut down the tree and develop the courtyard. His answer was: 'Over my dead body!' I think about how many generations have sat around or looked at that tree and found inspiration, creativity, peace or just a moment of respite from the urban craziness outside. Can't help taking a detour here and I find a website called 'Trees for Cities'. I read there that the London plane is a hybrid tree, and no one is absolutely sure about its origins. Most commonly it's thought to be the love-child of the oriental plane and the American plane, naturally hybridized in Spain and making its way here in the 1700s. Another version is apparently that it was indeed born in the 18th century, but in the Vauxhall garden of an English aristocrat who had both parent species planted there.

I can't help thinking that sounds a bit like the Imperial wishing version of the story, but who knows? I'll settle for the Spanish route because I think it's more poetic, and it fits well with all the natural hybridizing of music, art, electric manufacturing and metal bashing that was going on in our particular corner of North Kensington in 1983.

Back to the musical side of it all then. It's still Chaz's house, but more outside artists are coming to knock on his door. One who Philip remembers from that year is American trumpet player and composer Mark Isham. He played the trumpet solo on 'Ai No Corrida' and knew Peter Van Hooke and Chaz who were his connection to Eastcote. He came over to the UK with his producer Steven Miller to make his debut solo album *Vapor Drawings*. It was the first electronic album released on Windham Hill Records and it's a brilliant piece of music, taking its inspiration from early minimalist composers but performed with synthesizers and trumpet in a wash of echoes and reverb. Philip speaks very fondly about the project and says:

Mark is a world-class trumpet player. It was a wonderful album and I think it was the first New Age album Windham put out. New Age was known by musicians here as 'No Wage'.

For Mark Isham and Steven Miller though it was an early collaboration between two musicians who would end up having illustrious careers. Mark's compositions are highly regarded, and he has scored dozens of Hollywood films since then. And Steven, who is still very much active, went on in an almost Forrest Gump-like manner to make a huge impact in music across genres. His acclaimed ambient work with many of the artists on Windham led to working with Steve Jobs and with Andy Narell he created the music and sounds for Apple's early computers (the IIe, the Lisa and the Macintosh). He then worked as an engineer and producer with pop, rock and jazz artists as diverse as Suzanne Vega, Richard Marx, Pink, Dave Matthews Band, Michael Brecker, Bobby McFerrin and Manhattan Transfer. As one of the first sound engineers to fully embrace digital recording, he was at the cutting edge of developing and incorporating new technologies into record-making.

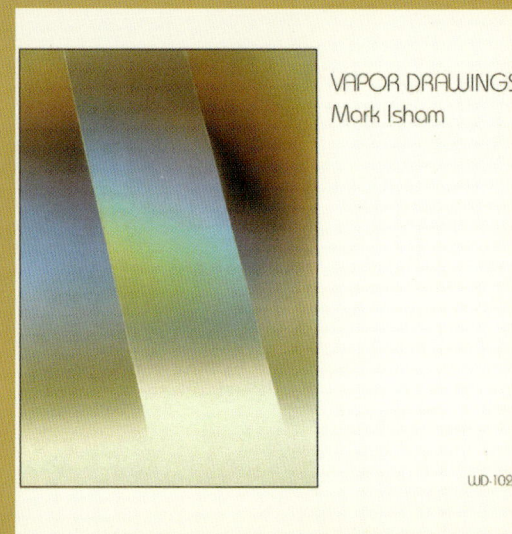

VAPOR DRAWINGS
Mark Isham

LUD-1027

I can see how Philip and Steven would have had many things in common and I imagine their conversations during those sessions. Maybe some in the courtyard, by the plane tree. Maybe with the Colonel and a bottle of whiskey. ∎

Mark Isham, *Vapor Drawings*, Windham Hill Records, 1983

Art director and graphic designer Peter Saville was Eastcote's upstairs neighbour at Walters Workshops. He had his design studio there from early to late '80s. He's seen here at the studio with his partner in Factory Records, Tony Wilson. (Photo: Peter Anderson)

WHO WANTS TO BUY HALF OF A HOUSE IN OXFORD?

When I first decided to sit down and write some notes and go through the photos in various boxes in the little workshop next to the Studio 1 control room, I was aiming to put together a photo document, a catalogue-style book of sorts for the 40th anniversary of Eastcote Studios. But most importantly I wanted to talk to Philip, with enough time to really hear his version of what made Eastcote what it is. I started, though, by reaching out to Charlie Seaward, without whom this project would probably never have actually ended up a finished book.

In 1984 the opening up of Eastcote to external clients continued and the connection was again Chaz's manager Andy. Andy was also the publisher of Man Jumping, a group formed in part from the remains of The Lost Jockey, a larger ensemble that performed systems music by composers like Philip Glass and Steve Reich.

Charlie played keyboards and flute in Man Jumping alongside Andy Blake on sax, Martin Ditcham on drums, John Lunn on bass, Orlando Gough on keyboards, Glyn Perrin on cello and Schaun Tozer, also on the keys. Charlie tells me:

I was a newly graduated solicitor and had a great job at a big firm in the City, and one of my clients was a man called Ronnie Bond who was a jingle producer. I decided one day that I wanted to take a break for a while, and I told Ronnie. He asked me: 'What are you going to do?' And I said 'I don't know'. He asked if I could write jingles and I thought, I can try. He gave me a reel and said you've got write 30 seconds of music for each one and I did. One was picked up by Quick Fix and it's still being played today! Anyway, Andy Heath and Ronnie Bond shared offices and when we started the Man Jumping project, he put me together with Philip.

Philip at work.

1984

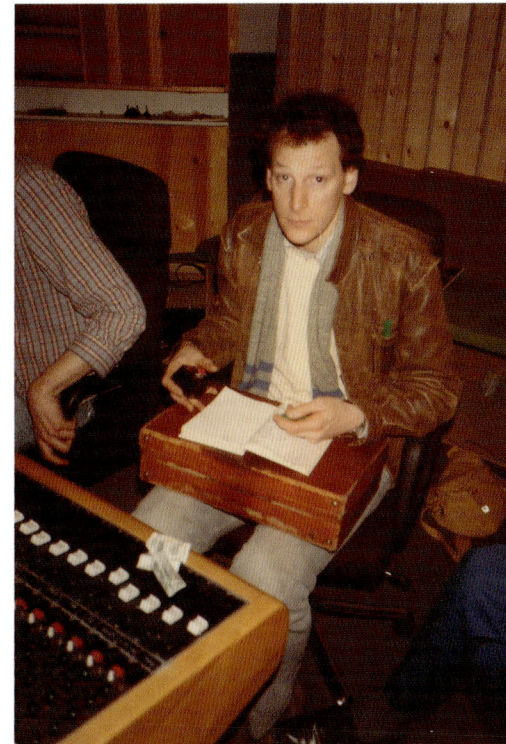

The new band started working on what would become their first album at Eastcote Studios together with Philip Bagenal. At one point Andy Heath came in and said: 'You need a well-known producer to help you finish so we can get a record deal'. He knew a young producer called Mike Hedges who was starting to make noise around town and was working in a studio nearby with Siouxsie and the Banshees. The Banshees would only work at night, so Mike came down for a couple of weeks in the daytime to help them and ended up producing three tracks on the album.

The album they made was called *Jumpcut* and it was released the following year on Cocteau Records. In my opinion it's a secret masterpiece, a curious one-of-a-kind record, decidedly refusing to adhere to any rules. It is systems-inspired in parts but without the stringent aesthetics of Reich, Glass or even Kraftwerk. Anything is possible on this album. The polyrhythmic percussion madness is soothed by beautiful keyboard patterns and melodies, only to be abruptly interrupted by surprises from the flutes and horns. And out of nowhere influences from the American West Coast are allowed to create funky backdrops to it all. It's crazy, wonderful and insanely ambitious.

After its release, the album was selected as one of the albums of the year by *The Times*, *The Independent* and *The Guardian*. Many members of Man Jumping went on to have impressive careers in music, notable examples being Gough's opera work, Lunn's BAFTA- and Ivor Novello-nominated TV and film scores including for *Downton Abbey*, and Ditcham, who was a drummer and percussionist for Sade, Elton John and Tina Turner among many others. Their producer Mike Hedges needs little introduction to anyone who is interested in recording credits. His award-winning production and mixing work with The Cure, U2 and Manic Street Preachers, just to name a few, made him one of the most successful British producers of his generation.

And Philip and Charlie? Well here's what happened:

Philip: *So I asked Charlie, do you know anyone who wants to buy half of a house in Oxford?*
Charlie: *Yeah, I couldn't hear what you were saying. I was recording piano and you said something in the talkback and I thought it had to do with my playing. Anyway, I was perfectly happy in Fulham, but when I got back home that evening my girlfriend said, 'I need a bigger garden for the dog'. I asked well, could the garden be in Oxford? Anyway, we went to see it*

43

Philip with Mike Hedges during Man Jumping session.

Martin Ditcham and John Lunn/Man Jumping 1984.

Charlie Seaward from Man Jumping making notes.

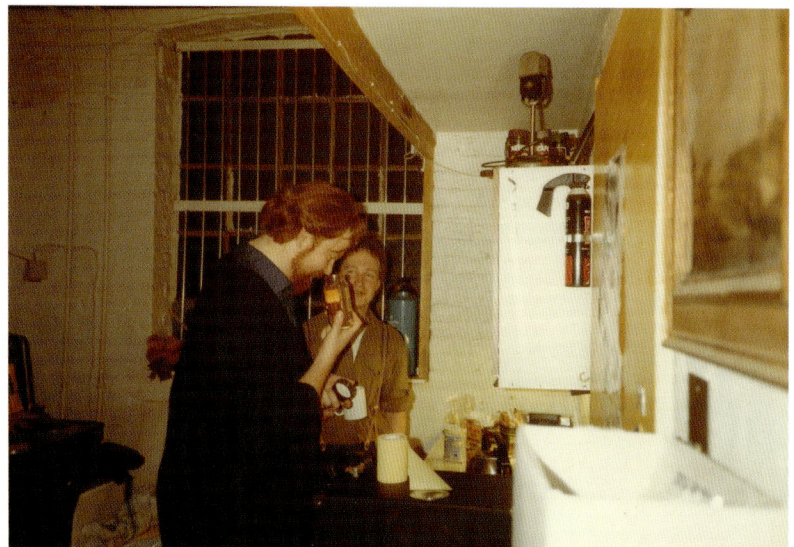

Man Jumping were back at Eastcote again in 1986 to record their second album *World Service*.

Martin Ditcham on the timbales.

Mike Hedges is not so sure about the Eastcote coffee.

Philip Bagenal was at his best when Eastcote was stretched, like a ship under full sail, out in mid-ocean, the wind tearing at the rigging, waves rolling over the bow, the control room awash with jack-to-jacks, discarded cables, reels of 2-inch tape and razor blades. But it wasn't the main brace he was splicing, it was arm full of carefully cut strips of magnetic tape. These were the last glorious days of analogue recording.

How come Man Jumping was one of the earlier bands to step through the hallowed wooden entrance into the world found, designed, built and managed by Philip? Our publisher Andy Heath, managed Chaz Jankel, who owned Eastcote at the time. Basta!

In those days, Philip was also the house engineer. Although we had no clear vision for our first album, Philip had plenty. He encouraged us to be less formal, more experimental, he challenged every note and every bar. He provided us with a kaleidoscope of sounds and colours with which to work. In that sense, he was as much a member of our band as anyone. We deferred to his imagination and to his intellect.

Richard Williams, who kindly provided the sleeve notes for the re-issue of Jumpcut, noted that "[Man Jumping's] legacy is demonstrably durable, a testament to their originality of thought and a commitment to an idea of what music might be rather than an imitation of what it already was". I hope there is truth in this. Anyway, it perfectly captures everything which Eastcote has stood for since the day that Chaz and Philip fired up the desk and the tape machines for the first time.

Why is it that the days at Eastcote, sharing the watches with Philip Bagenal, remain so vivid even and although half a lifetime has passed? They were days of adventure, days of discovery, days of industriousness, guided as we were, by the skilful hand of the kindly, thoughtful and generous man behind the desk. They were, as it turned out, the best days of all.

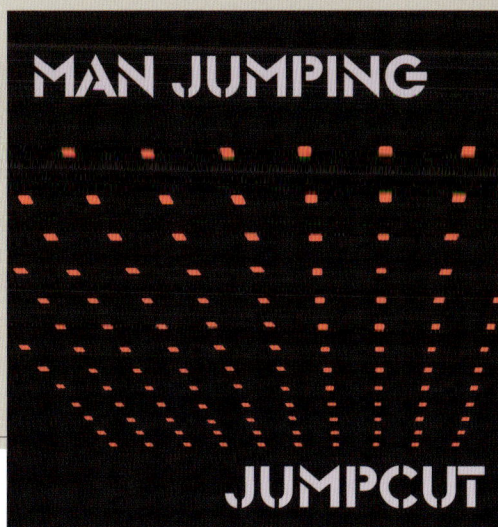

and immediately said yes despite some obvious challenges like planning, etc. Philip said, 'I'll fix it, I'm an architect', and we bid without really knowing where the money was going to come from. We ended up buying the place and me and Wanna, my girlfriend at the time and now my wife, have been neighbours with Philip and his wife Esther since then.

The conversations I've had so far with Philip, Chaz, Charlie and Nick Whitecross make me imagine not only the studio but also an atmosphere in which the only option was to push further, try and fail, and then try again. Fearlessness and commitment to their craft were what these young men were about. And what they created is a studio where this ethos is built in to the walls, and after four decades it's still there, steering new young artists away from the main roads and on to the winding ones that require more of the driver.

When I later ask Charlie to write down some words about the recording of *Jumpcut*, he returns an email and I think it's best read in its entirety. ■

Man Jumping, *Jump Cut*, Cocteau Records, 1985.

1984

Zeus B Held has arrived at Eastcote Studios.

I'm listening through an interview I've done with Chaz Jankel a few days earlier as he speaks about the time just before he moved to Los Angeles. It's 1985 and some early artists at Eastcote are coming back for seconds, with Kissing The Pink working on a new album and Man Jumping beginning the recording of their second and last album, *World Service*, with Philip producing. Several new clients have also started using the studio. One of them is a German producer and musician called Zeus B Held. His background is from the kraut-rock scene as a member of Birth Control, an institution of a band formed in mid-'60s' Berlin which Zeus joined as an organ player in 1973.

Zeus had met Philip through his management, Worlds End. Founded by Sandy Robertson and Paul Brown, Worlds End was one of the first UK management companies to focus only on producers, mixers and engineers. Zeus was hiring the studio whenever there was time available between Chaz's recordings, and an early project he worked on at Eastcote was Die Krupps' third album *Entering The Arena*. Jürgen Engler and his band from Düsseldorf were influential industrial music pioneers, but this new album had a heavy synth-driven sound and was a definite turn towards New Wave. By comparison, their first album, *Stahlwerksynfonie*, sounds more like what I imagine would have been the soundtrack while standing in the courtyard outside Eastcote when Chaz and Philip moved in. A curious mix of a loud live band from the studio and metal-bashing going on in the manufacturing plant next to it. It must have been their destiny to come and record there with Zeus a few years later.

Technology at Eastcote had evolved too, with the Trident console gone and replaced with an incredible-sounding MCI 500 console. It was modified by MCI guru Pete Clark and is still the beating heart in our studio 1 control room. The purchase was inspired by a trip Philip and Chaz

YOU KNOW WHAT, THIS GUY IS GOING TO BUY THE STUDIO

1985

ROUGH PRINT   NORMAL FILM

Philip Bagenal creating magic on the new MCI console.

made to Compass Point where they had the same board and Philip explains;

Island Records ordered two MCI 500 mixers, one for Studio 2, in the basement of their flagship studios in Basing Street, North Kensington. The other was for a smaller studio they had in St Anne's Square. The 42 Channel had some moments of fame and many could be chosen for early users. The most quoted are probably the Exodus *mix, 'No Woman No Cry' live version, and* Fables of the Reconstruction *– the R.E.M. album. But it rapidly became clear that, if you wanted a compact, slick and glossy pop mix, compressed to fuck by Alan Smart's remarkable stereo bus compressor that shot out of the transistors and nailed your ears to the wall, it had to be SSL. Livingston Studios in North London bought the MCI, but soon discovered the same problem. And the automation was very crude. They had to go SSL too. Eastcote took the desk, had it serviced and given the notorious Pete Clark's secret mod that doubled the action! Being primarily a tracking studio, we had got what we wanted and needed: a powerful fat sound that was inspirational for the musicians, our true clients.*

Eastcote had also taken on the lease for the first floor, above Studio 1. Here was now Studio 2, which Chaz describes as:

Amazing, it was a like a New York loft, I think because of the light coming in from the courtyard. I did a lot of stuff up there. I remember doing the whole soundtrack for a movie called War Party. *In the beginning you couldn't record drums up there, it was only over time it became a full-fledged recording studio.*

But despite new gear, a new space and a decade of successes both with Ian Dury and his own solo project, Chaz was getting restless:

At the time I was also starting to lose a bit of interest and felt like my whole world between 1980 and now had revolved between my flat on Penzance Place and the studio and I thought maybe it's time for a change. The world has to be bigger than Notting Hill.

Also, Eastcote had been my personal recording studio for years. But as time went by I think maybe Philip felt there wasn't enough money coming in and we both agreed on hiring out to other people. But the point was though that if you're going to start hiring out you got to be competitive and have new equipment and something to offer. And that's what Philip kept doing, he kept buying more equipment and making the studios better. And to cut a long story short what I felt was, it was becoming less of a personal space and more like a professional studio for anyone to use.

I actually remember the day I first saw Zeus B Held. I was in the main room in Studio 1 and he came in, and it looked like he wanted to eat the studio and swallow it. Like an animal about to devour the studio and I thought: you know what, this guy is going to buy the studio.

Later that year Zeus would be back in the studio, now as producer for Chaz's fourth and final album on A&M, *Looking At You*. Zeus says:

I had heard that Chaz wasn't very easy to work with, but with me and Philip it did kind of work. I had been hired by A&M as producer and arranger to take Chaz's music a little bit down to earth, but in the end I couldn't really do what I normally would have as the producer. I mean it was impossible. Chaz owned the studio and he and Philip were close friends. It would have been different if we had recorded in my studio, but I knew when I went home, Chaz would be straight back in the studio with Philip, changing things to the way he wanted them. But it was great, I learned a lot.

Something was brewing, and Chaz's prediction was right...

Zeus would go on to buy the studio. ∎

985

A new studio is open for business: Eastcote Studio 2.

THE STROLL BRO[S]

THERE'S A NEW SHERIFF IN TOWN

It's a time of division in Britain. Maggie Thatcher's political reign is in full swing and for the working classes around the country opportunities are closing at every corner. Unemployment remains near postwar highs after years of recession and rioting, but in the middle and upper classes there's another narrative. It's the '80s' boom and there is money to be made. With the punk and post-punk eras over and done with, gloss is the new finish of choice in record-making, and polished pop is dominating the charts and airwaves alike. Technically for studios it's the era of transition to digital recording and big consoles. SSL and NEVE are competing for the throne, making ever bigger and more complicated mixing consoles to go with multi-track digital tape machines. For consumers, CD is now the new music format of envy, although compact disc players are still so expensive that it will take a few more years before vinyl starts to give up ground. At Eastcote, it's a new chapter too.

Chaz has decided to make the big move to America and goes on to sell the studio to Philip and his new partner Zeus B Held. Although coming from a rock background, Zeus is getting recognition for his modern productions, heavy with arpeggiated synths and vocoders and certainly on the darker side of proceedings in comparison with the majority of the most successful artists around that time: A-ha, Madonna, The Pet Shop Boys, George Michael, Whitney Houston and R&B group Five Star were all frequent guests on the UK charts that year.

Also having number ones were soft rockers Bon Jovi and Europe, the thought of whom reminds me that I was only 17 then, just finishing high school and regularly permed my long hair before heading to the rehearsal room to practise scales on the guitar. Being able to play fast guitar solos was something to aspire to where I lived in a suburb of Stockholm called Upplands Väsby. Only a few years earlier both Yngwie Malmsteen and Force, who would later become Europe, were playing at Draget, our local youth music club. Europe had a great guitarist called John Norum who was a bit subtler than Yngwie, who had his unique ultra-shredding style, and it felt like an obvious career choice to play the electric guitar and keep writing songs as both John and Yngwie had become big stars. They, along with their bandmates, had escaped the depressing supermarket cafe at a nearby shopping mall, where we all used to watch the first MTV videos on a tiny TV in the corner. By some twist of fate and years later, I was playing 'Take On Me' on pump organ with A-ha at an '80s' celebration for Children In Need. The show at Wembley Arena concluded with Europe performing their biggest hit and in a 247 degrees of separation-type way... maybe it relates to this story like this: by the end of 1986, 'The Final Countdown' was number 1 on the UK charts and in many other countries across the world. I was a few months away from being an official adult when that Christmas I got my first CD player and a Toto album. I was very far away from the London underground scene.

Zeus tells me that his career as a producer had really got going when he was living in Cologne. After two solo albums he created a project with an art student called Gina Kikoine. The edgy, dance-driven electropop duo were called Gina X Performance. Their first single, 'No G.D.M.', did really well and they then made two

Philip and Zeus, 1986.

1986

albums in quick succession in 1979 and 1980:

All of a sudden everyone wanted that sound. Which was synthesizers and vocoder, and this coldness that I liked, because I was so bored of guitars and rock'n'roll endings and all that.

And because of that I was approached by Arista Records and they asked me to work with a band called Fashion and said 'Do whatever you want', and we went and recorded in Cologne, Paris and London. It took half a year to make that album. It was called Fabrique and it was a really good album. I met my manager because of that, and he said, 'We can help you to get more work', and it was then I moved to London. It was what I wanted after having spent six months in hotels and so that's what I did.

I was around town working in a lot of different studios. Small studios, like The Garden in Shoreditch, and big ones like Marcus Recording Studios And it was good. Things were happening. And from time to time I got to know this little studio on Kensal Road, and I liked there. And that's how I met Philip.

It was a busy year, and as winter was approaching Zeus was in the studio like most days, and was now making an album with Kirk Brandon's band Spear Of Destiny. Coming from a punk/post-punk background as the singer and writer in The Pack and later Theatre Of Hate, Brandon had a slightly more melodic approach with SOD. It was those times after all.

The first album they made with Zeus was called *Outland* and it was a big success.

We made a lot of the basic tracking at Eastcote but not the whole album because Kirk really hated that everyone was smoking in the studio. Philip always had a cigarette in his mouth. And Kirk Brandon, he was this kind of early days health freak. We worked on two albums together at Eastcote and the first one did really well.

Talking to Zeus I think that he must be a good producer. He's confident and engaging and I wonder what he thought that day when he first met Chaz in Studio 1. Maybe something like what they'd say in an old Western film: 'There's a new sheriff in town!'

He was the new energy to start the next chapter at Eastcote with Philip. ∎

Kirk Brandon of Theatre of Hate and later Spear of Destiny in the early '80s.

WE DID TO WARHOL WHAT HE DID TO BANANAS

'It is too early to be taking the tarpaulins off the lifeboats, and even signalling to other shipping,' said the Archbishop of Canterbury, Dr Robert Runcie, after the Church of England took a decisive step towards women's ordination when the General Synod voted by 317 to 145 to prepare legislation for the reform. And with the massive opposition in the church, including from the Bishop of London, he was right. It would be 1992 before a final vote was taken to allow the practice, and it wasn't until 1994 that any woman was actually ordained as a priest, still under massive protests. As many as 400 vicars of the Church of England flounced in a mass exodus to the Roman Catholic Church.

In the real world, however, women had long since lost patience with waiting their turn. The influence of women in every genre of popular music had been without contest since the 1970s, although the business of music was still largely run by men. The punk and post-punk movements of the previous decade had challenged old gender ideas and so did the club and dance scene of the early '80s.

It's 1987 and the world of mainstream popular music is now dominated by iconic women. The year kicks off with Aretha Franklin becoming the first woman inducted into the Rock and Roll Hall of Fame, the American foundation (and later museum) documenting the history of rock, founded by Ahmet Ertegun. Worldwide the charts are full of Madonna and Whitney Houston. But it wasn't only American women camping out on the UK top 10 that year. The siblings in Five Star, with the phenomenal lead singer Denise Pearson, were regular visitors. So were Alison Moyet, Kim Wilde, Mel and Kim, Pepsi and Shirley, Fleetwood Mac (Christine McVie), Keren Woodward, and T'Pau (Carol Decker), all British and having more than two top 10 singles during the year. And Taffy, she was from Deptford which brings us right back to the beginning of the story and Eastcote.

Yes, at Eastcote too there was a strong female influence this year. Wendy James lived in Ladbroke Grove and was often hanging out with other local musicians at the Warwick Castle pub on the Portobello Road. It wasn't far for her to walk up to Golborne Road, past Trellick Tower and around the bend on to Kensal Road and Eastcote Studios, where she and collaborator boyfriend Nick Christian Sayer were working. They had already released their first single, 'Revolution Baby', and at the end of 1987 Zeus was enlisted to help them finish their first album, *Pop Art*. From their collaboration came the second single, 'Tell That Girl To Shut Up', a cover of the 1979 single by Holly and The Italians. But it was the third single, 'I Want Your Love', that would change everything.

As if overnight Transvision Vamp were everywhere and the rebellious James, oozing sex appeal and always with a witty or provocative response to any question, had become a pop star and a style icon. In a recent retrospective interview, James explains the band name as 'Trans because it was all across the world. Vision, because we wanted to view the whole world. And Vamp, because you know... I was gonna be a vamp'.

Not liked by everyone and consistently questioned about appropriating and borrowing from artists before them, there was invariably a funny comeback. In a 1988 *Melody Maker* interview, when asked about the song 'Andy Warhol Is Dead', Wendy replied:

We did to Warhol what he did to bananas.

Zeus ended up producing both *Pop Art* and the band's second album, *Velveteen*, together with Duncan Bridgeman. And Philip was mixing, engineering and hosting the sessions in his usual way. With love and the occasional interruption at the right time. Or in Philip's own words:

I was in and out of the room, and I wasn't afraid to say what I wanted so I was always there. I didn't tend to keep my mouth shut.

When I later speak to Zeus about sessions in the late '80s and early '90s, he lights up and gesticulates with great excitement as he explains:

It was great. Those were the wonderful times. The band had a producer already who was a friend of theirs, but I was brought in by the label and given the wand to say what's on and not on. Some songs I produced from beginning to end and some they had already worked on, so we added to them, co-produced and got them finished. And then, you know, with Transvision Vamp I had the songwriter and I had Wendy. If they are not happy, it's not happening! But luckily, we had time, you know, it was good.

Zeus laughs warmly and continues:

Sometimes I had to think of psychological tricks, you know, to get the guitars in tune. And other times do some magicals overnight when no one was there.

It's October and late in the evening when I'm writing this, and rumours have been circulating for the past few days about a new national lockdown to keep coronavirus under control as winter approaches. It's raining and definitely getting cold and I think no way can I close a chapter about a year belonging to amazing women in music without a short story about how the year ended. Many will know it already.

Shane MacGowan, Jem Finer and their band The Pogues would find their way to Eastcote a few years later for a recording session with Philip in Studio 1. But this year is about a song they started writing in 1985 called 'Fairytale of New York'. The title was taken from that of a 1973 novel by Irish-American author J.P. Donleavy, and Shane had always intended for it to be a duet. It was put aside many times and reworked before in the summer of 1987 the late and brilliant Kirsty MacColl recorded the female part for the song at the nearby RAK Studios in St John's Wood. It didn't reach number 1 for Christmas; the best songs sometimes don't. But it did become one of the most loved songs of all time in this country, sung along to year after year at Christmastime in homes and pubs all around the English-speaking world. ∎

Transvision Vamp in 1988.

53

It's well known that Aretha Franklin would ever only sing the song once. She wouldn't allow the tape to be running while she was rehearsing and then she would say, right I'm going to sing it. That's it, you only get one take. Terrifying for an engineer because if her mic crackled, there was a problem. But I mean, a lot of the best music in the world has been recorded that way. Some records do take a long time to make, and you can't help that. Herding musicians into a particular studio, at a particular time, and a particular date... it's easier said than done.

Philip Bagenal

For every great quote or story from Philip, and there are many, one thing stands out more than anything else: his willingness to let things unfold without interfering until absolutely necessary. Many of the artists and producers tell me about Philip's smile as he was in the room but without saying anything. A smile out of sheer joy of hearing music coming together and filling the studio he had built with life. Like a great mother who is loving and encouraging but knows to let the child play and experiment to the point where, for the wellbeing of the child, it's no longer an option not to step in.

And when Philip did interject, he would be clear to the point where no one was left with any doubt about what his opinion was. And Philip didn't like when musicians and artists played it too safe. He couldn't see the point... and, arguably, in a studio setting there isn't one.

Having to revise his own ideas on how to make music over and over again, he wouldn't hesitate to move on and try different ways of working or new technologies as they arrived. This spirit is in the wiring of Eastcote. Even with a few marketing campaigns, like their own printed chocolate wrappers, and the odd year when there were so few bookings that Philip and Zeus worried about staying afloat, the studio remained open, and a safe space for artists to be artists in.

In 1988, Studio 2 had become increasingly popular and some artists and producers spent months at a time in the upstairs studio. One of the producers who started working regularly at Eastcote around this time was Cameron McVey. An early record he made there was 'Manchild', from Neneh Cherry's debut album *Raw Like Sushi*. I try to get hold of Cameron and Neneh and when I reach out by email to ask them about their time at the studios, I get an email back from Cameron who is with Neneh at their country home in southern Sweden:

Gosh we made SO many records in the old Studio 2!

Tim Simenon did his scratches for 'Manchild' there, & All Saints did stuff with us there.

I saw some photos of a few of us on the back couch in front of the window that used to look out on the back yard. Can't remember where I saw them though.

I broke the back of the upstairs reception room couch when Man U scored the winner against Bayern Munich in the Champions League Final (& I'm a Chelsea supporter... weird!)

I also remember the late great Jonny Dollar sending for loads of different grand pianos to get the right sound on a Neneh Cherry song called 'Feel It'. One of the team of piano humpers was a very big strong man & he got sick of humping so many pianos up & down those metal stairs & we heard him say:

'Who's this Jonny fucking Dollar fella then, where the fuck is he?!' Dollar evaporated!

I ask Cameron about how they ended up at Eastcote in the first place, what the connection was. It turns out to go back some years and to Chaz, who by now lives in Los Angeles:

My first wife Yvonne Roudette used to date Chaz & she took me to Eastcote & introduced me to him & that's when I first met Philip. Then a few years later I was working across the road in the Canalot complex & needed to find a nicer more friendly room & the upstairs room at Eastcote

LIKE TRYING TO CATCH LIGHTNING IN A BOTTLE

Tim Simenon of Bomb The Bass outside Hollywood Studios, Hackney, London in 1988.

Hard at work in Studio 1.

was available. I tried it out, then I believe I took it on a long-term rental & Eastcote became my home. I brought Jonny Dollar over there with me. He was my engineer from Canalot (but this was before he was called Jonny Dollar). My crew & I were always quite boisterous, but Philip was always so kind to us & so damn patient.

It was me that brought Tim Sim to the joint to record some scratch parts on Neneh's song 'Manchild' & years later I brought Tom Elmhirst there to engineer & mix for me upstairs in the days when the desk was 2 Mackie boards linked together. I still say that Tom's best-ever mix was 'Snakes and Ladders' by Virgin Souls done on that Mackie combo board upstairs at Eastcote.

Virgin Souls is Cameron's band with Paul Simm, Silvio Pacini and Neil Pearson, and Tom Elmhirst has since then become a very sought-after mix engineer with 16 Grammys to his name. Nowadays he's working out of Electric Lady Studios in New York and definitely on a rather

nicer console than a Mackie. I check out the track. Cameron is right. It's a great song and a brilliant sounding mix. The story reminds me of one of my favourite engineers and a good friend, Jan Ugand, who I made many records with at Atlantis Studios in Stockholm. The console there is a rare 1972 Neve with 32 x 1084 EQ modules and most engineers would probably be able to give a small lecture on why it sounds so good. But when Jan was once asked by the legendary Bruce Swedien about the module numbers on this mythical mixing desk, he replied: 'I'm not sure. It's a Neve. It's blue and sounds really great.'

Top-end gear makes things easier, but it's not the main ingredient in a good mix. It's the ears and skills of the engineer that create the magic in the sound, and no one knew this better than Philip. Cameron continues:

Philip is a one-off. He's an old-school seriously skilled recording engineer with the

sense of adventure normally exhibited by a five-year-old. His relentlessly positive vibes and influence on any session he engineered were worth more than any money could buy.

Neneh, Cameron, Tim Sim and Dollar became regular clients at Eastcote and will take us into a new decade at the studios. But before then, let's walk down to Studio 1 for a moment.

It was there in 1988 that Aswad recorded their hit single 'Don't Turn Around', a cover of a Diane Warren song originally cut by Tina Turner. It came more than a decade into the band's career when they were already an institution of UK reggae. Brinsley 'Chaka B' Forde and Angus 'Drummie Zeb' Gaye went to Holland Park School, just up the road from Eastcote and a stone's throw from Penzance Place where Philip and Chaz had both lived. Together with Donald 'Dee' Griffiths, George 'Ras' Oban and Courtney 'Khaki' Hemmings they released their first album as Aswad in 1976.

The following year they performed as Burning Spear's backing band at the Rainbow Theatre in London, a concert later released as a live album. They collaborated again in Kingston, Jamaica, on the 1978 album *Marcus' Children*.

By the time they were working on their album *Distant Thunder* at Eastcote they had already released 10 albums in the 12 years since their debut, and Philip says about the sessions:

I remember 'Don't Turn Around', which was their number 1 hit. They'd been working in the studio and I found it quite difficult to get used to their daily schedule, they'd turn up at about four in the afternoon and by six they'd all be fast asleep. And I'd sort of hang around and do a bit of submixing and sorting around and then put my feet up and read the newspaper. Then one by one, starting at around 11 o'clock at night, they'd wake up and by 2 am we'd have a working band and we'd be off.

And the other story that goes with that is Shane MacGowan. I remember recording a

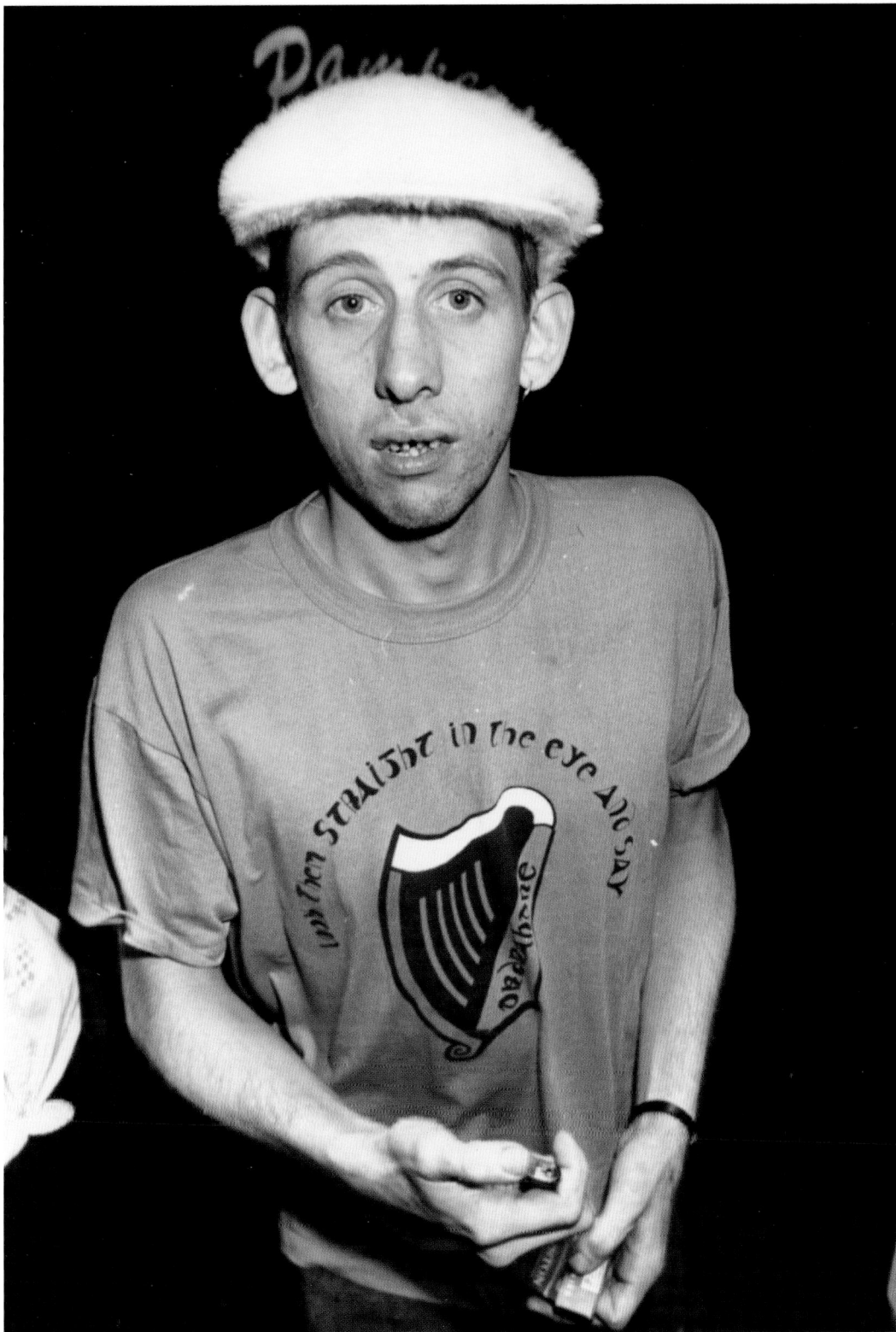

potential single for them and they'd all turned up at 12 o'clock when they were supposed to do so. We set up and Shane wasn't there at that point and so we spent time to get the balance perfect. And then Shane turns up, turned to his microphone and he put his cans on and then after four bars, he's supposed to come in... nothing happens! They try again... no result. It's just not gonna come. 'Okay Shane, take it easy'. And he gets taken into the lobby and laid flat out on the sofa, and the band then records the song; we spent about four or five hours working on it. With no singing, no voice. And Shane wakes up with the help of whatever, gets up and says 'I want to sing it', and he sings like a bird. Most amazing sound I've ever heard. One take.

And it relates to Aswad because Brinsley had been doing most of the singing with the band. But when we were recording 'Don't Turn Around', Drummie, who was the drummer and incidentally lived just down the road from the studio, was sort of singing along in the control room and I don't remember who was producing but he said, 'Drummie, go in there and sing the track'. So Drummie said, 'Well, I will'. And he went in and sang. He had not sung properly for the band before, and he walked back into the control room and everyone knew it was going to number one. It just had that sort of... well, that magic. When somebody hits a note, and his timing, holding back, jumping in and that great smile on his face. It wasn't even one of their own songs either, but you know, those moments... few and far between, are so memorable. It really illustrates that what you're trying to achieve in the studio are those moments. As much as possible. Like trying to catch lightning in a bottle.

In a later call with Zeus I ask him what he remembers about Aswad and those years. It was during what he describes as 'his best years in London'. He tells me:

I have such fond memories of that time, and how I hijacked Aswad to work with Udo

57

Shane MacGowan of The Pogues attending the release party for the film *Hairspray* at Hippodrome in London.

1988

[Lindenberg] for two songs. And it springs to mind because it was pretty amazing, even for Udo. He was already a star in Germany, but it was the first time he made an album that was not on his home ground. It was totally unhinged. And Aswad, they thought of it as their studio. If they were thinking of recording, they had a record label and they let them go to Eastcote. So, I got the songs from Udo and there was two he wanted to do with them, one was a reggae song and the other one more like 'Rainy Day Woman' by Bob Dylan, that kind of song. And I brought in The Kick Horns, who were an incredible horn section I was working with a lot, and then the bass, drums and guitar from Aswad. And Udo wasn't even there when I did it... and he's like the king, the maestro. Like the emperor. I came into the studio at 10 in the morning and the band were already there, in the courtyard smoking some dope. I said, guys can you not wait until a little later and they said, no that's our culture. And we record and later Udo came, and everyone was there, and I played him the track. I'll never forget. We were behind the console listening, nodding our heads and when the track was over Udo says, hmm... I don't like it...

I LOVE IT! And everyone first said 'What?' And then 'Yeah!' and celebrations. That was such a key moment, it was so great, I will always remember.

Zeus had had a lot of success with UK artists at that time, but he had made a promise to himself when he left Cologne for London. **There's two German artists I have to work with: Udo Lindenberg and Nina Hagen**. Zeus's collaboration with Udo at Eastcote resulted in the album *Casanova* and it's a really great listen. And when someone is already 20 years into a successful career one might be tempted to describe the timing as 'at the height of' or something similar. But Udo's is no ordinary career.

'The Godfather of German Rock' started as a jazz drummer, became a young rock star

58

Neneh Cherry – seen here in 1981 in a Ladbroke Grove squat where she lived – moved from Sweden to the UK when she was a teenager. By the late '80s she was at Eastcote working on her debut album, *Raw Like Sushi*.

East German rock star Udo Lindenberg worked with Aswad at Eastcote in the late '80s.

at 27, and was always a painter and activist for peace and for using the German language in rock. He long fought to be allowed to play in East Germany and became an embarrassment to the DDR government who didn't know how to handle the publicity situation. He early on described his sexuality as 'flexible' and has throughout his life been called eccentric, with his permanent residence being a hotel. Zeus explains that Udo arrived at Eastcote with *a whole entourage. He had his own chef, his own doctor and what he called his house intellectual that was forced upon me as a co-producer to help out with the lyrics. But I didn't care. The Udo days were great. He was very generous and loved champagne, he would always invite everyone to eat steak and drink Veuve Clicquot with him*. Lindenberg survived a heart attack in 1989, a year after recording at Eastcote, and describes the night when the wall came down that same November as:

> *The best party I've been to, ever!*

Now in his mid-seventies, he's still playing stadiums with his last three albums all reaching number 1 in Germany. His visual art is being exhibited at big galleries and maybe now is the time to say 'at the height of' but Udo still has work to do. In an interview with Robin Miller at an exhibition in Leipzig celebrating 30 years since the fall of the Berlin Wall he says:

> *I see today as an era of clowns. All over the world there's populism, nationalism, nationalist movements. Nationalism is never the way to go. It's all over the world. There are the Johnsons and Trumps, all ranting nationalism. Unfortunately, in Germany too. To me that's particularly awful because of our history.*

And in 2020, when we see more division across the world than I can remember ever in my lifetime, maybe the biggest takeaway from the events of 1988 at Eastcote Studios is not that such-and-such a song had success in the charts, or that any one artist came to record.

Instead I reflect upon the function that a place like Eastcote also has as a community space. Where cultures and opinions are exchanged, and hearts and minds expanded, I close my eyes and try to imagine a middle-aged German rock star celebrating with a group of young Caribbean musicians the music they've just created together. That they had just caught lightning in a bottle.

Was it Philip, Drummie, Neneh, Cameron, Udo, Chaz or Zeus who once said: 'Act according to your conviction, be an individualist. Don't just follow everyone else. Go down your own path'?

You pick. It really could have been any of them. ∎

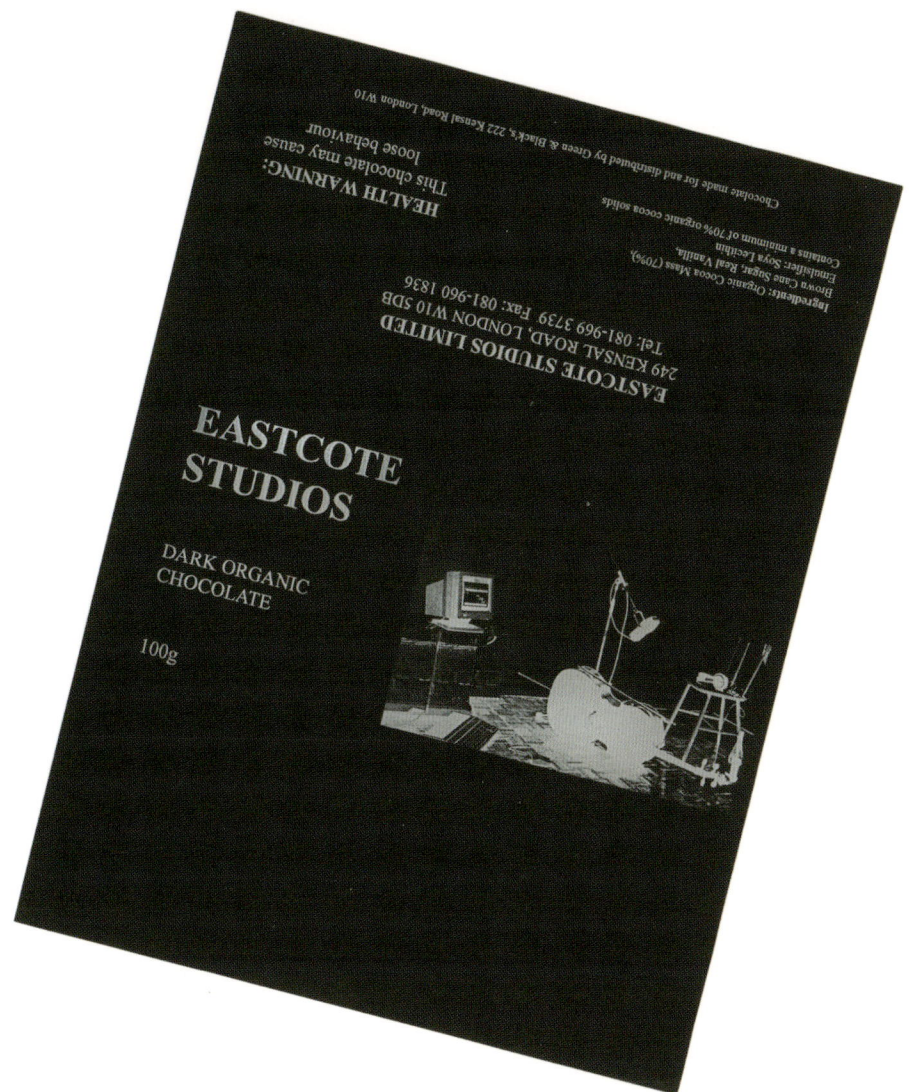

EASTCOTE STUDIOS

DARK ORGANIC CHOCOLATE

100g

EASTCOTE STUDIOS LIMITED
249 KENSAL ROAD, LONDON W10 5DB
Tel: 081-969 3739 Fax: 081-960 1836

Ingredients: Organic Cocoa Mass (70%), Brown Cane Sugar, Real Vanilla, Emulsifier: Soya Lecithin
Contains a minimum of 70% organic cocoa solids.

HEALTH WARNING:
This chocolate may cause loose behaviour.

Chocolate made for and distributed by Green & Black's, 222 Kensal Road, London W10

Philip made his own chocolate bar wrappers as part of a studio promotion.

1988

In 1989, Zeus fulfilled the second half of the promise he had made to himself when Nina Hagen walked in through the green door to start work on her eponymous fourth long-player as a solo artist. She had just signed a new deal with Mercury Records and Zeus says:

Her story is very, very colourful! From East Germany originally, she eventually came to Berlin and started a band, and she immediately became a star. Then after the band she wanted her freedom to do things on her own and she went to Amsterdam for a long time and then she started hanging out in London with her friends in The Slits, Ari Up and her mum Nora who was Johnny Rotten's wife. She was a big part of the whole punk scene. And that was sort of her wildest times. I met her actually when I was recording a duet with her and Udo for his album. A track by the way I love! It's called 'Vopo' (short for Volkspolizist = people's policeman) which she did in one, first take. The song is an important sign of the times back then: about an East German border soldier who is there to stop people going from East to West Germany, if necessary by shooting them. Udo sings it from the point of view of somebody living directly in a cheap grey mansard loft overlooking the border and always observing a particular soldier – good-looking, great shape, etc – I think Udo's house intellectual had helped with the lyrics. And it was sexy, full of homosexual innuendo.

A certain desire opens the door for the fantasy: throw away the gun and passionately bite his lips, etc. And Nina's part... it was outrageous! It's a great document, because a short while later people tore down this wall. And that's how we met. Her manager was there, and I said to him, I'd really like to do some more work with Nina. And he said, 'We can arrange that'. I started the first Nina album a few months later and we did the pre-production/soul-searching in my programming suite Voice Versa down the road from Eastcote at Portobello Green, tucked away under the Westway. Many songs were written between Nina, Billy Liesegang and me. After a few weeks we moved into Eastcote. First of all, Nina installed her personal altar upstairs in Studio 2. And I remember Philip liked it, he was really into it.

To say that Nina Hagen has a colourful story is not an exaggeration. Her journey from East Germany to London started at age 11 when her mother, Eva-Marie Hagen, who was an actress, married anti-establishment critic and dissident Wolf Biermann. He was a singer, poet and activist and became like a father to Nina. After being deemed a traitor by the Stasi, the long-time Communist Party member was stripped of his East German citizenship and exiled whilst he was playing a gig in Cologne (West Germany) in 1977. He had been given approval by the DDR authorities to do so, but the expulsion of Biermann had been planned beforehand and when trying to return home he was refused re-entry.

Eva-Marie and Nina soon followed him and emigrated, first to Hamburg and then spent time in London where she got to know The Slits and fell in love with ska and punk music. She moved back to Germany and found a place to live in Berlin, where she formed a band and made *Nina Hagen Band*, the album that when released in 1978 made her the German queen of punk. The band were wildly successful but made only one more album before Nina left, moved to Los Angeles, become a mother and released her first solo album, *NunSexMonkRock*. It was like a punk rock opera on vinyl. Mainly in English it was wild and unhinged.

When Nina started working with Zeus in 1989 she was already an international star, trendsetter and fashion icon. The first album they did together was called *Nina Hagen* and featured an eclectic group of musicians and creatives in the credits, including New Wave singer Lene

THE SORT OF PLACE YOU CALL IN ON YOUR WAY TO FAME

1989

Lovich, Lemmy from Motörhead, Martin Ditcham from Man Jumping on percussion and Richard Niles conducting an orchestra. Putting together the artwork was Nina's friend and enfant terrible of the fashion world, Jean Paul Gaultier. Zeus continues with a story about one particular song from the album:

When we were starting to work on 'Where's the Party' she invited her friend Lene Lovich. We decided to get the feel of a real party, and Nina asked me to get Lemmy to come along, which turned out to be possible. His then label Great Western Records was also just down the road and Doug Smith, the label boss and manager, agreed, and asked me to call Lemmy, but not before 7 pm. Lemmy happily was ready to contribute some vocals under the conditions: one bottle of Jack D, a big bottle of ice-cold Coke and the guarantee that after the recording he could take Nina out to a club. Well, it all worked out great – his vibe and voice fitted amazingly to the atmosphere of the track. When we were finished doing the vocal recordings, Lemmy looked at me and asked: 'Can I play some bass on this track?' How could I say no? What followed was the loudest bass guitar which ever came out of the studio – he basically played a solo from start to end; I used just a few little runs in the mix – and wish now I could get my hands on those multi-tracks...

I remember first hearing Nina Hagen in the early '80s when I was 13. I had just discovered some Swedish punk and New Wave bands through my music teacher at school. He was called Svante Nylund and was in a band called Stormakt Gul, and they had just released their own album. It was a great album: New Wave and ska, with Swedish lyrics. I was really impressed, and I still remember the album cover which was an appropriation of the sleeve for John Lennon and Yoko Ono's *Double Fantasy*, but with the photo being two of the guys in the band kissing. And the album title was *Ge Oss Pengar* (Give

Eastcote engineer Ingo Vauk with Billy Leisengang and Zeus B Held.

Nina Hagen in Studio 1.

Us Money). Svante played The Clash and Elvis Costello during music class, helped me start a band, and allowed us to rehearse in the music room after school. At band practice we listened to Ebba Grön, KSMB and the Dead Kennedys and I tried my best to write provocative lyrics. Although a lot of the American music I had heard as a young kid was of course protest music too, I was older now and understood enough for this to be my first real introduction to music with an activist edge.

Starting my own music career in Stockholm in the '80s I thought I knew Neneh's story quite well. I've always considered her an inspiration musically and also as a real symbol of strength and independence. When 'Buffalo Stance' was released, I remember seeing the video on MTV and couldn't quite believe that she was actually Swedish... she was too cool! And of course, when it came to her music, her references were from a whole other and much bigger world. Her musical inspiration came from so many places, from her family and from friends she made along the way.

Neneh grew up with her mother, Monika 'Moki' Karlsson, who was a visual artist, and her stepfather, the American jazz musician Don Cherry, who married Moki when Neneh was still a young child. The family lived in a converted school-house in southern Sweden, but when Don went on tour the whole family would often come with him. Although the house in Skåne remained the base, they moved around a lot, and in the early '70s to New York, meeting new friends and it's easy to imagine how that would influence the music she would go on to make. In 1979, Don goes on tour with the all girl punk band The Slits and through that connection Neneh, who is then 15, becomes friends with Ari Up, who she eventually ends up sharing a squat with in Battersea. After joining The Slits as a backing vocalist, she gets to know The Pop Group, which is where her connection to Bristol and the music scene there starts. It's a long and amazing story

in itself, but to sum up two-thirds of a decade in one sentence, Neneh would go on to join Rip, Rig and Panic, be part of the New Age Steppers, become friends with The Wild Bunch and collaborate on various projects including The The, before meeting Cameron McVey in 1987. The two of them became partners not only in music but in life. It's hard to exaggerate the influence they would have on UK music in the following few years, some of which connects with our Eastcote story in the coming chapters. At this point, it's 1989 and they continue the work on *Raw Like Sushi* upstairs in Studio 2. I can't help noticing the similarities and threads binding it together with Nina Hagen's story, who is also regularly at Eastcote at this time. I ask Neneh if they ever met at the studio and she says: *Yes, we used to see each other around and about over the years. She's always been good fun to hang with. I like her*.

My mind keeps going back and forth between trying to focus on the writing and memories of being a teenager in Stockholm. How alien I felt, but still convinced that all I had to do was 'figure it out' to fit in better. There are so many things I'd love to ask Neneh but one thing in particular is how she related back to Sweden having seen so much of the world and being part of such a big cultural moment and musical movement in the UK. She tells me:

There's two Swedens for me: 1) my family home in Skåne in the south where I grew up and where I'm writing this from now, which is a beautiful forest place surrounded by farms and trees and friends from my childhood, and people who (like all folks from the south) are very at peace with the way life is. And 2) Stockholm, which I found it a lot harder to relate to, having not grown up there. But eventually we went to live there in 2004 for a few years to put two of our kids into school and grew to understand and eventually love it, and in fact as a family we owe Stockholm a huge debt of gratitude for taking

us in at a difficult time in our family's life story. We never, either of us, managed to find our place in the Swedish music scene. I think most folks there find us quite 'quirky'!

And there it is. There are places where all the quirky folks belong. Even if at times it's hard to believe, and especially when you're young and trying your best to be a part of something. One such place could be a converted school-house in Skåne. One might be a youth club in a suburb somewhere that hasn't yet been closed for lack of funding. Another might be a club stage in New York where Billy Cobham slaps his Birkenstocks together at the Mahavishnu Orchestra's first-ever gig, with a young Philip Bagenal by the mixing desk, trying to get through his first-ever gig as their sound engineer. And without any doubt, one such place can be found on Kensal Road. Built by Philip and kept alive for decades by hundreds of quirky souls making music together. They are the ones he built it for and he tells me:

I wasn't really interested in what happens with a tape once it goes out the door. The whole doings of trying to market a product and put together deals with record companies, that was never my thing. I am simply not concerned about what record companies want. I want my bands and clients to leave the building with the music that they wanted to make. That's what it should be, and they shouldn't compromise. I mean, we had some pretty weird clients and there were some stories to be heard about what used to go on here. And studios are places of high excitement.

This was Philip's house. Open to those who found it and a safe port in the madness of it all. Or as I heard Philip call it once: 'The sort of place you call in on your way to fame'. ∎

Nina Hagen and Lemmy of Motörhead out clubbing (Photo: Derek Ridgers).

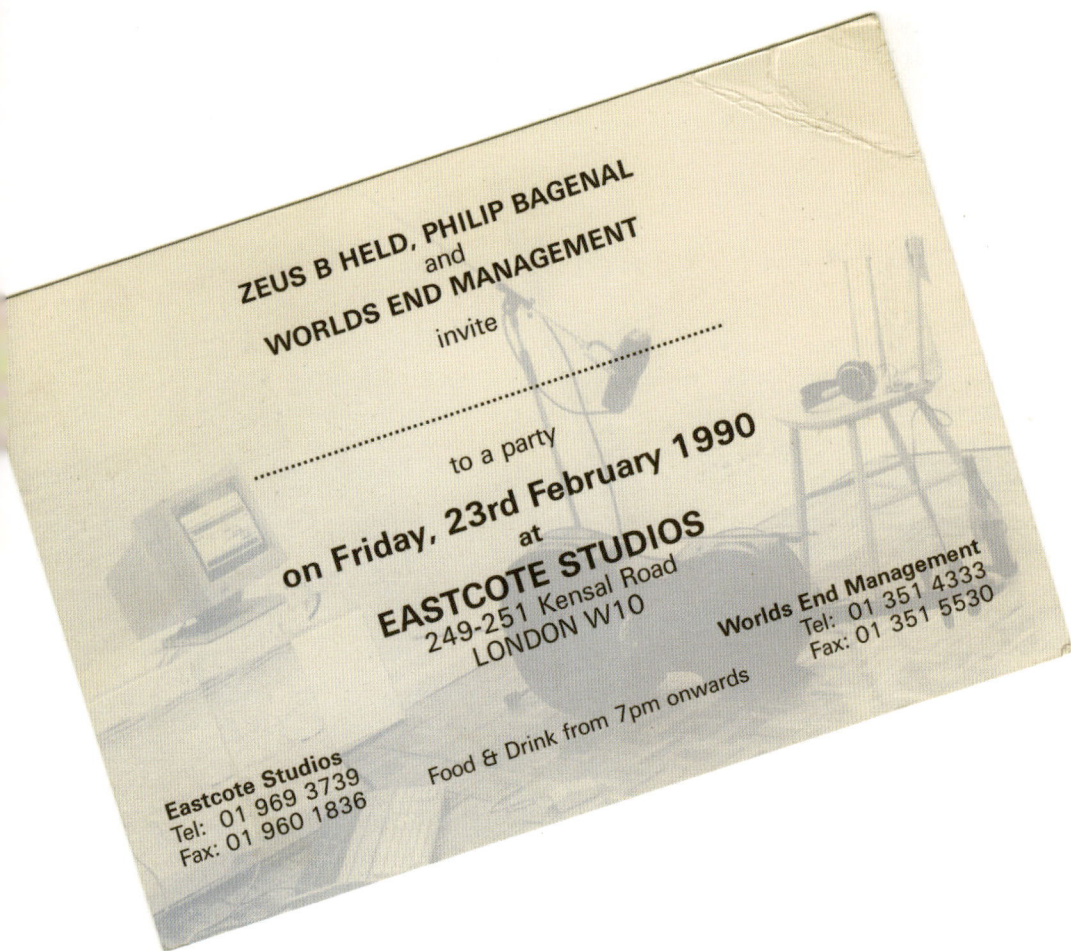

ZEUS B HELD, PHILIP BAGENAL
and
WORLDS END MANAGEMENT
invite ....
to a party
on Friday, 23rd February 1990
at
EASTCOTE STUDIOS
249-251 Kensal Road
LONDON W10

Worlds End Management
Tel: 01 351 4333
Fax: 01 351 5530

Eastcote Studios
Tel: 01 969 3739
Fax: 01 960 1836

Food & Drink from 7pm onwards

On 23rd February 1990, Philip along with Zeus and his management celebrated the 10th anniversary of the studios and I wish someone had taken pictures at that party. Who might have been here? Most likely many of the characters written about in the previous chapters and some who will feature in the ones to come.

From being Chaz's personal studio, Eastcote was now a regular destination for musicians and artists from around the country and beyond. Philip always put the artists and musicians first, but it seems producers, managers and labels alike were quite happy to let them spend their time and recording budgets there too. This is the time when Eastcote really became the preferred playground for many London-based producers.

Cameron McVey had made Eastcote his creative home, and together with Neneh they had brought with them Tim Simenon, Jonny Dollar and The Wild Bunch. Neneh and Cameron explain:

We knew Tim from the club scene and got to work with him when he produced 'Buffalo Stance', and then we toured with him on the Bomb the Bass tour. And Jonny, I brought across from Sam Therapy over in Canalot to engineer for me, then he gradually made it through the ranks in our production company and Cam gave him a production credit on Massive Attack's Blue Lines. We miss him (may he rest in peace). He was with us through a helluva lot of stuff for many years.

Jonathan Peter Sharp – 'Jonny Dollar' – was a recording engineer in another studio across the road when he met Neneh and Cameron. He first came to work at Eastcote with The Wild Bunch on *Raw Like Sushi* and when they started on *Blue Lines* it was as Massive Attack's producer alongside Cameron. The collaboration with Neneh continued through her first three albums and on the 1994 single '7 Seconds' with Youssou N'Dour. Jonny tragically passed away much too soon in 2009. Out of the many great records he wrote and produced over the years, perhaps 'Unfinished Sympathy' stands out as the special moment. In an article in *The Independent* following Dollar's death, Robert Del Naja writes:

Jonny was really important. There was a chemistry between us which made the first album. We were bringing the DJ world we were coming from – how we used to present music, cutting up on decks on a sound system, chucking instrumentals with vocals, very much a hip-hop way of sampling small pieces of music – and then linking them and making them into whole tracks. It was a completely new way of working. Jonny and Cameron were vital because they took something very raw and helped to fashion it into something a lot more sophisticated.

DRUMMIE? HE WAS ALWAYS THERE

90

He continues:

He was really integral to the whole project. He was the person who provided us with the key to finishing several tracks. Jonny had a very dry sense of humour which suited us because we're a bunch of piss-takers really. He knew how to handle us, he could take it and give it back.

Del Naja and the rest of Massive Attack had been camping out for months at Cameron and Neneh's house in Kensal Rise, writing songs. It was with their support and creative input that Tricky, 3D and Daddy G eventually signed a record deal with Circa Records. And via the same route, Massive Attack found their way to Eastcote during its 10th anniversary year, where they continued working on what would become *Blue Lines*.

Zeus was at work again with Nina Hagen and various other projects. And every other week another producer came through the doors who hadn't worked at Eastcote before. Toni Halliday and Dean Garcia's alt-rock outfit Curve were recording at Eastcote this year with producer Steve Osborne, whose relationship with Eastcote has continued for decades now. Through Steve, Alan Moulder and Flood entered the green door, and later so would Brian Eno and Trevor Horn.

When artists come to Eastcote, they often look around the site in amazement and say 'Oh wow, I never knew this was here!' After 40 years it's still a bit of a hidden secret, its existence spread through word of mouth. And it feels like making a spelling mistake to call the artists and producers who worked here our clients. They are more like a family. An ever-growing and changing one, from mixed backgrounds and musical roots. Some were here more than others. Cameron says: *Drummie was always there. And Eastcote's client list of West London music royalty puts Sarm to shame*. You can even trace the generations. Through Cameron came Tim Simenon, and between them they shared a 'living room' in Studio 2. Through Tim came a whole

new extended family of writers and producers to join or help out the Bomb the Bass project.

From the mid-'80s and well into the 2000s, the booking and administration office at Eastcote was run by Emma Feather. I ask her why she thinks it was that so many artists and producers came back to Eastcote again and again. She tells me: *This question is simple to answer: Eastcote was a family. The studio was comfortable and in a way I suppose it could be considered Bohemian.* She tells me about when Philip first decided he needed help with the office and took out an ad to find the right person, and I get a perfect example of just that:

Philip interviewed me for the book-keeping job he had advertised sitting in front of the MCI in Studio 1. Studio 2 did not exist at the time. I didn't really say much, he sat there divulging his vision for the studio, which included his wish that it would one day be as successful as the Townhouse. Unfortunately, this was somewhat lost on me at the time as I wasn't then aware of the Townhouse – not that I let on. A few weeks later he called and offered me the job, prefacing it with the fact that I was not his first choice. The person he originally had offered the job to asked for more than he was prepared to pay! After a couple of days' consideration I accepted the job as I needed the extra work. On my first day at the studio, I arrived to find Philip had forgotten I was starting. He rummaged around and found some bricks and a piece of hardboard, placed it in what became the lobby to Studio 2 and that was my desk!

Some in the Eastcote family would keep re-finding their way here by various routes. Like Kerry Hopwood. He was exceptionally good at programming synthesizers. Zeus had always kept his smaller studio under the Westway as a place for his synthesizers and to do writing and pre-production. When he first set it up, he had been told that Kerry was someone who could help him. They bought gear for the studio and Kerry kept working with Zeus for years and of course got to know Eastcote very well in the process. On a Zoom call that starts with some technical difficulties he tells me:

I remember one day working with John Fox, who was in Ultravox, up at his house in Highgate. And there was a knock on the door, and it was a chap called Tim Simenon from Bomb the Bass who was there with his record company owner. And basically it was Emma Feather, who worked at Eastcote, who had put Tim up to trying to find me. He needed a guy to help him out in the studio as an engineer and to do programming. So that's how it happened that I went with Tim for years and we ended up producing stuff and being Bomb the Bass and doing all sorts of silliness.

Soon Kerry would not have time to work with Zeus anymore, as he became an integral part of Tim's crew. They would spend a lot of time at Eastcote and in Digiland, their own space at Walters. And talking to Kerry, it sounds like from that point they didn't have many days off during the better part of a decade. ∎

Power nap before that term was invented.

Producers, engineers and others from pinboard in studio lounge. Among those pictured are Kerry Hopwood and Dave Clayton (Bomb The Bass, Depeche Mode), Giles Martin, Anti Uusimaki (Eastcote engineer), Jonny Dollar (in winter hat), Dave Holden (by big modular synth), Shiro Sigasu (film composer), Phil Vinall (engineer), Richard Norris (The Grid), Peggy (Eastcote receptionist) and a picture of Lulu, Philip and her producers in Studio 2 in the late '80s.

EASTCOTE STUDIOS LIMITED

249 KENSAL ROAD, LONDON W10 5DB   TEL: 0181-969 3739   FAX: 0181-960 1836

Artist   Client

Title

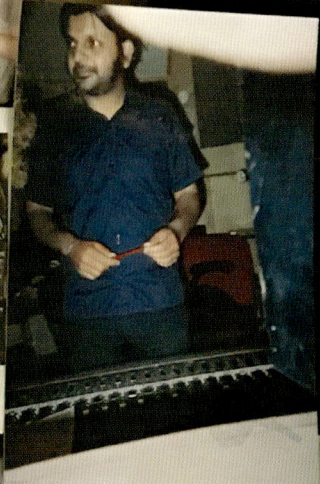

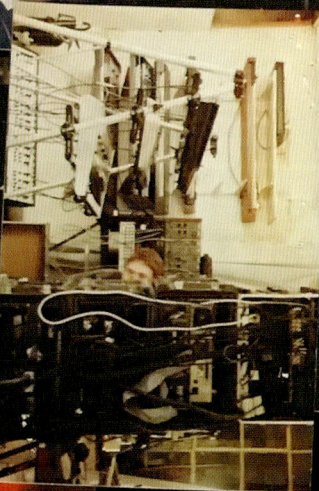

DAVE CLAYTON

Startled of London

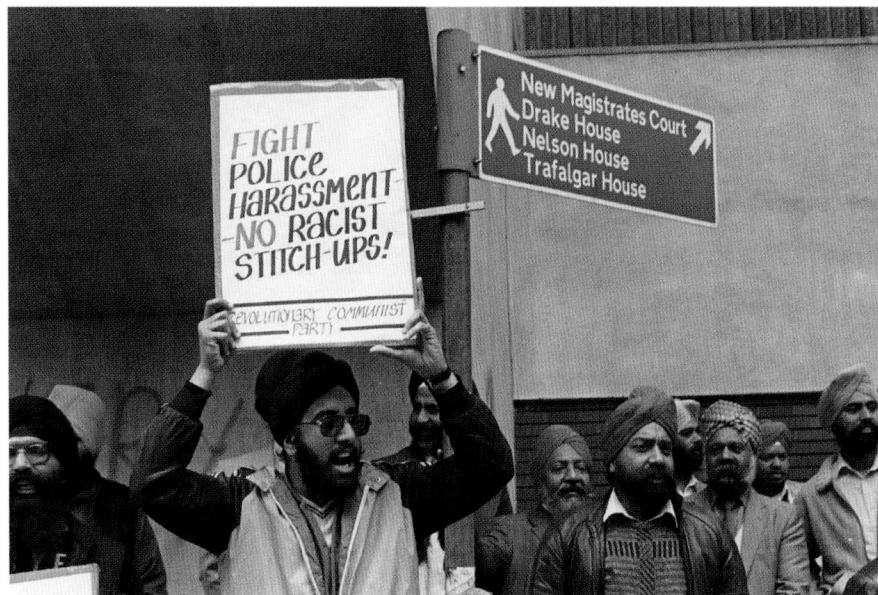

TRIP HOP AND SYNTH RIFFS

In 1991, Massive Attack released their album *Blue Lines* and in doing so put Bristol's vibrant and multicultural music scene firmly on the world map. Bristol has a murky and unresolved history as the busiest port for the British slave trade, and deep connections to the Caribbean. The music made there at the time had a distinct and subversive sound that was different from what went on in London. With its roots in dub and reggae but also in post-punk and ska, the Bristol underground scene flourished through its sound-system culture.

Throughout the '70s, race relations in the city had become increasingly strained because of local campaigning by the National Front, poor housing conditions and more frequent use by the police of Stop and Search laws, disproportionately directed at Afro-Caribbean youth. After this culminated in 1980 with a riot in the St Pauls district of the city, the authorities had to act on the discontent, and by

the following year the so called 'sus' law was repealed and new rules were brought in. Now it was possible for the community in St Pauls to self-police and sound systems started playing music all night. On the streets and in derelict buildings, parties were going until the early morning, and with the freedom of not being regulated as strictly as in other parts of the UK the scene gained its own momentum. Both art and music in Bristol have an intriguing history. Despite the racial tensions and the city's troubled history, it was an inclusive scene. Teenagers who had grown up with the sound-system culture, black and white, were all partaking. In 1981, the influential post-punk pioneers The Pop Group split up and in their wake several 'collective' bands like Rip, Rig and Panic and New Age Steppers followed, blending influences wildly. US hip hop was now also in the mix and the sound systems played ever more eclectic music. You can probably see here the threads to the Wild

St Pauls Carnival, Bristol, 1985. (Photo: Beezer)

Anti-police demonstration in Bristol in 1984. (Photo: Beezer)

Bunch and Neneh Cherry, and how they run all the way through this brilliantly innovative time in British pop culture. *Blue Lines* would bring Jonny Dollar to Eastcote, and also connect the studio with several other Bristol artists in the years to come, including Portishead.

After the successes with Bomb The Bass and a worldwide hit with Neneh Cherry's 'Buffalo Stance', Tim, who was still only 24 years old, was quickly becoming very in demand. He needed more space and was relying on help from the main Bomb The Bass 'band members' ('collaborators' might be a better description), to keep up with the increasing workload. Kerry Hopwood was working with Tim full-time now and this year they teamed up with another young talented writer and producer, Guy Sigsworth. Apart from recording at Eastcote, Tim and Kerry also built their own studio facing Kensal Road. Philip had first set the room up for George Kajanus from the glam-rock band

Sailor, but when Bomb the Bass took it over it was gutted and reconfigured in the same 'living room' style as Studio 2.

One of the records Tim and his team worked on in 1991 at Eastcote was Seal's 'Crazy'. I remember listening to it on repeat when it came out. I loved the song and the sound was amazing. One of those genre-defying records, it was neither rock, pop or soul: it was all of them and the production by Trevor Horn and Guy Sigsworth was ambitious to say the least. I had no idea that it started on Kensal Road and when Kerry tells me about the beginnings of that record, I'm all ears. And something he tells me about Guy Sigsworth sums up the fact that regardless of studios, equipment or any one particular way of working, a great record can be made in many different ways. And sometimes the limitations might inspire the outcome:

Do you know Guy Sigsworth? Well, he was in Bomb the Bass as well and did at least

Tim Simenon at Communiity Arts Centre The Tabernacle in Notting Hill, London, in 1986. (Photo: Beezer)

The Wild Bunch at the Dug Out, Bristol, in 1984. Left to right: Milo, Daddy G, Nellee, Willie Wee, 3D. (Photo: Beezer)

Massive Attack, *Blue Lines*, Wild Bunch/Virgin,1991

one album with us. And because of the link to Guy, Seal was very keen to be Bomb the Bass's singer, and we were of course very keen for Seal to be our singer. We thought at long last we'd actually have a focus.

Guy and Seal were working in a small studio on the other side of the road. I can't remember what it was called. Seal was Adamski's singer, you know, and was singing in clubs and doing weird sketchy gigs around London. But we saw A) a superstar in Seal. And B) Guy was a very interesting writer. And really, he did everything on a D110 and a little sampler. I mean he literally just had two 1U racks and he came to us and played 'Crazy' that they had written. It was all there, you know the catchy synth riff, all with system exclusive, in the shittiest little Roland boxes. It was all he could afford, but he'd essentially made the entire first Seal album on those small machines. He got his head completely inside them and created some amazing sounds.

But then I remember being in a kebab shop in Notting Hill Gate with Seal and he said, 'You know, Trevor Horn is very interested in me'. And I said, 'Well we don't have Trevor's pockets, we're sort of an indie band and I'm sure he's offering you the sun and the moon and the stars. But in the end we did Crazy at Eastcote. I can't remember if we did anything else with Seal there, but we moved down to Sarm, and Trevor would waltz in and out and listen to things and then bugger off. We sort of left it, and when it came out it sounded completely different. There are bits of what we did on there somewhere. The arrangement was much the same and a lot of the things were in there. On the 12-inch there's a remix which is exactly where we left it, but the thing with Trev is, he had to go through so many incarnations of the song. It was a kind of surreal thing, because he was a huge hero to Tim and me, but a very strange person to work with.

Trevor Horn is another producer who came and worked at Eastcote from time to time. His own studio, Sarm, was the crown jewel of West London studios and he was already an almost mythical figure. His production of 'Crazy' is in a different key from the track Tim Simenon recorded. It's glossy in that restrained and cool way that became his signature sound. On the 12-inch you can listen to the earlier incarnation named 'Krazy', which is actually quite similar. I ask Trevor about his memories of Eastcote, Philip and the recording of 'Crazy':

Philip is one of those people that seems likes he's content, he built his place to a level, and it was working. He seemed like doing something he loved to do. If you look in to great studios there's often someone like that, keeping it all together. I came to Eastcote mostly when Sarm was booked out, and always with my own engineer so I didn't work with Philip in the studio. But he was always around.

One of my clearest memories of coming to Eastcote was when we were working on 'Crazy'. I'd hired Tim Simenon to produce the record with Guy Sigsworth. Guy was at that time a great keyboard player and programmer and a very interesting guy. Tim had done something I really liked, 'Buffalo Stance' with Neneh Cherry. But I don't think either of them knew how to handle Seal. I remember coming to the studio a few times, and then I ended up taking it to America with me. The session had 160 tracks. The most I'd ever done. I don't know how we managed to do it, because back then it was not all digital, and it was a lot of stuff. I spent ages finishing the version that Tim started, using Guy's synth arrangement. But then I started again. I had played it to a few people over at Warner Brothers, and they were interested, but I knew it didn't have 'that thing'… yet.

So I went back to it. I kept the middle bit and I slowed it down. And to compensate for slowing it down I took it up a key. And then I got them to rewrite parts of the song because it wasn't complete. There was a part they were jamming in the end, and I got them to write some lyrics for it… 'in a sky full of people', that bit. It was brilliant. I had the first-ever sound tools rig, and I was in LA working on a film soundtrack, and 'Crazy' was my hobby. It took ages to finish, to get the middle 8 right, and finish a specific one bar link back into the chorus.

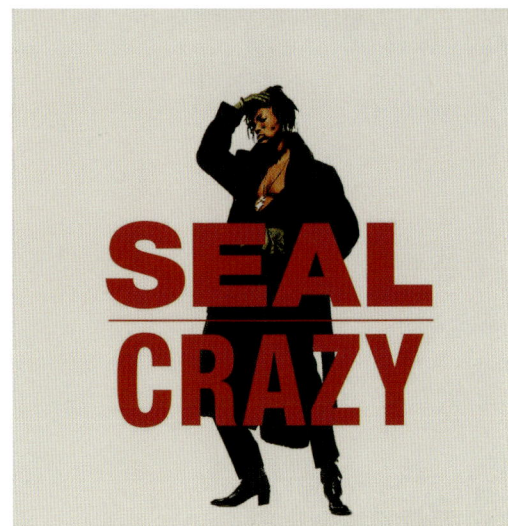

Trevor Horn had created a road map of sorts for contemporary pop music with 'Video Killed The Radio Star'. Tim Simenon and the production team he had assembled were just getting started. They would make many incredible records at Eastcote over the coming years, and Philip had found a group of technology-savvy musicians to talk to about all kinds of synthesizers and equipment. Recording technology was evolving quickly and Philip was never a conservationist. The studio was known for its wealth of analogue recording equipment and instruments. But this is the era of sampling and samplers. And in the UK in the early '90s, more than any other piece of equipment, it's about the AKAI S1000. ∎

Seal receives a disque d'or for 'Crazy' in Paris in 1991.

DON'T GO SHOPLIFTING AT VIRGIN RECORDS

It's a rather rough week and late October by now. Another half-lockdown has been announced by the government and I've just received some bad news about a relative who's passed away suddenly. I've concluded that writing is an obsessive pursuit, much like music, and days and nights are blurring together whilst I'm getting some familiar signs that I'm drifting away from the day-to-day world around me. But in the sobering reality of Covid London anno 2020 it's quite nice floating around in this exciting research project about glorious days gone by. Records of studio bookings and administration have been hard to find from the '80s and 1992 is the first year where we have a complete booking calendar filled out and it's in front of me. A big wall calendar showing how the studios are so fully booked that the entries are mostly abbreviations instead of full names, and not even Philip can remember what they all mean. I find some interesting threads to follow:

Maxi Priest made his third album, *Fe Real*, at Eastcote that year. Maxi is one of only two UK reggae artist to have a Billboard Number 1 single (with 'Close To You'). *Fe Real* won a Grammy for best reggae album and featured a long list of top musicians including Sly Dunbar on drums and as one of the producers.

Nina Hagen is back in the studio again. Probably to do some writing with Zeus and Billy Leisegang this time, as she was now recording with a new producer, Phil Manzanera from Roxy Music. I know Phil has a connection with Eastcote going back to the beginnings with Chaz, and I get a message through to him to ask if they recorded at Eastcote. He says his Nina recordings in 1992 took place at another studio in London.

Brian Eno recorded his 12th studio album, *Nerve Net*, at Eastcote in 1992.

Maxi Priest made his third album, *Fa Real*, at the studio in 1992.

'1992

But he did record at Eastcote twenty years later with the late and legendary Kevin Ayers. He was an influential part of the English psychedelic music movement that started with Soft Machine in the late 60's and went on to have a long career. They worked on Ayer's last solo album *The Unfairground* at Eastcote.

Also back in the studios are electronic dance outfit The Grid with David Ball from Soft Cell and Richard Norris. This is the year they released the album *456* on Virgin Records. They were already regular clients at Eastcote and would continue to work here for many years, including on the album *Evolver* and the single 'Swamp Thing' that became a big dance hit for them on Deconstruction Records.

One of the songs on *456* is called 'Heartbeat' and that year it was remixed by Brian Eno who was spending a fair bit of time at Eastcote working on his album *Nerve Net*, which he had started recording the previous year. An insistently rhythmic album where Eno features guitarist Robert Fripp on most of the songs and where he collaborates with his protégé and engineer Markus Dravs. I'm on a call with Dravs and he tells me that *Nerve Net* was the first recording he remembers where he was credited as producer. And it is as a producer he will go on to become another important part of Eastcote's history. About the sessions that year with Brian he says:

I think that was my first co-production credit. It started with Brian doing a lot of remixes. He would come in and do some ambient tracks and a bass track, and a track of this and that. But sometimes he wouldn't finish putting it all in a structure before he left and would leave me to work on it. And he introduced me to a lot of the Eventide effect stuff that he was doing at the time. He would leave at around five or six and I would 'stay behind', which was great, because I could sit there and try things out. It was the early days of the H3000 with all those dreamy sounds, string modular and it was

74

1992

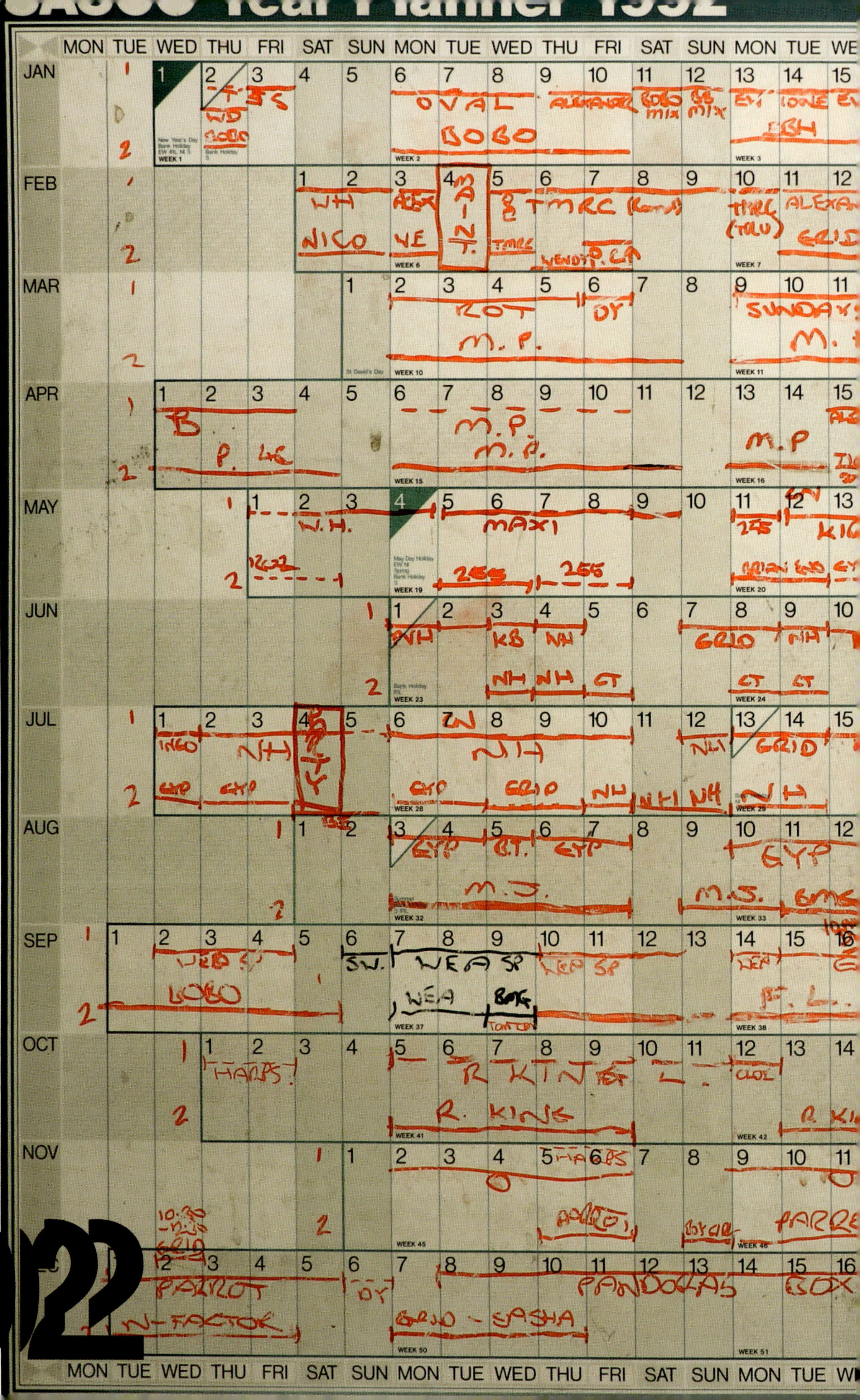

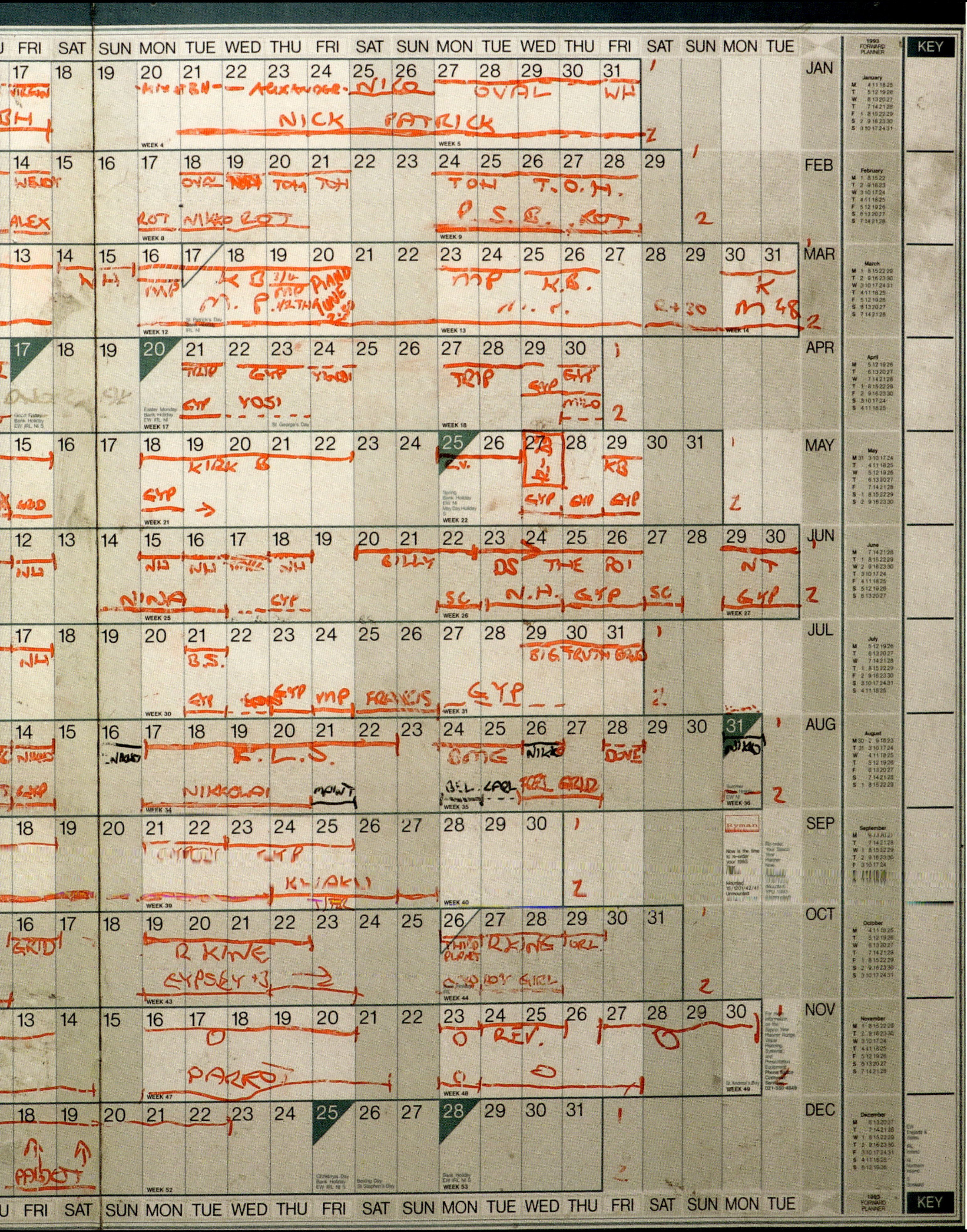

1993 FORWARD PLANNER — KEY

JAN	
FEB	
MAR	
APR	
MAY	
JUN	
JUL	
AUG	
SEP	
OCT	
NOV	
DEC	

WEEK 4, WEEK 5, WEEK 8, WEEK 9, WEEK 12, WEEK 13, WEEK 14, WEEK 17, WEEK 18, WEEK 21, WEEK 22, WEEK 25, WEEK 26, WEEK 27, WEEK 30, WEEK 31, WEEK 34, WEEK 35, WEEK 36, WEEK 39, WEEK 40, WEEK 43, WEEK 44, WEEK 47, WEEK 48, WEEK 49, WEEK 52, WEEK 53

75

1993 FORWARD PLANNER — KEY

very exciting, especially having Brian show me all of that. So we would spend loads of time fucking around with the sounds... well, I used to call it fucking around. Brian would probably say 'exploring the aural spectrum' or something like that.

Markus laughs and tries to remember who else he recorded at Eastcote early on.

Definitely with Einar from The Sugarcubes, we did more stuff too for One Little Indian. I think maybe with Björk. I think we were in there with her. But what I remember most about Eastcote is Philip and Zeus. I met Zeus when I was assisting at Westside. He was there with Nina Hagen and we were both German and started talking. So I started going to visit them at Eastcote. You know, coming to a place like that as an assistant or engineer and really be treated like a human was great. Philip always took his time to explain things, he was patient, demanding but not unnecessarily strict like some other producers, you just wanted to do things right for him. And Zeus, I really got on with both of them. Philip is a great cook. Do you know Schwarzbrot? I mean now you can get dark rye bread everywhere but back then you were kind of stuck with whatever they had at Greggs [bakery]. But Philip baked fresh Schwarzbrot for us, and you know being from Germany, it was amazing.

To me that sums up one important aspect of what Eastcote and in particular Philip are about. He is a teacher in an education system that should be the template for all schools. No fear of making mistakes. No forceful imposing of authority. No bullying of the new kid.

Imagine going to that school.

Maybe because of where my head is at on this particular day, or just because I'm looking for another angle, I get stuck in reading about the '90s, both in music and society. And it's clear that the glorious times gone by were not always that glorious. These were days of hardship, challenges and tragedy too. The Gulf War has just ended and the last fires burning from oil wells on the fields of Kuwait have been extinguished. But rage in the aftermath of the invasion of Iraq is brewing. And if we should ever feel that ours are times of extraordinary division, just consider the furore around Salman Rushdie in the early '90s and how positions were taken, not only between cultures but within our own, trying to be a liberal, Western and democratic society. Fear of contracting AIDS is rife everywhere and recreational drugs are getting heavier. In clubs, the weighing scale is moving from the old hashish, booze and weed and tipping rapidly towards pills, skunk, cocaine and cheap opioids from the Afghan poppy fields. Heroin addiction is now at an all-time peak and in a few years between the late '80s and the early '90s in the UK opioid overdoses increase almost five-fold. And our oasis on Kensal Road was not immune to the times. For each musician trying to get clean, there's a dealer, waiting outside the NA meetings in the area, ready to re-supply. There are new protest singers with new politics, competing for space in the media with easy-listening pop stars, and the booming success of hypnotic dance tracks. All kinds of music are being made at Eastcote, successful, interesting, generic and some forgotten. And from my own experience of making records for three decades I believe that it's in that relentless pursuit and tireless ambition where now and then magic happens.

Amongst the things I find along the journey of researching this year is a story that puts the focus on the hundreds of records made at the studio that no one has ever heard of. On all the creative effort that ended up in someone's collection of old tapes, floppy disks or maybe remaining only as a musician's distant and blurry memory of something they once were part of. The Grid have made many successful dance records at our studio, and as I put their name along with Eastcote into my search engine, a recent and nostalgic Facebook post by Richard Norris sums up the randomness of it all. It's funny and reminds me of all the records I have worked on that for one reason or another never saw the light of day. Quoting from the post:

The lockdown does strange things to your brain. Today for example, I woke up with a song in my head that was squatting and wouldn't leave. It featured a sub On-U sound dub backing, alongside a messed three-part harmony vocal, singing 'Shoplifter! Shoplifter!' in a melodic and soulful way. 'What fresh hell is this?' I wondered and then it all came slowly back. It was the long-forgotten Grid track 'Shoplifter', one of the only tracks myself and Mr David Ball made that never came out. Here's why.

'Shoplifter' was recorded at our favourite studio, Eastcote in Kensal Rd, London W10. The road was home to Eastcote, and also our publishing company, record company, design department, club promo company and many more. We spent a fair amount of time during the recording sessions at The Village Inn, a plain-looking boozer a few doors down from the studio, where we had regular 'meetings'. These invariably led to dreaming up some insane ideas for the album. At one point we decided we needed a tap-dancer on it. Then JJ from the Art of Noise came down in a fetching bow tie to play the saw.

This brings back memories. The Village Inn was our local too when I started recording on Kensal Road regularly. And some mad ideas were certainly born there, along with some rather painful hangovers. We sat in the steamy and loud indoors in the winter, and in summer we'd be outside, around the wooden tables or on the pavement. On occasion artists or producers who had consumed a few too many drinks would pay 25 quid for one of the little bedrooms they had upstairs to get some sleep before being back and ready to record the following morning. Now it's gone. Bought by someone who also

'19.

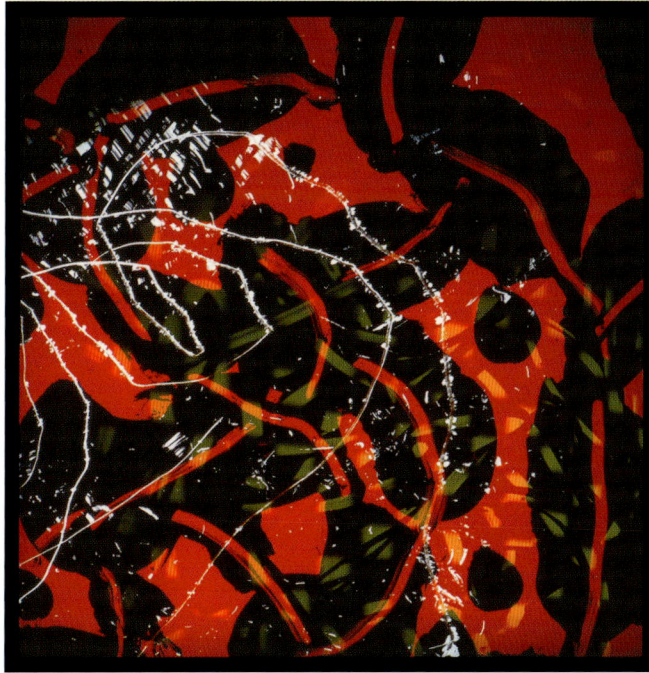

bought the only other watering-hole in close proximity, The Cobden Club. A brilliant place, an old working-men's club, with booze, decent food and live music across several floors that had been there for a century. Its fate was to become a private residence, and as for The Village Inn, rumour has it that it was bought to be the oversized granny flat. The story about 'Shoplifter' continues like this:

So, we devised a plan to record a song entitled 'Shoplifter'. I have had a rather senior Shakespearian actor friend with a voice like Laurence Olivier after a couple of shandys. Straight out of the sitcom Toast. *We persuaded him that his next lead role was to be the singer and main character in 'Shoplifter'. He played the part of a gentleman of a certain age with a large coat and a twinkle in his eye who liked to roam along Oxford Street stealing things. His favourite place to steal was, as the lyric tells us, 'Mr Branson's shop' – the Virgin Megastore, from which he stole prodigiously, without snobbery of taste. He describes going into Mr Branson's shop and stealing 'Elaine and Jimmy Pa[i]ge', and then lists a whole litany of other recording artists in the style of a Hamlet soliloquy. Added to this, we decided P.P. Arnold should come in and sing the 'Shoplifter' refrain, which she did with great style and grace. We thought we were on to something. The Village Inn sessions hadn't been in vain! We would only have to hand it in to the record label and wait for the limo to* Top Of the Pops. *There was only one problem. We were signed to Virgin Records. Proprietor – one Mr R. Branson.*

The label took one listen and said it would never be released.

It's languished in the vaults ever since. ■

Brian Eno, *Nerve Net*, Warner Bros. Records, 1992.   The Grid, *Evolver*, Deconstruction, 1994.

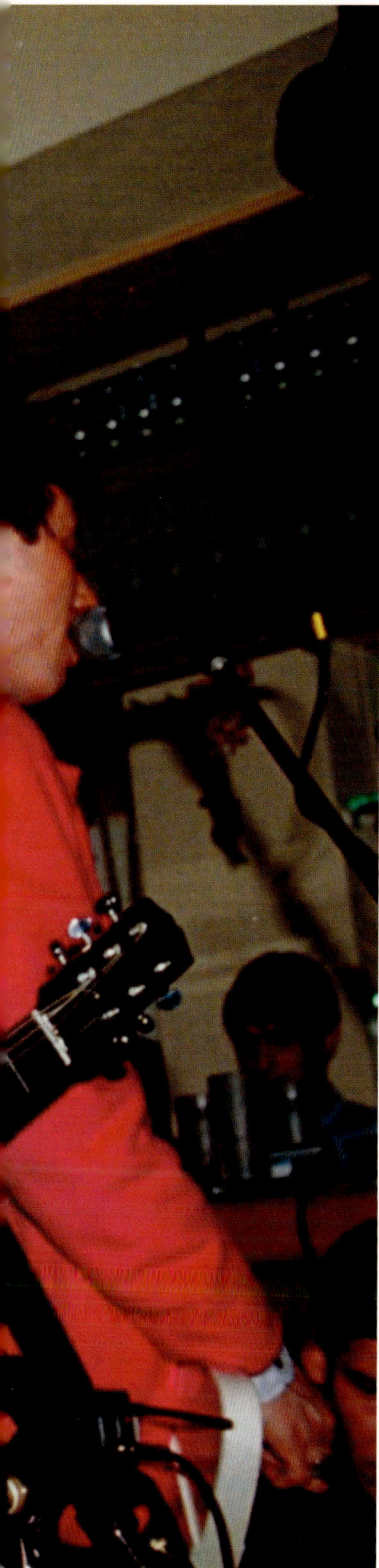

MIND THE BUZZCOCKS AND HOW TO FIND A BIG GOOD ANGEL

The diversity in music genres among the bookings in 1993 is astonishing. Looking at the calendar feels like walking from Notting Hill Gate to Eastcote Studios. Down Portobello Road and taking a right on Golborne, then across the railway bridge past Trellick Tower and following the bend onto Kensal Road. So many impressions. It was around that time I had started making regular trips to the UK together with my music publisher and a young Swedish singer called Sara Isaksson. We had been recording a bunch of demos together, teamed up with Nick Whitecross from Kissing The Pink and would end up getting signed to a record deal with Nick Philips at MCA Records. This would soon lead me to Eastcote, but not quite yet. For now, we were confined to the little demo studio in MCA's publishing office, and coming from Stockholm, it was a culture clash of sorts. I remember someone had written: 'MUSICIANS ARE DEAD, LONG LIVE SAMPLES' on the door to the studio which had an Amek console and a rack of Akai samplers: S900, 1000 and even an 1100, which was the newest one at the time. I remember saying sarcastically to the guys in the studio, 'Did you kill the musicians that played the samples?' Truth be told, I didn't quite get it at the time. So much effort and hours of work to create something you could just sit down and play on an instrument and record in a few minutes. There I was, just arrived from Stockholm with a vintage Telefunken I'd rented and brought along. I had meant to use it for vocals and as an overhead mic for the drumkit, but there wasn't one. It was a whole new way of making music; MIDI wasn't just an addition to an analogue recording setup. It was the setup. Even singers were recorded in bits on the samplers for easy-to-move-around backing vocals. And you could record different bits of a guitar part, assign each bit to a midi note, and then tune, time and program the whole guitar take on a keyboard. What eventually converted me, though, was the unexpected things that happened because of the shortcomings with the technology. I loved sitting in the room and watching my new English friends light their joints and fiddle with the Akai toggle wheel late into the night. It was a case of opposites attract. Being a novice in this way of making music, happy mistakes would happen every time I tried to do something on the sampler, and it was great fun. In the end I adopted a hybrid way of working that I love to this day.

Had I stepped in to Eastcote that year I could just as easily have ended up in a room with a reggae band, a group of DJs with racks full of samplers, a punk rock band making their first new album in 15 years, or a combination of all of the above. And Philip as always wasn't looking to the past around this time and says about the arrival of samplers in the sessions:

It was great. You could do all kinds of magic. Just the fact that if you sampled something off tape and then played on a

The Buzzcocks performing at Zeebra Bar in Frith Street, Soho, London in 1993.

119

19

keyboard, both time and pitch changed as you went up or down the octaves and you could create some fantastic sounds.

Philip and I look at the calendars together and try to decipher the various abbreviations and decide that 'Gypsy' in 1992 doesn't mean the Gypsy Kings but one of Zeus's development projects. But producer Nick Patrick was there, and he did make an album with the 'Bamboleo' singers that year, so maybe they were there after all. Anyway, on to 1993: 'A.T.R.', 'R.S.', 'L.T.', 'T.H.'; lots of initials. Moonshake. Not the CAN song. The band. I get curious and find an absolute gem of a mini-album. And one that illustrates perfectly what you could achieve by playing around with samplers. Something the band and their engineer Philip Bagenal were clearly spending time on when making this record. Moonshake consisted of Dave Callahan and Margaret Feilder and the album was called *Big Good Angel* and it is great experimental work. I read a bit about the record and the people involved. The music press called this 'post-rock' and Margaret's dark and melancholic singing makes me think that one of my favourite artists, P.J. Harvey, must have found some inspiration here or vice versa. And following along the thread it doesn't take much digging to find the connection. Feilder would leave the band after this album and form her own group, Laika. And on Moonshake's follow-up album, *The Sound Your Eyes Can Follow*, I find P.J. Harvey in the liner notes. Polly and Margaret would end up collaborating in the years to come and I make myself a P.J. Harvey, Moonshake and Laika playlist to listen to as I continue writing.

Ralph 'P' Ruppert is a German record producer who lived in London and worked on several projects at Eastcote that year. One was the acid house duo Messiah who were in the studio working on their album *Thunderdome*. Another one is the first new album in 14 years from punk legends The Buzzcocks. Their previous album was released in 1979 in the glory days of British punk. If they had been a trio with the Sex Pistols and The Clash, The Buzzcocks were the ones with the melodies. And they were great players, too. They were a major influence on the whole Manchester rock scene that would follow, and, some would probably say, the future of rock'n'roll. At the very least the boys who would become The Buzzcocks arranged a gig with the Sex Pistols at the Lesser Free Trade Hall on 4th June 1976. It has been described as 'the day the punk era began'. In the audience that night were, according to music journalist and author David Nolan, only 35–40 people. Not all of them were musicians or connected to the music business as has been described. In a BBC interview where he talks about his brilliant book *I Swear I Was There: Sex Pistols, Manchester and the Gig that Changed the World*, we learn that: **They were schoolboys, schoolgirls, they were people who worked for the Manchester Dock company, they were plasterers from Denton. A lot of them were ordinary people.**

But then some of them weren't.

We know that Morrissey was there, who went on to form the Smiths. We know that the lads who went on to form the Buzzcocks were there because they organized the gig. We know that two lads from Lower Broughton were there who went out the next day and bought guitars at Mazel Radio which used to be on Pendleton Station Approach, they formed a band called Joy Division; we know that Mark E Smith was there who went on to form The Fall; we know that Paul Morley was there who went on to become a writer and wrote about the scene for the NME etc.

The Buzzcocks were also the punk band that the Americans loved and many rock'n'roll stars from across the pond cite the late remarkable Pete Shelley and his band as a major influence. During three weeks in March 1993, Bagenal and Ingo Vauk worked with the Buzzcocks and Ruppert in Eastcote Studio 1. The album, called *Trade Test Transmission*, was released later that same year. A long-player with 15 songs just as the CD age would have demanded. It's in my opinion a great listen, and CMJ describes it as 'a brilliant record that got oddly lost in the shuffle'. When I sit down with Philip to listen and reminisce he says, 'That is really great sounding bottom end'.

Shortly after the release of the album, Kurt Cobain, who was a big fan of the band, invited them as special guests on what would end up being Nirvana's last tour.

I did promise a chapter full of diversity in genres and a few months after The Buzzcocks, All Saints are in Studio 2 for one of their very first recording sessions with Cameron McVey. Their first album would take three years, dozens of studios and an army of producers and songwriters to complete. And indeed, this would become the decade for the most expensive recording sessions of all time. The transition from vinyl to CD sales over the previous years had made record labels wealthier than ever before, and pop albums regularly took years and a nearly bottomless purse to finish. Often they made the money back too, and when All Saints finally released their self-titled debut album in 1997 it sold 5 million copies worldwide and went 5x platinum in the UK. I think to myself, do mind The Buzzcocks. And that there are many ways of making music. Most of which are worth trying at least once. ∎

Melanie Blatt, Nicole Appleton, Shaznay Lewis and Natalie Appleton – the All Saints. They worked on their first album in Studio 2.

Where to start... can it really get any busier? Without even trying to decipher all the letter codes in the calendar, I start looking into what happened this year at Eastcote. Neneh is back, working on *Man* with Jonny Dollar, who kept asking for pianos to be hurled up and down the metal staircase. Remember? D-influence are working on *Prayer for Unity*. Guy Chambers, Tricky, Howie B, Mark Saunders, Tom Jones: they were all in the studios. There's a Polaroid of Leigh Bowery and Richard Torry in Studio 1. What were they recording?

And Tim Simenon. He's working on a new Bomb the Bass album, *Clear*. I would love to talk to Tim. How do I get hold of him? No one knows. Okay, just a small dive deeper in the calendar. On Google I type in 'BTTP, abbreviation, band'.

Back To The Planet – an anarcho-punk band from Peckham recording their last album, *Messages After The Bleep*. They formed while they were squatting and ended up playing four times at Glastonbury. It's going on the playlist. This might end up a long chapter....

In July 1994 I got married. Most probably, had I not met my remarkable wife Tia, I wouldn't have ended up moving to London. She was born in Nekemte, in the Oromia region of Ethiopia, but grew up in Sweden close to the Norwegian border in a small town called Arvika. We met in Stockholm where I was already making music, but in the confines of the local area, and on the occasional short tour around the country to play with my band. Tia was into art, photography and music and quite literally lit up my world. We were

IT'S A GIANT BLENDER

1994

Performance artist Leigh Bowery was renowned for his extraordinary and risqué performances and club nights. Shortly before he died in 1994 he recorded his only record at Eastcote.

Tricky first recorded at Eastcote with Massive Attack for their album *Blue Lines*. In 1994 he was back to make his seminal first solo album, *Maxinquaye*.

Leigh Bowery & Richard Torry
27/3/94

and Sven Lindvall was inspired by Neil Young, Tom Petty, Daniel Lanois and Joni Mitchell. It had simple lyrics and a really organic sound. Although a lot of it was written during trips to London, it sounded just right when we pulled up the tracks at Quad Studios in Nashville. Richard Dodd, an amazing English engineer from Luton, was mixing some songs for us. He had ended up in Los Angeles after working extensively with Jeff Lynne and Rick Rubin, and the sound that came out of the console was just how we wanted it. England seemed much more foreign then, and when we continued mixing the album a few months later at the Strongroom in London it felt like we were on another planet. And we were. The UK is its own world when it comes to music. Like a giant blender that although you may have put in some American soul, hip hop or rock, African drumming, or even Indian sitar-playing, there's no way you could ever mistake its country of origin. And it wasn't only the clash between playing live and chopping things up in samplers that formed me as a Swedish music producer and songwriter, living in the UK and making records with what would end up being a majority of American artists. It was about balance. In the lyrics. Between earnest simplicity and abstract poetry or sheer nonsense. It was between the 'let's do it' attitude of the Yanks and the default resistance of the fashion-driven London scene. Between guitars and drums versus synthesizers and samplers. But I found my spot. It was in North Kensington and it was Tia's spot too. We were in the right place. And it was a place for the whole eclectic collection of artists I mentioned at the start of the chapter. For Philip Bagenal who speaks in perfect Queen's English and Zeus B Held with his broken German accent. It was a place for punks, dancers, divas and steel bands. For music from around London, from the Caribbean and Africa, from the US and Asia, and from Manchester and Bristol.

both young and restless and wanted to explore more of the world, and so it was that a few years later we packed up and left for London. I saw it as a place to start from, and certainly neither of us thought we would still be here 25 years later, less than a mile from our first flat in Ladbroke Grove and with our children Hanna and Noah, who are now steadily closing in on the same age we were when we arrived here. I didn't know then who Tim Simenon or many of the artists I

see in the Eastcote booking calendar were, or that I would end up recording in Studio 2 the following year and soon live around the corner. But looking back, it all seems almost like a well-laid plan, which it really wasn't, or at least we didn't make it.

It would probably have made more sense musically for me to end up in America. 1994 was the year I went to record there for the first time and the music I was making with Sara Isaksson

Leigh Bowery and Richard Torry were in Studio 1 with their band Minty.

1994

One session that Philip remembers from 1994 is the only one in his 40 years of recording where he walked out of the studio because of the lyrical content. And Philip is not very easily offended. Which shows us how good Leigh Bowery was as the ultimate provocateur. His whole life was a work of art, pushing the boundaries of the accepted and as an LBGT icon and activist. His talent as a fashion and costume designer and his mind-bending performance art show won him awards and a place in modern art history. But it also saw him banned from performing at all in parts of London. Which he probably considered an award in itself. He started the legendary nightclub Taboo in Soho and was a major part of the New Romantic movement. He is probably most famous for being Lucian Freud's model and muse, and one of his least-known projects must be the band he started with Matthew Glammore, Nicola Bateman and Richard Torry, a fashion designer who worked for Vivienne Westwood before starting his own label in the early '80s. They were called Minty and found their way to Eastcote to record their first and only single with Bowery, 'Useless Man'. The lyric was the following words on loop: *Bootlicking, piss-drinking, finger-frigging, tit-tweakin', love-biting, arse-licking, shit-stabbing, motherfucking, spunk-loving, ball-busting, cock-sucking, fist-fucking, lip-smacking, thirst-quenching, cool-living, ever-giving…* Philip did end up finishing a remix of the track and as much as Leigh Bowery did and continues to divide opinion he made a big impact on the club and performance art scene. He was the canvas and the exhibition, but one thing that he kept to himself until only a few months before his very early death was that he was ill with AIDS. He passed away just a few months after the recording session and was one of the true originals who brought his creativity to Kensal Road that year. Another one came from a radically different background to Bowery, but

had no less of an explosive impact on the club scene of the early '90s.

I'm sitting with a copy of Tricky's autobiography *Hell Is Round the Corner* next to me. It's a tough read, and also the title of one of the songs on his debut solo album *Maxinquaye*, which he recorded at Eastcote in 1994. It's a moody and dark masterpiece, mostly produced by Mark Saunders and Tricky. Featuring Martina Topley-Bird throughout, the album is painfully beautiful at times, outrageously 'I don't give a fuck about what you think' at others, and a poignant example of a record that probably could only have been made in England. But it's more than that. It's Tricky's first solo album and his life has been all but a smooth ride. The name of the album is that of his mother, Maxine Quaye. She committed suicide when he was four years old. When he started working on the album that year, Topley-Bird was only 19, and pregnant with her and Tricky's daughter Mina-Mazy. In May 2019, she too took her own life. May they rest in peace. I feel quite upset and wonder whether I should take a break from writing or go on, because the only way to continue is to divert into another conversation altogether. I decide that it's got to be done, partly because I can't stop, but also because Philip, in our interviews, over and over repeats his sadness and concern about the state of world:

Has anything changed since I started? No! The country is still run by Etonians.

In relation to Eastcote that applies to the world right outside the green doors. A rapidly gentrifying neighbourhood with historical struggles very similar to the Bristol streets where Tricky grew up. The music business adheres to the same rules as society in general. Maybe that's why Philip felt it was so important to make it a place for musicians, not for the business. And in 2020, Tricky's childhood on the streets of Knowle West where he lived, is repeating itself all over Britain and around the world. More than 50

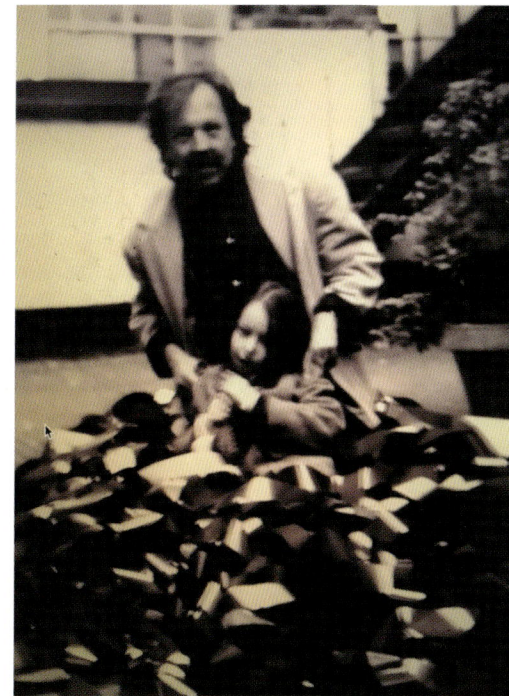

years after Dr Martin Luther King was shot, black friends and my own family are out on the streets asking for the most basic of understanding. They don't want to be stopped and searched, and potentially beaten up or killed, because of the colour of their skin. And they are asking that I, and others like me, liberal white people, immersed in a multicultural urban world, really acknowledge that racism is embedded deep in our system and support them in working to make that unacceptable both on the streets and in our schools and institutions. How does this relate to *Maxinquaye*? Because it's an album that is the culmination of work that can only come from reality. It has no veneer on it and isn't adjusted to fit in. Yet it did. It became a success and it touched all kinds of people in many countries around the world. That's another thing music can do. And the artists and musicians are the ones who can pass on that gift. Philip knew that. And Tricky too. ■

Zeus and his daughter. For her birthday party, Philip rolled hundreds of meters of old tape off their reels to make a giant tape mountain in the courtyard.

THE FUTURE IS MEDIUM

It's proper detective work at times to try to make sense of decades'-old memories, sometimes wildly conflicting, from the various participants in any one recording. Calendar entries that no one can decipher, like who is 'A.J.'? An early entry reading 'U2' leads nowhere as Philip says: 'I know for a fact that they never recorded here'. But 1995 is the year the great Irish poet Seamus Heaney won the Nobel Prize for Literature, and I decide I want to find out what connection the studios might have had at that time to the island on either side of the border. I remember Zeus mentioning an Irish artist during one of our calls and I track back and re-listen to the recording: 'There was an Irish artist working with Tim upstairs. Bono came by with four bottles of beer one evening and we all had a drink. Kerry [Hopwood] would remember who it was.'

Someone who knew Tim and Kerry and the rest of the crew around them at that time is another producer and composer I was recently

Tim Simenon at work in Studio 1.

1995

introduced to, Ivor Guest. Mainly known for his film work, he also produced Grace Jones's *Hurricane*, which in 2008 was her first album in 19 years and her most recent to date. They would pass through Eastcote in the process, but I'm not going to give it all away here... we're still more than a decade away from that. I speak to Ivor over the video-phone-miracle-no-wire thingy and he asks me:

Do you know Atticus Ross? Me, Tim and Atticus had been working together on Bomb the Bass, and then we decided to do our own little thing, called 'Strange Cuts'. The only thing that ever came out of what we did together was in the movie In The Name of the Father. *There was a Sinéad O'Connor track at the end of that film called 'Thief Of Your Heart', and we did some of that in Eastcote. And we also did a Bono track for the same film.*

So, there is an Irish connection. And here is the slightly longer version. Dik Evans and his brother Dean were two of the original members of Feedback, five teenagers from Dublin. Dik was a few years older than his little brother David 'The Edge' Evans, and when he went to college the remaining members of the band would continue as a four-piece, and after a brief stint as The Hype they decided to call themselves U2. They were all part of a surrealist imaginary world called Lypton Village, dreamt up by Gavin Friday and that also included Giggi and Peter Rowan. Peter is the face on the cover of U2's *Boy* and he, together with Giggi, Gavin and Dik would start a new band called Virgin Prunes. I'll send the roll of thread out on the motorway for a bit here because, let's face it. This book is about Eastcote. And how it all connects is through the Tim Simenon sessions that both Zeus and Ivor told us about. In 1993, Tim, Atticus and Ivor worked on two songs written for Jim Sheridan's biographical courtroom drama about the Guildford Four, based on Gerry

Claudia Sarne and Atticus Ross from the band 12 Rounds.

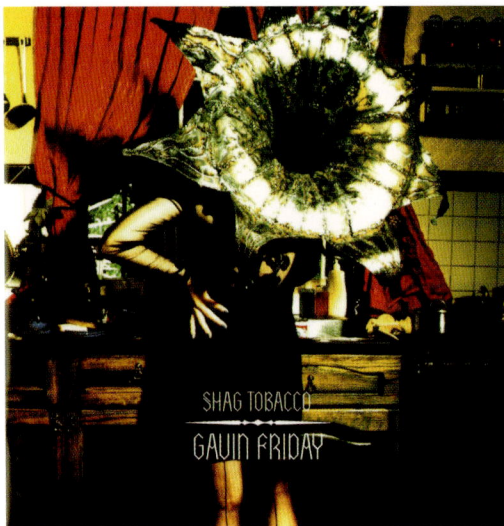

Conlon's autobiography. The songs were Sinéad O'Connor's 'Thief Of Your Heart', and the title track 'In The Name Of The Father' was by Bono and Gavin Friday from the Virgin Prunes.

The following year, Gavin is back at Eastcote with Simenon and Kerry Hopwood working on his album *Shag Tobacco*, and it's released in 1995. Twenty-five years later and a few days before the American Presidential election in 2020, I'm at home writing. It's 1.06 am and it's been a long day. I decide to listen to the album they made and can't help laughing out loud in a moment of overwhelming joy. It's a dark, weird, theatrical and wonderfully eccentric body of work that I would probably never have come across had it not been for deciding to write this book. It was a long time since I felt so childishly excited about discovering new music. Bono and The Edge do appear here too, on track four, 'Little Black Dress'. There's also an unexpected

arrival of a jolly accordion player on 'The Slider' that makes me decide to pour myself a whiskey and keep listening. Gavin Friday's talk-singing is quite a hypnotic affair.

So, who is Atticus Ross? Well to start with he and his family are from Ladbroke Grove and I know a couple of his siblings. His brother, Milo, ran a record company out of Walters Workshops until only last year, and regularly recorded his bands with George Murphy down in Studio 1. His dad was one of the three founders of Radio Caroline, the '60s floating pirate radio station that inspired the Richard Curtis comedy *The Boat That Rocked*.

Atticus is often at Eastcote and has worked here for many years, mostly on his film and TV assignments. He won an Oscar for his work alongside longtime collaborator Trent Reznor with the score for *The Social Network*. They also won a Grammy for their soundtrack to *The Girl with the Dragon Tattoo*. Atticus is also a member of Nine Inch Nails and a record producer. Around this time in the mid-'90s he was at Eastcote working with Tim Simenon and Bomb the Bass, with Barry Adamson and also with another of his long-time collaborators, Claudia Sarne, his wife and partner in the band 12 Rounds. Apart from Claudia and Atticus, the band also included his brother Leopold Ross and in 1995 they recorded their first album, *Jitter Juice*, at Eastcote.

The stories from the mid-'90s weave backwards and forwards between adjoining years, and into previous chapters that I thought I had already finished writing. Ivor continues talking about Eastcote:

It's a vibe really, and everyone comes around there. I mean, during that period when we were all mucking about there were so many ties between Ladbroke Grove and Bristol and the reggae music and the punk stuff, and the jazzers. It was a melting-pot period in the '80s and the '90s. And my kind of first proper way in was when I met Sean Oliver who was part of Rip Rig + Panic, and that whole posy. I met Bruce Smith and Mark Springer, Bruce was in The Pop Group and was in PiL Public Image at the time, and Tessa from the Slits. There were quite a few hard drugs around, and some people were into that and some people weren't. After Sean tragically died from sickle cell I cleaned up my act when I was 22, so back in 1990. They all had close ties to Bristol, because everybody came from Bristol and those were the roots of Massive Attack, and all those things were bubbling and melting away during that period around Ladbroke Grove. And I was sort of in the fringes of it all, as a young guy who just came out into music and met some of these people, and I got involved in different things. I wasn't even aware of Bruce and the work that he had done in The Pop Group, and that he'd done with Public Image and New Age Steppers and all those worlds. I wasn't even aware of it at the time, but now that I've looked back at it, which was relatively recently, I thought, wow that was all bubbling up. I can't claim to be in the centre of it, but I was definitely on the fringes. I was young, and watching and listening and trying to learn how you make records and what it's all about. There were a lot of drugs around – I think it's safe to say some dangerous Class A drugs have been taken in the room you're sitting in.

I end up having a really good and candid conversation with Ivor and tell him that through

1995

Gavin Friday, *Shag Tobacco*, Polygram Records, 1995.

Gavin Friday of the Virgin Prunes.

Guitarist Garret Lee (aka record producer Jacknife Lee) performing with the Irish punk band Compulsion who recorded at Eastcote in 1994. Lee would go on to produce for The Killers, Blur, REM and U2.

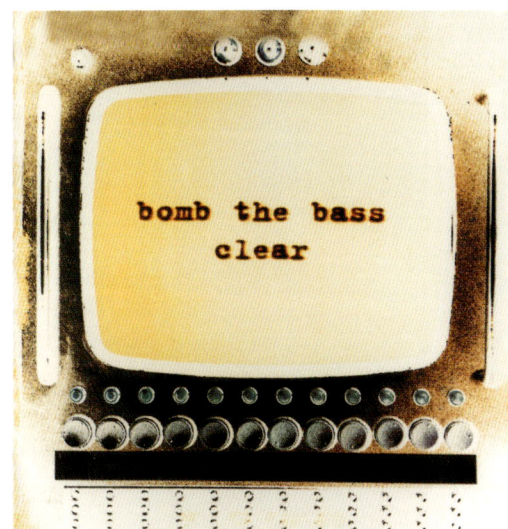

researching this book drugs have indeed been a recurring theme. And without going too deep into a wider conversation, one thing worth acknowledging is that unlike the romantic myth sometimes portrayed in retrospectives of this kind, in relation to recording music most of those I speak to feel that drugs more often work as an inhibitor, as opposed to a facilitator, of creativity. Ivor says:

By the early '90s a lot of us got clean and there was a real recovering community around – everyone trying to get things done, which was great and really creative. But at around the same time, and I think this is common knowledge, Tim was having to deal with producing Depeche Mode who were going through a hard time as a band, which must have been tough for him. That experience and the fact that he had been constantly working for so long must have contributed to him stepping back from music entirely shortly afterwards.

And that of course explains why most of those I speak to have lost touch with Tim, which is a pity because his legacy as a producer is undeniable, and I would love to hear his take on this era in music. I have tried, and so far the closest I got was on a detour to the Czech Republic. A friend of mine called Miro, who runs a music company called Brainzone in Prague, tells me that Tim lived there and owned a fancy meatball restaurant around the corner from his apartment, and that he regularly used to go and eat there. One night he and a group of friends got talking to Tim over a few drinks and he told them in a very humble manner that he once worked with music. The restaurant closed in 2019 and that was the end of that lead. Ivor continues:

He's a wonderful guy, Tim, we were very close friends back then. When I finished the last Grace Jones record, the Hurricane one, Tim did dip his toe back into Bomb the Bass. He did make an album in 2008 and we got back in touch and spoke about maybe starting a label at the time. He played me his Bomb the Bass record, and he did a remix of something, but the thing with Tim, he was a very interesting producer in the sense that I can't remember ever seeing him touch anything. He never touched a drum machine or an S1000, he always had Kerry and a bunch of musicians that he worked with a lot. And the Tackhead crew. Really interesting musicians. That crew were always with him and he was truly a producer in the true sense of the word. At that time he was so successful that it seemed that hardly anyone who made a record via a major record label didn't come to Tim. I'm sure I even heard talk of Bowie. Tim was sort of offered everything and he was so young at the time, couldn't have been more than 25 or 26 during the Depeche album. But I remember working with Tim, because he called me one day, and he came round to my studio that was at the Pall Mall Deposit down on Barlby Road. Tim never touched any piece of hardware, he just said to me, 'Like this, like that', and when I listened to it the next day, I was like, that's really incredible because this really sounds like Bomb the Bass, or something that only Tim could've done, but he's done it entirely through me somehow, just by making decisions. It was amazing really, Tim is very talented, and he is a sweet and lovely guy with a quiet charisma and a huge musical imagination.

I feel like I've almost got to know Tim Simenon a little bit by talking to Ivor. There are another couple of calendar entries that I notice too. Portishead are in for a few days in August and September and that keeps the link to Bristol going. A whole month in Studio 1 says 'Compulsion'. They were an Irish punk band which reconnects us nicely to the beginning of this chapter. Compulsion made their second album at Eastcote this year and it was called *The Future Is Medium*. A great album title, and in the end the future turned out quite bright, at least for their guitar player Garret Lee, who would soon become Jacknife Lee and go on to have enormous success as the producer for bands like Snowpatrol, Kodaline, Blur, The Killers, REM and... U2.

And in December that year there's an entry for Studio 2 that reads: 'Maidi'. Her full name was Maïdi Roth, a French songwriter and actress who was in London writing music for a solo album and a film by Gérard Kravcwyk called *Heroines*. Together with Nick Whitecross, I was enlisted for a writing session, and Nick suggested we'd go to his friend's studio in Ladbroke Grove. That session is when I first stepped in through the green door to Eastcote and met Philip Bagenal. Exactly 25 years ago this winter. ∎

Marshall in the 'old room' in Studio 1.

1995

Bomb the Bass, *Clear*, 4th & Broadway, 1995.

SITAR AND MAGIC STONES. TO MAKE THE SOUND MORE MAGIC

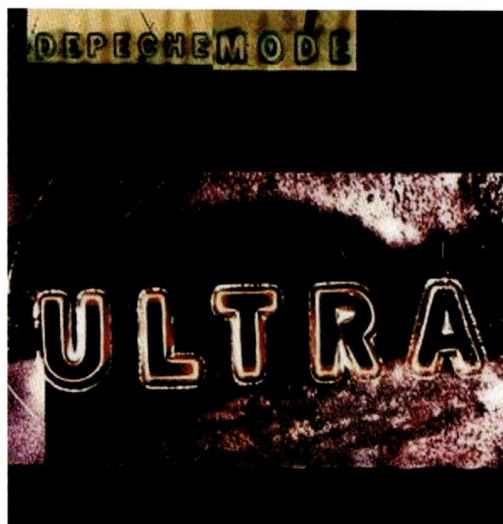

In 1996 different music cultures would continue to intertwine. Cornershop, Wah Wah Watson, Tindersticks, Aswad, Trevor Horn, Atticus, Placebo, Dreadzone and Kula Shaker were all recording at Eastcote that year. And for a significant part of the year in Studio 2 the booking calendar reads: 'Depeche Mode'.

They were at Eastcote to work on their ninth solo album *Ultra* and it was their first time back in the studio after Alan Wilder had left the band. They had decided to work with Tim Simenon and the darker and quite smooth electronic production connected well with the late-'90s' dance scene. The album debuted at number 1 on the UK charts when it was released in April 1997, but it wasn't an easy recording and it took around 15 months to complete. I start talking to some of those involved and their memories are blurry. Philip doesn't immediately remember the details either, but he shows me a great picture he took of Martin Gore playing sitar in his boxers:

I can't quite remember. 1996. Studio 2, yes I think so, I can easily work that out and get the dates. I have a nice list of all the materials I used and how much they cost which I had to provide to give to their accountants, it wasn't that much, I think it was about 20 grand.

At Eastcote on the wall in the upstairs lounge there's a promo picture of Depeche Mode sitting on the back couch in Studio 2, by the window. The picture is taken by Anton Corbijn, who has been a friend of the band and documented their career through the years. After some digging into the dates it seems like Tim started working with Depeche in the fall of 1995 on a handful of tracks. By Christmas they had decided to make the whole album together and Tim with the rest of his production crew set up an electronic music control centre of envy. Ivor Guest had told me:

At that time, Tim Simenon was the hottest producer in the world. He really was. I remember

1996

Depeche Mode, *Ultra*, Mute, 1997

Depeche Mode photographed by Anton Corbijn at Eastcote.

Tim only being in that room [Studio 2], he literally lived there. And Kerry was with him the whole time and there's no doubt that he was working right on the edge of what the technology was capable of back then. It was right at the edge.

I've still not been able to track down Tim Simenon, but in 2018 he posted a note about the making of *Ultra* on Depeche Mode's Facebook page. It reads:

At some point during the summer of 1995, Daniel Miller called me to say that Depeche Mode were looking for a producer to start work on some new songs. I think Martin and Dave had enjoyed the Gavin Friday album Shag Tobacco *I had produced the year before and the interest began from there. So, I went in for a meeting at the band's offices in London and met with Daniel, Martin and Fletch. We listened to a demo of 'Useless'. It was a very bare-bones version of the song with Martin singing but the melodies, structure and main guitar riff was all there. The meeting went well and so in the autumn of 1995 I assembled a small production team, and we went to a recording studio that I worked at often called Eastcote in West London and started experimenting and reworking the first three songs Martin had written.*

There were a lot of mixed emotions during those first few weeks – excitement, pressure and uncertainty were the ones that leapt out the most. Excitement at the prospect of working with the band I had enjoyed listening to for so many years. Pressure in knowing that with Alan's departure, those were going to be some big shoes to fill! And uncertainty looming constantly in whether the album was going to be made

95

Lee 'Scratch' Perry performing in France in 1998.

Martin Gore playing the sitar during the making of *Ultra* at Eastcote.

or completed at all due to Dave's recent health scares. We were just simply going to take it slow and see how things would progress. The first three songs that we started on were 'Useless', 'Insight' and 'Sister of Night'. The production team included Dave Clayton on keyboards, Kerry Hopwood as programmer and Q as engineer.

I decide to talk some more to Kerry Hopwood, who was there through all of the *Ultra* sessions. Later and for almost 20 years he became an integral part of Depeche's touring crew and a close friend of theirs. Kerry begins:

We started at Eastcote because we needed a big room for all the equipment. We had lots of gear, system 700 modulars and samplers, and Dave Clayton, our keyboard player, had a ridiculous amount of stuff. More modular synthesizers, lots of Roland stuff, and Martin [Gore] came in with three Arp 2600s that he had on top of each other in a rack. The upstairs room was just so perfect for us, lots of space where we could spread out. We kind of did the album in phases. Martin would come in with demos. The band had been through some rough times. I think it's all well documented. Tim and I were big fans of Depeche, I mean, I don't know anyone who isn't really, but we were enormous fans. But it was hard, Dave Gahan doesn't remember making that album. He actually has no recollection of it at all. And it was generally a bit of a basket of problems to get through. So, it was slow, but we were really comfortable at Eastcote and took it in phases. We'd be working on Martin's demos, and also did some writing up there. We wanted to make a statement album for them to comeback with. 'Barrel of a Gun' is one we did up there. We tried marrying a bit of

what we [Bomb the Bass] were doing with what Depeche did. So beats-driven, a bit fruity and a bit of a statement.

He talks about the project and those involved with great fondness, but it's clear that it was also a challenge and some rather stressful times too:

It was a very tough 15 months because of the ups and downs the guys in the band were going through, but Eastcote was pivotal in the process. We'd come and go, do some prep work, do some song-writing, some recording and then we'd have a break. Live with it for a couple of weeks. And then we might mix some things early, just to see where we were at, the budgets in those days allowed for that. I also remember we went over to Electric Lady in New York, primarily to do vocals because Dave lived there. But I'll tell you, it was an emotional time. I remember we went to Abbey Road to mix the album, and when I came home after it was all

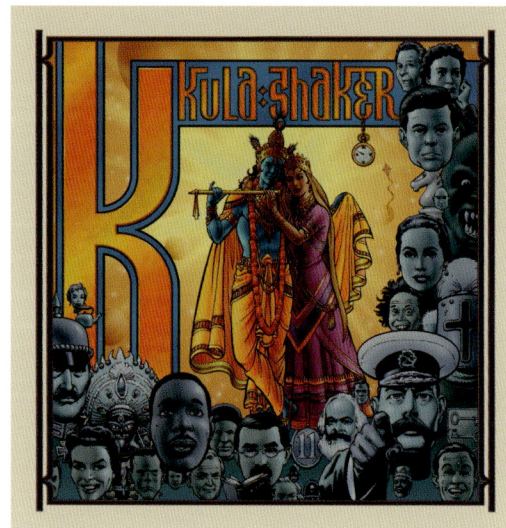

1996

Wah Wah Watson recorded at Eastcote in the '90s. A brilliant guitarist and session musician, he was famed for his use of the wah wah pedal.

Kula Shaker, *K*, Columbia, 1996.

done, I sat down to have a listen and I was just cheesed off. I was really upset and thought, it's terrible, rubbish, and after all that time we spent on it. But looking back, of course it was all those feelings, we were so close to it. It was all the things we'd been through with it. I mean we lost Dave. Dave died on it for a bit.

After all the hard work though, they had made an album that really did capture the mood of the times and it remains much loved by fans and critics alike. A few years after its release, Russell Faibisch and Alex Omes started an electronic music festival in Miami Beach that grew to become one of the biggest yearly music festivals in the US. They named the festival Ultra after the Depeche Mode album that inspired them. It's been running every year since and is widely considered one of the most important events in the electronic music calendar and one of the sparks that detonated the explosion of EDM in the 2000s. (The ongoing Covid pandemic has led to a near-total shutdown of live music events across the world, and this year Ultra was cancelled for the first time since 1988.)

Whilst Depeche were working away upstairs, Aswad were in Studio 1 working on their album *Big Up*. Their first record after signing to Atlantic Records. And there was other reggae royalty in the house too. Zeus was recording many of his projects in other studios at the time, and when he was at Eastcote, it was mostly in Studio 1. He tells me about this period:

I remember Wah Wah Watson, I was a fan. And the crazy dub guy... that worked with Bob Marley... Lee Scratch Perry. He was there in Studio 1. I remember he took the speakers apart to put magic stones in them. For a more magic sound. Philip and I were saying oh no... he's wrecking the studio.

One particular album that Zeus made that year at Eastcote once again illustrates the incredible musical diversity at Philip's studio. Yulduz Usmanova has been one of the most loved artists in Uzbekistan and across Central Asia through the past three decades. In 1996 she recorded her third album *Binafscha* in Studio 1. What an unexpected detour it is listening to it. It's Uzbek folk music with pretty full-on beats, arpeggiated 303s and great-sounding bass lines. A refreshing change of scales and chords and I can imagine Martin Gore playing his sitar now, with Uzbek folk music being recorded downstairs. And then, Scratch Perry coming in on a Sunday with his magic stones.

The Asian influence would appear in a much more westernized version on another album recorded in Studio 1 this same year. Crispian Mills and his band Kula Shaker went straight to number 1 on the UK charts with their debut album *K*, which became one of the fastest-selling albums ever in this country. I vividly remember the first time I heard *K*. It was blasting out of the speakers of one of the record stalls on the Portobello Road. We had moved to London just a few months earlier. It sounded different and quite psychedelic and I bought a copy on CD. Like every time I bought an album back then, I immediately tore off the plastic, checked the credits and discovered John Leckie's name as the producer. Having spent most of that year wearing out my copy of Radiohead's *The Bends*, Leckie was one of my favourite producers, so I went straight back to my bedroom studio on St Charles Square to lay down on the carpet to listen through the album. ∎

Aswad recorded at Eastcote throughout the '80s and '90s.

Cornershop stopping for refreshments with guest guitarist Noel Gallagher at Eastcote's 'conference room': Village Inn, the local pub.

EVERYBODY NEEDS A BOSOM FOR A PILLOW

It was the sort of oddball jobs like Cornershop that I fell for.

Philip Bagenal

On most sessions at Eastcote, Philip wore many hats, sometimes engineering, sometimes cooking and a lot of the time he was fixing gear that had broken down. But perhaps his most important role was, as has been described by many, his patience and understanding of the dynamics between the various people in a room. He wasn't afraid of friction; quite the contrary, he sometimes would go to some lengths to encourage it:

It's the whole business of working in a studio. You need a bit of friction: not too much, but a bit. And if you take the friction out, it all stops. People get bored. There's got to be a bit of tension in the room, and sometimes you have to help out. Stir things up. Create a bit of controversy to get things moving.

Many sessions at Eastcote started late and ran through the night. One of Philip's recording assistants, Al O'Connell, tells me: 'Philip used to have a way of working which he called loop-the-loop. It meant we'd start mid-morning and work all day, then all night and then the following day too. A 36-hour shift.' Philip always wanted to be there, whether engineering or being the host. Sometimes, of course, it all got too much, and Philip left. One time he came to regret it, but as usual there was a genius solution to the situation that followed:

I'll try to remember the name of the record, but we were making a record for an English artist, and they had got a very famous New York DJ as one of the producers. Sly was playing the drums, and he had it all programmed on an Akai MPC and he used to lock the box with the discs in it every time he went home. He was very paranoid about people ripping off his sounds. *The New York DJ kept saying we gotta have fours on the floor, we gotta have fours on the floor, and there they were working with the most amazing drummer in the world pretty much, apart from Steve Gadd. It kept dragging on and I had something I needed to do back in Oxford, so I left the tape op in charge and left at midnight which was quite early for those sessions. And I got into trouble with the local environmental health department because not long after I left most of Ladbroke Grove were migrated to the second floor of the studio and there was a wild party that went on through the night. The vicar from the church on the corner, the one that's still there opposite the playground, he called Kensington and Chelsea Council and complained. The next day I got a visit from the environmental health officer who, it turns out, was an amateur guitarist. So he had a go at all the guitars in the room and he was very friendly, and I said 'Look', and I showed him what I'd started building that morning, which was a box with some relays on it. And if someone would open the side door, which was the problem that previous evening, it would shut down the speakers. So, you weren't able to play any music as long as the door was open. I still have the box somewhere, I keep coming across it. And the officer was quite happy with the solution. I apologized and told him that normally we would have been more respectful to our neighbours and off he went. But that really was one party they all had!*

For every technical problem there was a solution. That was what Philip was about and that's what he thought the studio should be about. There's a short exchange between him and Charlie Seward that I think illustrates not only his ability to build great technology but also how, by prioritizing the artists and musicians, he created a space that was made for making music. As a producer, I actually find it quite liberating to hear about his pecking order:

Charlie: *How did the word spread that Eastcote was the place to record? Was it via producers? Or artists? Or engineers?*
Philip: *It was all three of those things. I think there are a couple of things that are really important, one is that I wanted it to be a place for musicians, not for record companies, executives or A&R men. And in my mind, musicians came before producers as well. Therefore it had to be a place that inspired the making of music. That was the important thing for me. All my attention was focused on that, and to give you one obvious example, it's that I always placed emphasis on the sound that the musician gets in the headphones. We just have a far better foldback system than any other studio in London.*
Charlie: *That you designed?*
Philip: *Yes, I put it together. I learnt over the years that the more freedom you give the musician to adjust the sound, the better the result you get. Also, a lot of the big studios didn't see it from the musician's point of view. They saw it in terms of, selling a certain technical... professional attitude to recording. A lot of the musicians that came to Eastcote, had not been in a studio before and studios can be quite intimidating when you first go in and plug your headphones in. Eastcote has a sort of welcoming and human approach and that's why we got a lot of projects. Some which were successful and some not. I think the artists were very much responsible, I think they felt at home because the sound in the headphones was incredibly good, and because they had an enjoyable time. I used to cook lunch for them when I had time. I wanted it to be a very human place, I come from a family of musicians, I play the cello, and I've played enough to know how it feels when you get it right and how it feels when you get it wrong.*
Charlie: *And as you say, the way that you built the studios around the control room with the windows, it enabled people to have a sense of recording live, and a lot of eye contact with everybody from the control room and with the other players. So the musicians were key allies, but you've also had some producers who have been supporters over a long period?*
Philip: *Yes, we have. But again, producers change. The scale of what they are doing either goes up or it goes down. There were a lot of American producers and engineers who had a very fixed way of working, but the fact that we tended to roll up our sleeves – 'Have you got so-and-so mic'; 'No I'm afraid we haven't'; 'Oh well that's fine, what else have you got that might do the job?' – you know. That was our attitude.*

In 1997, Philip did get that oddball job. Cornershop. The band from Wolverhampton consisted of Tjinder Singh and his brother Avtar Singh, along with David Chambers and Ben Ayres. The band name was a swing at the stereotype that British Asians often own cornershops. Philip liked them:

I really liked Cornershop. Early on, their live show was so bad that the audience walked

out. But they went for it and ended up having a number one record. When it comes down to it, a few famous singers might have airs and graces and make a fuss, but more often people realize that they have a limited time and a job to do and they do get on with it. Although there used to be a bit of playing around in the studio. Some fun and games. At least in the days back when we made whole albums. And sometimes great music came from it.

'Brimful Of Asha' is one of those songs that everybody loves. It is, inasmuch as anything can ever be objective, quite simply an outstanding and unusual piece of music that will continue to be played for the longest time. And to be honest, I hadn't made the connection between the band name and the song title and the song I knew and loved until I saw the gold disc alongside only a couple of others in the Eastcote lounge some years ago. Which piqued my interest, because Philip was very restrictive with putting up any awards on the walls, as his philosophy was to make the place feel like home to every new artist who came through the door. Sometimes music is like that, a moment of brilliance that connects with the world in such a big way that it overshadows its creator(s). Either way, I am happy to report that the album that Cornershop made that year at Eastcote, *When I Was Born For The 7th Time*, is a whole long-player of brilliant playfulness.

There was a whole lot of things happening at Eastcote in 1997 apart from Cornershop of course. It's the Britpop era and Suede are in the studio, and so are a bunch of more obscure bands. These are the heydays of British indie labels, whilst they were still (more or less) independent. And for the first year in the studio calendar, the bookings are marked as labels instead of artist names or initials. Apart from Mute, there's Nude, Wiiiji, Gut, Hut, etc. Some entries have only label information, so it's hard to know which of their bands were in the studio, but we had Barry Adamson, Aswad, Curve, Placebo, One Inch Punch, 12 Rounds and Tindersticks in there that year amongst quite a few others. In Studio 2 it's still Tim Simenon for extended periods. And somewhere along the way, either this year or around this time, Philip and Zeus decide to go separate ways. Zeus is interested in developing artists and Philip is happy the way things are. Philip says:

Zeus was producing and getting stuck in, and he had somebody who was working with him called KP, a German guy. What KP had said to Zeus was, 'Studios don't make money, artists make money, and the studios that are successful and make money are all studios that have signed artists or produced demos and encouraged artists that have later been signed by record companies'. I wasn't really interested in anything else than the recording side of things, so at that point Zeus was saying 'I want to get out there and move on'. So, I borrowed some more money and took over the place.

Neither of them remembers exactly when that happened, but they remained friends and collaborators for years and even decided to share 4 voices each of the beloved Oberheim 8 that they had acquired together. From this point, Eastcote was on paper what it had been in spirit from the day Philip started making the drawings for the studio in 1979: Philip's house. And for the following two decades he ran the show. I imagine his ethos for the future of the studio, once he had signed whatever paperwork that needed to be signed, was something in the style of 'There's a brimful of Asha on the 45... And everybody needs a bosom for a pillow.' ∎

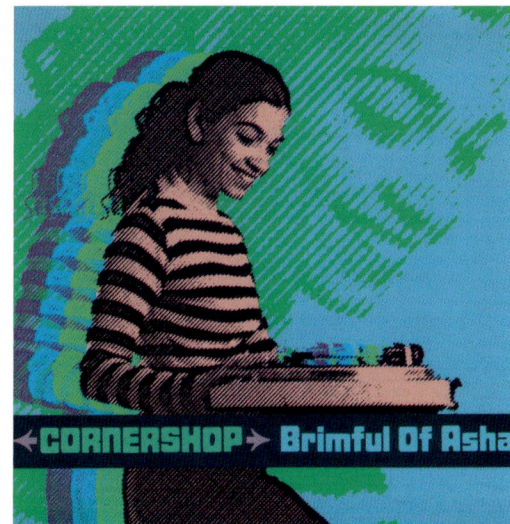

The famed Eastcote RCA microphone in Studio 1.

Cornershop, 'Brimful of Asha', Wiija, 1997.

Drugstore, *White Magic for Lovers*, Roadrunner, 1998.

The years really are weaving into each other now and so are the band names. Cornershop and Drugstore share booking calendars through the mid- to late-'90s. And this year, in 1998, the latter are releasing their album *White Magic for Lovers*, produced by Clive Martin and recorded at Eastcote through '97–'98. It's a rather American-sounding album for coming out of Eastcote at that time, which makes sense when I see that the band are signed to Roadrunner Records, the originally Dutch hard-rock label that came to be the home of choice for American metal bands with loud guitars and pop choruses. But this is not a pop album. And White Magic? The voodoo dolls on the front cover, made by the band's singer Isabel Monteiro, and the dark songwriting suggest that all kinds of magic are allowed. To give you an idea of the mood of the music, let's put it this way: the most singalong and up-tempo moment on the album is when Thom York sings 'They killed the President' on the chorus of the single 'El President'. This is around the same time that I went to a Radiohead concert, and someone in the audience cried out: 'For God's sake, somebody give that guy a hug!' The duet reached the top 20 on the UK charts.

Daniel Miller at Mute Records regularly sent artists to Eastcote when they ran out of space in their own studio across the canal or needed a bigger space. This year the band Add N to (X) came to Eastcote to work on their album *Avant Hard*. When I was a kid in Caracas, if someone had asked me 'What do you think music might sound like in the future, at the end of the millennium?' I would have first asked what a millennium was. And that would seem very, very far away. And then I might have made up some imaginary sounds in my head that were so futuristic that I couldn't really explain them. I think those must be the sounds Philip heard at Eastcote when Barry 7, Ann Shenton and Steven Claydon connected all the synthesizers together and got going. When Alison Goldfrapp appears on the album, singing mournfully on 'Revenge Of The Black Regent', it becomes for a moment that perfect harmony of machine and human sound that... hmm, who makes that kind of sound? Well, certainly Add N to (X). The theme of human and machine integration continues on 'Metal Fingers In My Body', which is accompanied by an animated video depicting the loving act between a woman and her robot. At least in 1998, this band were definitely on the futuristic tip. And if you want to double up on the experience, try listening to *Avant Hard* whilst reading Stanislav Lem's *The Futurological Congress*. That ought to prepare you mentally for any future world possible.

A less controversial record on Mute that year was Depeche Mode's compilation album *The Singles 86 > 98*. It's an amazing collection of music and it sees the band reunite with Tim Simenon at Eastcote to record the only new track on the album, 'Only When I Lose Myself'.

Listening through the compilation I think of my friend Flood who I haven't seen for years. He lives around the corner from me, and his studio is not far from Eastcote in Willesden.

He produced two of Depeche's most famous albums, *Violator* and *Songs Of Faith and Devotion*. Julie Bateman, our studio manager, had reached out to him regarding the book project and I decide to call Flood and see if he has time for a chat. He has recorded at Eastcote several times through the years and knows Philip.

Before I get to it Julie calls and says: 'Flood just came by the studio! I told him about the book, and he says he'll come by on Wednesday'. What perfect timing! I'm excited about reconnecting, and haven't really seen him much since we worked together on an album I produced with Norwegian pop legends A-Ha in 2005. It's a sunny day when he comes up the stairs to the room above Studio 2 where I'm working on the book. We catch up and he

LEARNING FROM THE MAESTRO

Drugstore singer Isabel Monteiro performing in 1997. That year and the following the band recorded *White Magic For Lovers* at Eastcote.

I always love the stories of what the engineers back then were doing with tape and how with ingenuity they overcame so many limits to the technology. It required some serious skill and it's also great to think of the bond between the engineers and assistants. Assistant was the worst job in the studio, but most often someone had their back. Like Flood. Everyone had been an assistant themselves and knew how it felt and how hard you were expected to work. But the difference was they were all being taught along the way, and the skills they acquired were so specialized that they'd soon go on to be the engineer and from there, mixer or producer. The sky was the limit. It's more unusual now with that kind of mentoring of young technical talent. A combination perhaps of fewer opportunities, but also different expectations from new graduates from the music tech colleges. The idea that some skills take many years or maybe a decade to perfect is daunting in the soundbite era. Great engineers – who have come through the 'old school way' and really know, live and breathe audio and recording – are far and few between. And on top of that you can open your logic system and click a pull-down menu to find a fairly decent simulation of an old Wurlitzer EP200 through so and so amp simulator. Not the real thing but close enough, especially if you don't know what the real instrument – through an actual amp, picked up by a good microphone into a good mic pre – sounds like.

One of the albums Flood produced and worked on at Eastcote was Curve's *Doppelgänger* in 1991. On guitar was Flood's now longtime friend and studio partner, Alan Moulder, a legendary producer and mixer. The duo consisting of Dean Garcia and Toni Halliday had met through Dave Stewart from the Eurythmics and became one of the early electronic-leaning indie-rock bands. They worked in Studio 2 and Flood continues:

then tells me a story I'm hopeful Zeus will laugh about almost 40 years later. It was in 1984 so before Zeus became a partner in Eastcote. He had been producing an album with the band Fashion called *Twilight of Idols* and Flood was engineering and mixing it at Trident studios. Flood says:

I'll tell you a great story. Something I never told Zeus had happened. There were so many drugs going on, and it was almost 24 hours-a-day of recording. And the night before we started mixing we had one of those stupid conversation like, oh yeah, it's amazing, what day of the week is it and wouldn't it be weird if like, stuff got wiped, after all this work. And the next day I started mixing. It was a good size mix-room, the console was L-shaped and the tape machine to the side of it behind me. And there was a solo matrix in the centre section, and I pressed it, and everything went into solo. And then I went out of solo mode, but everything was still in solo. I turn around and the assistant had lost his mind and put all the drum tracks into record. I leap to the tape machine and press stop. He was totally fucked, I mean the working hours were ridiculous. So I said, you better go home. Luckily it was in the middle of the day on the first mix and Zeus and the band were out of the studio. I just sat there. The assistant had wiped about a half verse of drums. But luckily there was an identical drum pattern in the second verse. This was '84 so I meticulously recorded bass drum and snare to the 2-track tape recorder, lined it up manually with the multitrack machine and flew it into the right place. And the next two tracks and so on. All 8 tracks of drums. I never told Zeus. Just said I'd had a technical hitch.

Ann Shenton and Steven Claydon of Add N to (X) performing at the Knitting Factory in New York in 1998. That year the electronic band used Eastcote to record *Avant Hard*.

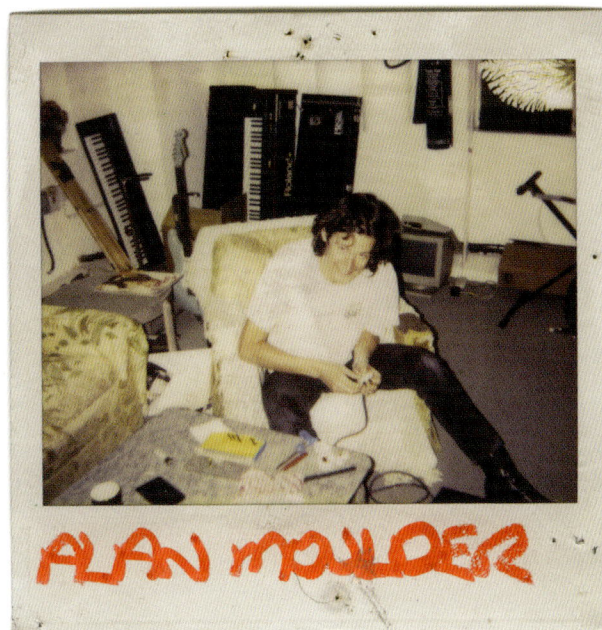

There was always something different about this place, something unexpected. The idea that you were in someone's front room, you could be working and walk over to the lounge area and sit down, having a listen. And my technique of not being right in the middle of the speakers, always listening from the sides, I definitely developed that here. In Studio 2.

I'm reminded of the summer in 2005 when we were mixing *Analogue*, the A-ha album. How as a young(ish) producer I really enjoyed sitting in to see Flood mix. And listen to his ideas. Through the years as a producer, engineer and mixer he's responsible for some of the best-sounding albums I know of. From Depeche and U2 to PJ Harvey and Sigur Ros. And listening to him talk about sound and studios is learning from the maestro.

This year in the story, in 1998, Curve are back at Eastcote again. After a short split in 1994 they are back to make their third album, *Come Clean*, this time working with Tim Simenon and Steve Osborne. This is the last album project Tim works on at Eastcote, and he is slowing down on record-making altogether. At this point he's just turned 30 and has already achieved what other successful music producers might hope to over a lifetime. His style was unique both because of how it sounded and the way he did things. On one hand he was a DJ who had figured out how to use samples and marry that with conventional artists and songwriters. On the other, and despite his young age, he was almost the classic old school record producer. With a team of musicians and programmers that he conducted with a bigger-picture vision. Finding Tim has become its own parallel story in this book. I love the records he made and am curious about his time at Eastcote. Amazingly, Ivor Guest sent me a message saying he'd got hold of Tim and a few days later I am on the phone with him. He is In London! I tell Tim about the book and what

is happening at Eastcote, and how I've tried to track him down for the past couple of months. Here is me, talking to Tim Simenon:

Martin: *Where are you these days?*
Tim: *I am in London. Well, I wasn't for a few years. To be exact, I left the UK in the summer of 2000. I've been living abroad in various different countries around Europe up until the first lockdown. I came back here actually, to take care of some business with my flat. Then the lockdown happened, and I've just stayed on since.*
Martin: *How did you meet Kerry Hopwood?*
Tim: *We met through Zeus. I met Kerry because I was working with John Fox, I think that's how it all came together. I think Kerry was there or helping John with something and that's basically how we connected.*
Martin: *When you came to Eastcote, when did you start using the upstairs room?*

Alan Moulder and Flood at work in Studio 2.

Tim: *I was about to start on the second Bomb the Bass album, that's what it was. I think we were just looking for a studio and Philip rented us a room where we set up our own studio, we called it Digiland. That's why we were at Eastcote. I think it was the first project that we did there, and then we also did the remix of Björk's 'Play Dead'. And the pre-production for Seal's 'Crazy' with Trevor Horn started there too. Then we went down to Sarm with a keyboard player called Bruce Woolley, we did a session with him there. Gota Yashiki played drums and Kenji Suzuki did some guitar stuff. He was living at my flat for a while, and both of them ended up in Simply Red. A few years down the line, these guys also guested on the second Bomb the Bass album. As did the guys from Tackhead. So all those guys and I became quite close, especially Keith LeBlanc and myself, so we did a lot of work together. From the third Bomb The Bass album we had got rid of Digiland and did everything in Studio 2, upstairs. Then that led on to Gavin Friday's album. We spent a few months there with Gavin, and later Depeche's* Ultra *was*

done there as well. I brought Daniel Miller in to Eastcote, maybe he knew about it or maybe he didn't, but the band seemed to all agree that it was a good place. And it was close to Mute, which Daniel liked so I sold it on that. I was very keen to keep him as close and in the loop as possible. I was drafted in as the producer, but it was a very tender situation within the band. I think we were all like, 'Where's it all gonna go; how is it all gonna go?' And Daniel knows the band so well, and having him a few minutes away definitely was a bonus and obviously his ears too. That was all a plus.*

Martin: Ultra *must've been a massive project to take on at that time?*

Tim: *Yes, I think in more ways than one. The band, you know, Martin and Fletch seem to be getting on okay. I think it was just that Dave, well… he was fighting his own demons obviously during that time. It's all very well written about, that period in his life and the band's life.*

Martin: *There is so much of that album that I love.*

Tim: *That's good, it's actually been a while since I've heard it. Maybe, it's time to drag it back out and have a listen.*

Martin: *Then you went on tour with them?*

Tim: *Yes, exactly. We finished* Ultra *and then we went back to Eastcote and I did a few more sessions. I did 'Only when I lose myself', that EP. We did the production there and I believe we mixed it in Abbey Road. And then we did the singles tour, which I think that was '98. I did the European leg of the tour as the DJ basically. So, seven weeks on the road with the band. On the private jet. That was really fun. I had a fantastic time during that period. It was a great experience and by that time Dave was clean and on the right track. Martin, Fletch and… yeah well we spent a lot of time going to after-parties, and it was all quite a raucous seven months, from my recollection. Then after that, after the tour finished, I started on a new Bomb*

the Bass album, but I did that in San Francisco with the guy from Meat Beat Manifesto called Jack Dangers. So I was out there for a couple months. Then I came back to Eastcote again and started working with a band called Curve. With Alan Moulder's wife Toni and Dean Garcia. They dragged me in to give my twopence worth and that was the last session I did at Eastcote, '98 I think that was.*

Martin: *There were a lot of S1000s weren't there?*

Tim: *[Laughter] I guess Kerry would have told you but we were the guys with the most S1000 samplers. Everyone was saying why do you need more than one? I think we had four.*

Martin: *You worked with Cameron McVey and Neneh as well.*

Tim: *Yeah. I did 'Buffalo Stance' with Mark Saunders. Okay, actually it's all coming back now. Kerry and I had a studio across the street before we had Digiland. It was on the top floor of the redbrick building, in Canalot. This guy had a spare room in the back and it was tiny, 20 square metres or something. That was where we had our first studio and that's why I first met Cameron and Neneh. Then Virgin Records was around the corner too. It connected so much of that stuff going on at the time, it was so vibrant with the music and Virgin being just across the street, it seemed to be quite a buzzy area.*

Martin: *What you guys did with the sound, with the samplers, was something that everyone was doing a few years later.*

Tim: *It was the sound for sure, for a while. For a couple of years it definitely resonated. It was an '88 sound. It felt like it went on till '95.*

Martin: *What was your relationship with Philip?*

Tim: *Really, really good. I mean the main reason why I think we worked at Eastcote was because I was very fond of him. I developed that relationship with him through having Digiland as well. We were renting from Philip, and he kind of oversaw the projects and just made*

Steve Osborne set up for making sound in Studio 2.

'19

sure everything was going smoothly but he also stayed out of our way, and we appreciated that as well. The help was always there when we needed it and because we spent a good few years there that relationship became closer. It really did become my second home. A good five or six years I spent there. Upstairs in Studio 2 by the window there was a couch and that was my little setup area. I would just sit there and stare out the window and daydream, listen to music and then when I turned my head back, it was the studio. Oh yeah, here we are again. And the tree. Is it still there?

The tree is there and Tim says he would like to come by sometime to see the place again. It's been so nice chatting to Tim. I realize there may be some discrepancies on dates and years between the different interviews, calendars, books, magazines and record sleeves that I've been through to piece the story together. A lot of projects took place across several years and it was a long time ago and so many sessions. It's humbling to think of all these great producers and sound magicians who have come through the studios. Philip and Zeus, of course, Flood, Tim Sim, Daniel Miller, Cameron McVey, Dollar, Alan Moulder, Jacknife, Steve Osborne, Eno, Trevor Horn and all the others I've written about, and who have been through the doors so far in our story. And how they all connected, worked together and crossed paths in different studios across town. Just one year left of the '90s now. Have you prepared for the Millennium Bug? ∎

Studio 2 in the late '90s.

In the late '90s Eastcote was in the midst of many big changes. Technology meant that more recording could be done in an artist's home or rehearsal space, and another wider threat to the music industry was about to rattle it to its core. Napster and its P2P file-sharing platform arrived. Now it was possible to download near-CD-quality audio files from the Internet for free. This would fundamentally change the distribution of music and eventually kill off the CD format in favour of streaming. And despite total revenues for music creators in 2020 now being back at an all-time high, it largely favours major record labels with big back catalogues and a handful of best-selling contemporary artists at any given time. I doubt many of us miss the CD. But as most artists were forced to spend more time on the road and play for their supper, the ambition level and available budgets for recording were decimated during the decade-long transition from illegal downloading to legal streaming platforms.

At Eastcote this wasn't really a problem yet as much as a storm brewing. More noticeable was probably another change of regular clients. It was the days of Britpop and with Placebo, Suede and Elastica came a new group of producers and engineers to the studio. And some enjoyed it more than others. I'm talking to Bruce Lampcov on the phone from LA and he tells me that after many years of living and making records in the UK with some significant artists, this era and his time at Eastcote were the catalyst for a move to California. Originally from Detroit, Bruce cut his teeth as an engineer and mixer at the Power Station in New York. Dylan, Springsteen, Neil Young and David Bowie are just a few of the artists he recorded there at the beginning of an illustrious career that would eventually see him move to London. He talks openly and very candidly, and tells me:

I remember Philip as being an incredibly supportive person, an awesome guy to have around. He was rock-solid, dealing with any issues that I had. I didn't really spend a lot of time talking to him because, you know, I was extremely overwhelmed at the time dealing with Elastica. I have a lot of memories of the sessions, very deep. In fact, I can say pretty certainly that those sessions helped clarify that it was time for me to move on to do something different with my life. There was a lot of chaos and stuff that happened. It was just really challenging, from all perspectives, their moods, their creative ability or inability. Some light memories too, of course. Damon Albarn would come around all the time to hang out, with him and Justine being a couple. And Donna, she was a real talent, I think the most talented in that band. And there was some good music being made at that time. But what made me question what I was spending my time doing, was all the drugs. I have a really weird memory of someone I was supposed to be doing a session with, that like many in the London scene back then was a smack addict. They all had this one doctor who would help them with their addiction. There's a drug you can take that basically makes you sick if you take heroin, to help you get off it. But of course, a lot of times they wouldn't take it. So, he came up with this new idea, of putting in implants of the drug instead... one day, not to ruin your day, this person is in the lounge when I get in, and actually with a knife had dug the implant out of the stomach, and there I was having to deal with that... You must know what it's like dealing with heroin addicts? So, these are my Eastcote memories... they were dark times. I also remember when Mark E. Smith came by the studio and we were doing a track with him that he was singing on. One strong memory I have of the building, the room, is a carpet or rug, in the control room which was really old and quite disgusting; obviously, everything fell on it and Mark was completely off his head and his cocaine dropped on the ground, and

BLOW THEM AWAY. FLY THEM TO THE MOON

he got right down on his hands and knees and sniffed the cocaine out of the carpet... it really happened.

I'm slightly lost for words but tell Bruce that the carpet has definitely been changed. And he really did move on. I first met Bruce at a concert when I was working with Jason Mraz. He was Jason's publisher and through the years our paths would keep crossing. He is now at Downtown Publishing and the reason we got on the phone this day is a project we are both involved in around Miles Davis's experimental masterpiece *Bitches Brew*. I think to myself there's probably bits of all these conversations I'm having with producers and artists that I should leave out of the book, and of course there are some details I choose not to include, because really they are just more of the same. But it would make it a rather pointless account of Eastcote's story and of the humans who are part of it to leave out the uncomfortable bits. A recording studio can be a sanctuary, a vibrant place where creativity flows freely, but sometimes it can also be a place where pressure and expectations make the job at hand very difficult. For Bruce, it was at Eastcote he decided that enough was enough. And regarding drugs, they are of course everywhere, in every part of society. Experimenting and questioning the perceived reality around us is a part of being alive. A really positive recent change for musicians and the music industry in general is that the younger generation consider it much less of a taboo to talk about drugs, sexuality and mental health. Both as part of their lyrics and art, but also just more straight up. Person to person.

Talking to Philip about the late '90s makes me realize he wasn't particularly fazed by it all. And I believe one of the reasons Eastcote has become what it has is his shapeshifting ability to be the needed, missing part in most any situation. I think of a book I read during a short stint studying philosophy at Stockholm

Brian Molko from Placebo in Studio 2.

Producer Phil Vinall with Stefan Olsdal and Brian Molko of Placebo in the upstairs lounge.

University. Let me explain and feel free to turn the page if you suffer from dizziness or have a tendency to get car-sick.

I was 19 and not quite earning enough money to get by from making music, so I took all kinds of odd jobs, driving a small truck, moving furniture and bashing metal at a local workshop. Sweden at that time had very generous government grants and loans for students and I decided it was much easier to combine writing songs and practising the guitar with a few hours a day at university than getting up at 5 am to drive a truck across the country. So, I enrolled. The book was on an extended reading list and it was called *Lila: An Inquiry Into Morals*. I remember it arguing the need for both Static (conservative) and Dynamic (progressive) energy in any functioning community system. So, veering swiftly off-piste here... if someone like me who after 35 years of making music might say (and feel) that music was better 'back in the day' or something similar... it does have a function. And when a young musician hears me say it and replies 'Fuck off', that has a function too.

Or in the words of my eloquent psychotherapist Jerry Hyde, when he once compared the inner workings of aging with *The Wire*: *You know, first you need to be McNulty, and go out there to knock some stuff over and stir things up. But then eventually you're going to have to be Lester and sit down by a desk and work on your daughter's dollhouse. That's when you'll solve the case.*

Last time I was up to see Philip in Oxford he was working with his son-in-law on the dollhouse he once built for his kids. They were refurbishing it for the grandchildren, and I haven't seen anything quite like it. It's beautiful. The detail is extraordinary, with plank wooden flooring, hand-built furniture and electric wiring. But it wouldn't be Philip's project if it wasn't a work in progress. We were talking about the dollhouse and then Eastcote and I said, being the new owner feels

like a big responsibility. Like being the guardian of something that has great value. And all of a sudden Philip lights up and exclaims:

NO! You can't be a caretaker. It's got to be funky. It's got to have passion, or else it has no value. It has to be a place where people can say what they mean. Blow them away, fly them to the moon!

Philip could be the Static or the Dynamic energy. He was interested in the outcome, not in any particular details. And despite the difficult circumstances around this time, great music still came out of the studios. I can see Philip cleaning up after trouble as much as instigating it.

Always with care and with a bigger picture than most of us in his mind. Definitely Lester, but with the ability to play McNulty for a while too if required.

During this period, roughly '97–'00, Britpop had moved into Studio 1 and brought its energy and excitement with it, along with some challenges and drama. Elastica were working on their album *The Menace*, Suede on *Head*, and Placebo came several times during these years, starting off with working on their '97 single, 'Bruise Pristine'. Brian Molko said in an interview with *Marshall Amps* magazine that year:

I think one of the reasons that Placebo have been so successful is that British rock for a long time has been devoid of danger really, devoid of perversion and devoid of provocation, which is intrinsic in the personality of this band and I think it has been crushed down quite a bit, it's been a bit limp-wristed really recently. We just want to be a powerful rock band, we are an emotional rock band and a band that will merge with you – but will also play with your head. I think that there was a reaction against the anti-star and anti-glamour of grunge basically, and that the kids wanted something that was by its very nature dangerous really.

Cameron McVey was also back in Studio 2 again this year, this time working with three

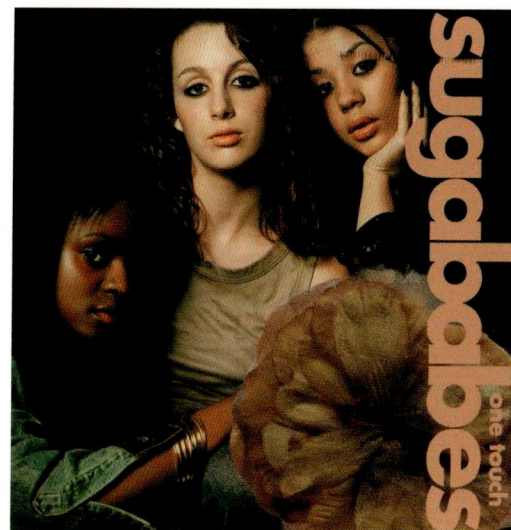

teenagers, Mutya Buena, Siobhan Donaghy and Keisha Buchanan on their first album *One Touch*. The Sugababes would go through many incarnations, but this first line-up was the start of the group. They wrote much of their own material, together with McVey, and the single 'Overload' set them up to become a much-loved act in this country.

I've discovered when researching and writing this book how much I enjoy following the leads where I have no references and here again I find a band name I'm not familiar with in the calendar. Suckle were recording at Eastcote this year and their only full-length album has been on repeat since the first listen. Frances McKee is from Glasgow and better known for her band The Vaselines and their connection with Nirvana, who covered several of their songs. She is an absolutely brilliant songwriter and *Against Nurture* is a fantastic record where she shares vocal duties with her sister Marie McKee. I'm struggling to find full credits but 'Saturn' that also appears on an EP called 'The Sun Is God E.P.' is engineered by Philip, gloriously open-sounding and like a mixture of indie rock and the Scottish wilderness. ∎

Donna Matthews, Sheila Chipperfield and Justine Frischmann of Elastica in the *NME* offices in London in 1996.

Sugababes, *One Touch*, London, 2000.

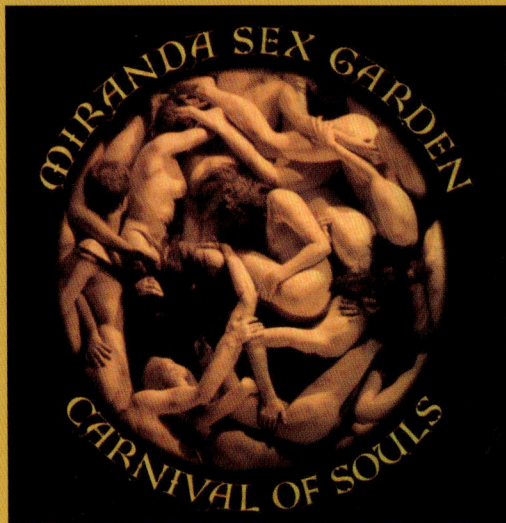

A BIG CRANE AND THE RIVER OF FIRE

It's a foggy morning in London when I wake up and immediately turn on the news. Two days after the US Presidential election, armed Republican voters, trying to enter a ballot-counting centre in Maricopa County, Arizona, have forced the centre to shut with its staff locked inside. These are surreal scenes, but the gun-carrying lunatics are supporting the most corrupt and dangerous politician in modern American history. For four years, with the incomprehensible support of half of the American people, the Republican Party and its financial institutions alike, Donald Trump has been allowed to significantly erode the idea of a working democracy in the US by continued questioning of its media and its institutions and by spreading an impenetrable amount of lies. Had someone told me this story in 2000 I would have thought they were out of their mind. But of course, madness breeds madness and 2020 is a mad year. I decide there's not much I can do

from where I am, in London on the first day of the second national Covid lockdown of the year. I'm just going keep thinking positive thoughts and continue writing.

On New Year's Eve 1999 I'm aboard the old RAF rescue ship *Carimuda* that Tia and I had bought and were living on, close to the flood barriers on the Thames in East London. We'd made a fire, lit some candles and were planning to have an evening in before going for a walk later to watch the 'river of fire' that had been promised and was supposed to make London's Millennium celebration the most ambitious anywhere.

There's a knock on the door to the wheelhouse, and our friend Pascal Macaigne has come by impromptu with a bottle of wine. He plays with The Bisons, a band I've just made an EP with, and when I say come in and ask if he wants to go and see the fireworks with us, it transpires that he's totally forgotten that tonight is when the world is celebrating the start of the 2000s. We all laugh about it and drink some wine and talk about whether the world will actually collapse in the morning with the Millennium Bug. Something doomsday prophets had told us it would, resulting in more than 300 billion dollars being spent worldwide by governments and companies to reprogram their computer systems. In the end we escaped the mostly fictional bug unscathed. And the ring of fire? Well, it didn't quite ignite. As we walk back to the boat along the river, I keep thinking about a bigger problem: how am I going to get my new Trident B-range console, three meters wide and weighing almost half a tonne, into my new studio on the top floor of Walters Workshops?

It's with some sadness I realize that from this year in the story I will start to recognize and remember much more of what happened at Walters and Eastcote. I've enjoyed diving into the colourful history with few ties and kind of incognito. The 2000s seem a bit more familiar

2000

Miranda Sex Garden, *Carnival of Souls*, Cleopatra, 2000.

Film composer Shiro Sigasu (left) working in Studio 1.

and… Well, I am at this point Philip's everyday neighbour, so working through what happened at Eastcote from now on feels more of a potentially solvable puzzle than a magic mystery. I didn't have a name for the new studio, and because I also had my old place, Electric Earth, across the road, I didn't quite need all of the space I'd taken on. I decided to split the space in two and let one half to Alan McGee at Creation Records and two of his producers, Felix Tod and David Ayers. And so began my tenure at Walters that would lead to building Kensaltown Studios a few years later in a brand-new building on the site.

The Trident made it up with a big crane, lifting it first onto the roof of the old bomb-shelter building and from there rolled in to what had been the live-room part of the new studio that became my second open-plan recording space. It was great to be back in the building where I had made my first London recordings and to see Philip and his crew at Eastcote regularly.

The first year of the new millennium was one of big block bookings at Eastcote. Atticus Ross and 12 Rounds are in the studio on and off all year. And in Studio 2 there are months

booked by Japanese composer Shiro Sigasu, who is another long-time client at Eastcote. Most known for composing the scores to dozens of anime films, he has recorded much of his award-winning work at Eastcote.

Also in the studio that year is the jazz saxophonist Gilad Atzmon and his Orient House Ensemble. As a member of Ian Dury and The Blockheads he had already recorded at Eastcote many times over the years and he is largely responsible for bringing through our studios a generation of British jazz musicians, lovingly referred to as 'the jazzers' by Philip and his

Gilad Atzmon at Eastcote.

Miranda Sex Garden recorded their first album in six years at Studio 1 this year – *Carnival of Souls*.

engineers. There has been a wealth of brilliant recordings of improvised music made in Studio 1 through the past few decades, including an incarnation of the UK jazz institution that is Soft Machine.

There are a few pop projects in the studio, most notably All Saints, who are back with Cameron McVey again, just after the winter break, working on the song 'Dreams' for the album *Saints & Sinners* that was released later in 2000. I've picked out three other artists too who I think help kick off a new decade at the studio in true Eastcote spirit. One is Miranda

Sex Garden. The classically trained madrigal singers were discovered by Barry Adamson and turned... well, they are like many of Daniel Miller's signings to Mute Records, a genre of their own. Philip is mixing Miranda S G's album *Carnival Of Souls* in Studio 1 this year, and their first album in six years is quite a trip somewhere between prog rock, folky vocals and grunge. And there is Mick Hale, the Mod Fun guitarist, songwriter and DJ from New Brunswick, NJ. Looking into his releases, it's probably to work on his dance outfit, Croc Shop, with Bobby Strete and v.Markus.

One of the albums I really enjoy from that year at Eastcote is Transglobal Underground's *Yes Boss Food Corner*. As the studios turned 20, Philip recorded the album together with one of his Eastcote engineers, Tim Rixton, who also mixed the album. It sounds just like I remember East London sounding and feeling then, as we entered the first calendar year with three zeros in a full ten centuries. The Natal-born Zulu vocalist Doreen Thobekile Webster sounds incredible on this record, and emotionally I remember these days as a time of hope. But that year too there was a contested election in the United States. Tia and I had been talking about moving to New York as we'd both spent a bit of time there and liked it, but we made a pact to stay in London should George Bush Jr win the election. After a Supreme Court intervention to stop an ongoing recount of ballots in Florida, Bush Jr became the President, and we stayed aboard the *Carimuda*. We did move though. A little bit further up the river, to Chiswick. ∎

Transglobal Underground performing at the Buttermarket in Shrewsbury, UK, in 2005.

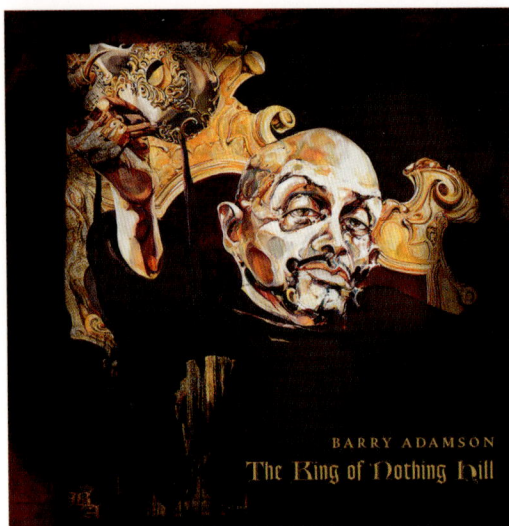

BARRY ADAMSON
The King of Nothing Hill

HAVE YOU INVENTED A GENRE LATELY?

I've always been very anti-presets of any kind.
Daniel Miller

Get up, get on up, it's 2001. At Eastcote Philip is doing what he's always been doing. Keeping the house open for those who want to take a turn off the main road. There are always a few of them recording at Eastcote, but perhaps the most unusual album made there this year, and one of my favourites from the early 2000s, is Barry Adamson's *The King Of Nothing Hill*. The album was released by Adamson's long-time label, Mute Records. It was recorded at Eastcote and Philip was engineering the sessions assisted by another of the brilliant engineers from the school of Bagenal, Antti Uusimaki. Barry had already worked in Studio 1 many times in different bands and constellations. He had his own room at Walters in the courtyard and it was his go-to live room. The album was released in 2002 and its opening track is called 'Cinematic Soul'. Joe Tangari wrote a brilliant review in *Pitchfork*,

where he suggests that it should perhaps be the name of a whole new genre. The review starts like this:

Have you invented a genre lately? It's probably safe to bet that you haven't, and there's really no shame in that – not many people ever do. In fact, these days it may be impossible to even do it at all, given how much ground has been covered and how much exposure we all have to so many different forms of media every day – chances are it would just turn out to be a subgenre of something else. Still, I'd like to posit that Barry Adamson has come pretty damn close to pulling it off.

At the very least it was another deep dive into the unknown. With soulful tracks and dreamy sound experimentation as backing, Barry is sometimes singing and sometimes whispering, and the dark mood is regularly interrupted by violins, saxophones and inventive orchestrations. It actually sounds to me like the perfect soundtrack to what Notting Hill was really like in the early 2000s. It was rapidly changing, with posh estate agents now in every corner and American coffee franchises moving in to prime spots along the Portobello Road. But at the end of 2000 started the collapse of the dot-com bubble, and the bankers who had only just moved into the area were escaping reality along with models and popstars, drinking cocktails and champagne at 192 on Kensington Park Road until the early morning. Eastcote is a few blocks north of Portobello, and around there it was decidedly rougher, with drug gangs fighting it out over territory and police helicopters circling over Kensal Road and Kensal Rise almost every night.

Mute Records had their offices and two studios on the Harrow Road, parallel to Kensal Road on the other side of the Grand Union Canal.

In the summer of 2001, Tia and I had decided to move back to Ladbroke Grove after a few years living aboard our converted navy vessel. In February that year our son Noah was born and

Barry Adamson, *The King of Nothing Hill*, Mute, 2002.

Barry Adamson recorded at Eastcote and in his own studio in the courtyard at Walters for many years from the '90s onwards.

at the end of a beautiful summer on the boat in Chiswick we felt it was time to put a pause on the river life. It had been a pretty stressful time: I was working a lot, Tia was pregnant, and we had been on and off the boat whilst it had been docked to repair and prepare it for us living aboard with a baby. We had all just come back from New York where we had set up camp at the Royalton Hotel. In the mornings I would take Noah, who was still just a few months old, out for a long walk so Tia could get some sleep. And then I'd be off to work. We were mixing an album with Leona Naess at Quad Studios around the corner from the hotel whilst also doing some final overdubs at Sorcerer Sound on Mercer Street. The album was called *I Tried to Rock You, But You Only Roll*, and looking back on that time it feels like a suitable title because I don't really know how we pieced it all together. But Tia was the anchor that somehow kept us from drifting too far from the coastline, and now the focus was to find a good place to live. On shore and close to the studio. We were house-sitting a friend's place close to the Portobello Road, and after having spent a good few weeks looking for somewhere to rent long-term we found a nice Victorian cottage on Barlby Road, a stone's throw from Eastcote. I was scheduled to fly to New York for another recording session, but the house we'd found was perfect and available right away, so I cancelled my session so we could move in as soon as possible. On the morning of September 11th I got up and started packing the van we had rented: it was the day we were moving into our new place. I drove back and forth with a couple of loads and just before 2 pm I was back to where we lived for some lunch. I walked up the stairs to the lounge and was met by Tia with tears in her eyes. The TV was on in the background and she says, 'A plane has crashed into one of the Twin Towers'. We sit down on the sofa and a few minutes later we are both stunned to silence. It was as if the world as we knew it had come to a standstill.

There is definitely a before and after 9/11, just as most probably there'll be a before and after Covid for the young adults of this generation. Nineteen years after the attack on the World Trade Center my son is now a grown up, making his own music and working a lot out of The Shed, the little annex to Eastcote, on the courtyard where Barry Adamson had his studio. Apart from feeling incredibly proud, it is really inspiring watching Noah's generation making music. Discovering sounds of the past and creating those of the future. And listening to their thoughts and conversations on what to do with their music. Many have already decided they have no intention of signing with any major corporation. The various new platforms, for raising funds, connecting with fans and distributing music means a big record label is not the only way to reach an audience anymore. Just as was the case with the explosion of independent record labels in the UK from the late '70s to the early '90s, this new generation are writing their own chapter and it looks like it could be a very good one.

I've made had so many calls, writing sessions, interviews and even family dinners on Zoom throughout the lockdown, and the mere thought of opening the app normally makes me feel exhausted. But today I have a Zoom call I'm both excited and oddly nervous about. I am going to interview Daniel Miller for the book, and he is someone I've always admired, both as a producer and the founder of Mute Records, one of the really great independent record labels. Like Philip and Eastcote, Daniel has always kept a space for those interested in exploring and pushing for the boundaries of modern music and technology. On the call, he explains:

We were just a two-minute walk from there, across the canal on Harrow Road. I wouldn't say I know Philip well. But we worked there a lot. The biggest project was Depeche Mode's Ultra, we were in the upstairs studio for a very

long time. I really enjoyed it. It's a great working environment. And it's not, how can I put this politely... it wasn't, at least not back then... the highest end in terms of technology. But I never thought that was important anyway, not in any context. It's more about the passion and the music you put into it. And Ultra was a huge seller and we got great results at Eastcote. Philip tended not to impose, he just left us alone really. And if we needed something or something went wrong, he was there, but basically he was very discreet and let us get on with it. We did a few other things, some Polly Scattergood work, and we used the live room sometimes. Because you know, we were in the building a lot, and Barry Adamson had his studio there too.

The first time I really heard about Eastcote was the echo time thing on Filofax, and I think that was before we moved to Harrow Road because we moved to Harrow Road in '83. It felt like a really, really good home studio rather than a formal structure like how studios were in those days. It was very unintimidating, and I think that was really important. For all artists really, but even more for younger or less experienced artists. If you walk into a more conventional studio it's easy to feel like you are kind of in an alien space somehow. Whereas Eastcote felt like an extension of a home studio, especially the upstairs room, which is what we used the most.

Depeche at that point were used to working at very high-end studios, but they weren't bothered in the slightest, I think they enjoyed that kind of homey atmosphere.

Daniel says that one thing about Eastcote is that it was incredibly good value for money. Especially comparing it to other commercial studios at the time. The proximity to his and the label's office was another reason they kept coming back:

Had it not been because we had two studios of our own, we would probably have lived at Eastcote. The thing for me was, I was the head

2001

of A&R as well as running the company, and this was before the Internet and swapping files and that kind of stuff. I didn't want to spend half of my time running around London to a studio in East London just to listen to a mix. So, it just kept the artist closer to me, and not just with me but with the company.

I ask Daniel if he feels that, apart from the obvious changes in technology, the way records are made now has changed in any significant way.

It's different, but it depends on the artist, a lot of stuff is still very similar. Probably the majority of our artists are more electronic-based and they tend to have their own facilities. But we have quite a few artists that work with their bands and musicians in the studio. Personally, I haven't produced a record in years now, but I think one of the most important things in the process is the fresh ears, just like it has always been. At the beginning of the project, it is about deciding what kind of record we're going to make and understanding what the artist wants from the record. And making sure they are on track. When you're in the studio, you get lost and you can listen to a song a thousand times. Sometimes you'll have been working on the hi-hat sound for three days. It's best if you come in fresh, not knowing the politics. That way I can go in and just listen to the music. And maybe I hear something and say, look, that hi-hat is shit. Why don't you just simplify it. You know, I haven't heard the arguments, I haven't been there for the trials and tribulations. These days nearly everything I say is just strip it back, there's too much stuff going on. Just because you can, but ten tracks of synth pads? You know what I mean?

I do know what Daniel means. It's much more common to do too much than not enough when making a record. I think this applies not only to producers and artists, but to the rest of the creatives around the making of a record too. Over-thinking is rife at labels and managements alike and everyone likes to think they know how it should sound. And especially how it should sound if it is to have any chance of success. After 35 years in the studio making records, some you've never heard of and some wildly successful, I've come to believe that you never know. But you can create an environment where magic can happen. And if it does, sometimes it will translate to commercial success and sometimes it will just be... magic.

Mute was founded in 1978 and, to learn the ropes, the first single Daniel put out was his own. I think every creative at labels and managements should read what he has to say about his process when being involved in records from the label side. He explains there's a beginning, a middle and an end phase. And his advice?

In the beginning:
– How are you going to make the record?
– What are the songs?
(Or If there are no songs? It's not a song, etc.)
– What's the process?

In the middle:
– How is it going?
– If it's going well, let them get on with it.
– If not, if there's an issue, if there's a problem. Ask, have they got questions?
– Listen and get involved.

In the end:
– It's in the end really that I prefer to get stuck in. I'm not a mix engineer, but I tend to get involved then, for the mixing.

So back to whether making records has changed over the years:

Actually, the basics of making records is the same really. ■

THE COOK AND THE RACONTEUR

I wish I had enough time to really follow every single thread in the amazing web of creativity that unfolded at the Studios and the intrigue that came with it. I could see myself continuing this project for a long time, but I still do have a day job and we're already a week into November. The plan was always to finish this document during Eastcote's 40th anniversary. So whilst the show must go on, the writing has to conclude at some point before the end of this month. Today, as I begin the 2002 chapter, I find a calendar entry reading 'H. Crew'. After some digging, I learn that most likely it stands for Heartless Crew. They are a garage outfit from London consisting of a trio of MCs called Bushkin, Mighty Moe and DJ Fonti. They started out in the early '90s as

The Blockheads at the Islington Academy in 2004.

Heartless Crew, who released their first single and compilation album this year.

2002

a mobile sound system, playing around North London, and were an early part of the UK garage scene. It took until the early 2000s before they signed to East West records and this year they released their debut single 'The Heartless Theme a.k.a. The Superglue Riddim' as well as their first compilation album, *Heartless Crew presents Crisp Biscuit Vol. 1*.

The Spanish punk rockers Reincidentes have blocked out a whole lot of time to make their album *Cosas De Este Mundo*. Reading about the anticapitalist quartet from Sevilla I find another link to Venezuela. Lead singer Fernando Madina Pepper is born in Valencia, Venezuela, and has commented on local and world politics through their three-decades-long career. Around the time of *Cosas De Este Mundo*, Fernando said, regarding music piracy, that not only was he not against it, he thought it could be a great tool for bands and artists that are not funded by commercial interests to find a wider audience.

A rebel of another kind who I also see in the calendar that year is my friend Ed Harcourt. I didn't actually know him back then, but we

would meet a year later when he came in to play piano on an album I was producing. My grandmother's old August Hoffmann piano, built with some serious weight, has followed me from my childhood to every studio I've set up over the years. When I drove it in Tia's dad's van from Stockholm to London in the middle of the winter in 1996 we had a terrible storm on the ferry crossing and everything in the van tumbled around like in a dryer. We arrived at Kensal Road late at night and it was raining cats and dogs. I'd asked a few friends to meet us, and we carried the piano up an outdoor metal staircase and into my studio. I immediately sat down to play it so I could see if it had been damaged. Not only had it escaped unscathed, it was also pretty much still in tune. The only pianist who has ever been able to knock it out of tune was Ed when he took a crazy solo on it that made the storm during the Channel crossing seem like a gentle breeze.

There are also many long-timers from Eastcote's extended family back at the studio. I've given up on trying to tie projects to an exact year, as by this time the 'two months in the

studio and an album has been made' days are long gone. Most projects are in and out of the studio for a few weeks or sometimes months at a time. Some recordings that don't end up on one album show up on a later one, in a different incarnation, or with another artist. And thus some of the early bookings this year are made for putting final touches on records that were started in 2001.

Cornershop are back with Philip in Studio 1 and will soon release their ambitious 13-track album *Handcream for a Generation*. Despite fuller instrumentation and Noel Gallagher playing guitar on a track, they definitely haven't lost their brilliant laissez-faire attitude to making music. And 'Lessons Learned from Rocky I to Rocky III' must qualify as one of the best song titles of the decade.

Tindersticks are back in Studio 1, putting the finishing touches on *Waiting for the Moon*, which will end up being their last album before singer Stuart Staples embarks on a solo venture that would lead to the end of the original line-up. The band formed in the early '90s and they immediately set their own tone in an ocean of indie bands playing around the country at that time. Careful and minimal was the musical setting Dave Boulter, Neil Fraser, Al Macauley, Mark Colwill and Dickon Hinchliffe created for Stuart's thoughtful storytelling. It's open and cinematic-sounding like big landscapes, and it seems obvious that Dickon would be back regularly at Eastcote after the Tindersticks, as a film music composer. He tells us:

I first met Philip when I was in the band Tindersticks recording at Eastcote Studios. Once or twice a day he would come into the control

Tjinder Singh from Cornershop in Studio 1.

2002

room to listen to what we were doing. He would often say little but would stand for a few minutes with a huge smile on his face. I later realized this was his joy at listening to live music being recorded in the studio. This joy and passion for music and people is what I always think of when I think of Eastcote.

Since those days I have been returning to work with Philip – he has recorded and mixed many film soundtracks with me over the years. He has been a teacher, a friend – and a wonderful cook and raconteur – on this journey. His ability to articulate complex musical and sound-related ideas is truly unique, as is the studio he built. From vintage outboard and microphones to furniture found in skips, Eastcote creates an atmosphere that gets the very best out of everyone who steps through the door.

Stuart A Staples by the classic MCI 500 in Studio 1.
Philip helped Stuart install an MCI in his personal studio
a few years later.

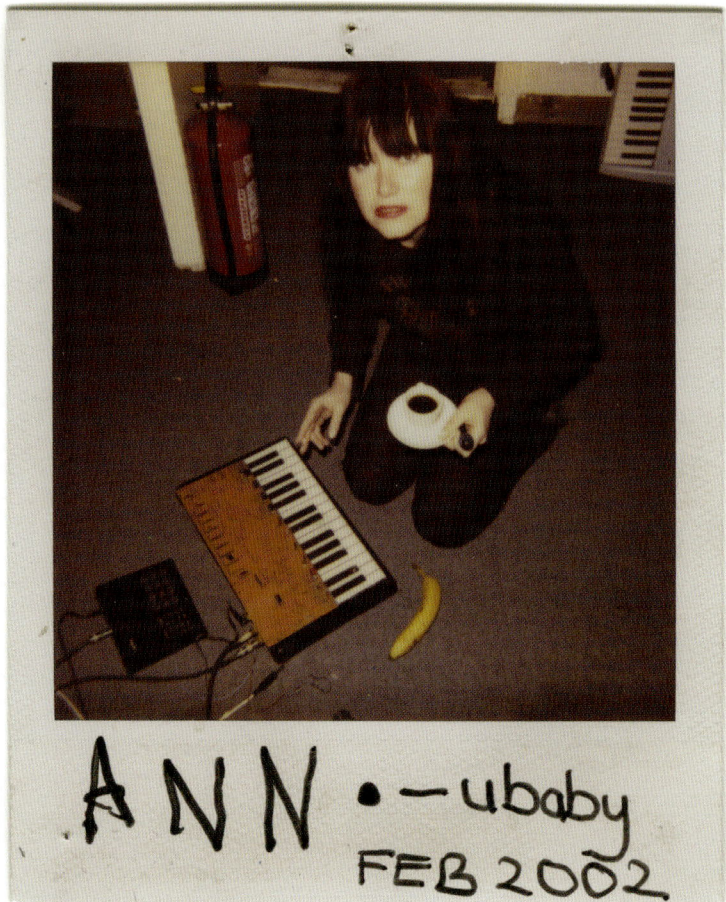

ANN •—ubaby FEB 2002

Philip's creative skills in the studio and his energy to go the extra mile to help the recording process are legendary. Sometimes this will be in the form of a lovely handmade piece of electronics and at others – such as my request to set up surround sound in the studio – a few breeze blocks and some gaffer tape to hold it all together. In my mind this combination of engineering skill and innate practicality sums up both Philip and his studio.

This is also the year The Blockheads are back at Eastcote to work on *Where's The Party?*, their first album since Ian Dury passed away. Chaz was again living in London and had been back to Eastcote a few years earlier to work on his jazz album *Out Of The Blue* that also featured Blockheads' saxophonist Gilad Atzmon. But this was the beginning of a return for The Blockheads. They've made another three studio albums since and still tour together. I'm having lunch with Chaz at a small Sardinian restaurant called Panella that opened a few years ago in the Trellick Tower just a few moments from Eastcote. He has come by to see the newly refurbished Studio 1 and to leave me a brilliant Polaroid photo of him and Philip in the late '70s. We order the home-cooked ragu, arguably the best one you can get in London at the moment, and Chaz says: 'This is what I always loved about being around here. The people, and all the great little places that would pop up'.

Marc Almond and David Ball had revived their electro-pop band Soft Cell for a tour in 2001 and were in the Studio 1 this year working on their first album since *This Last Night in Sodom*, released 18 years earlier. The album is

124

Ann Shenton from Add N to (X) playing with a synthesizer in Studio 1.

2002

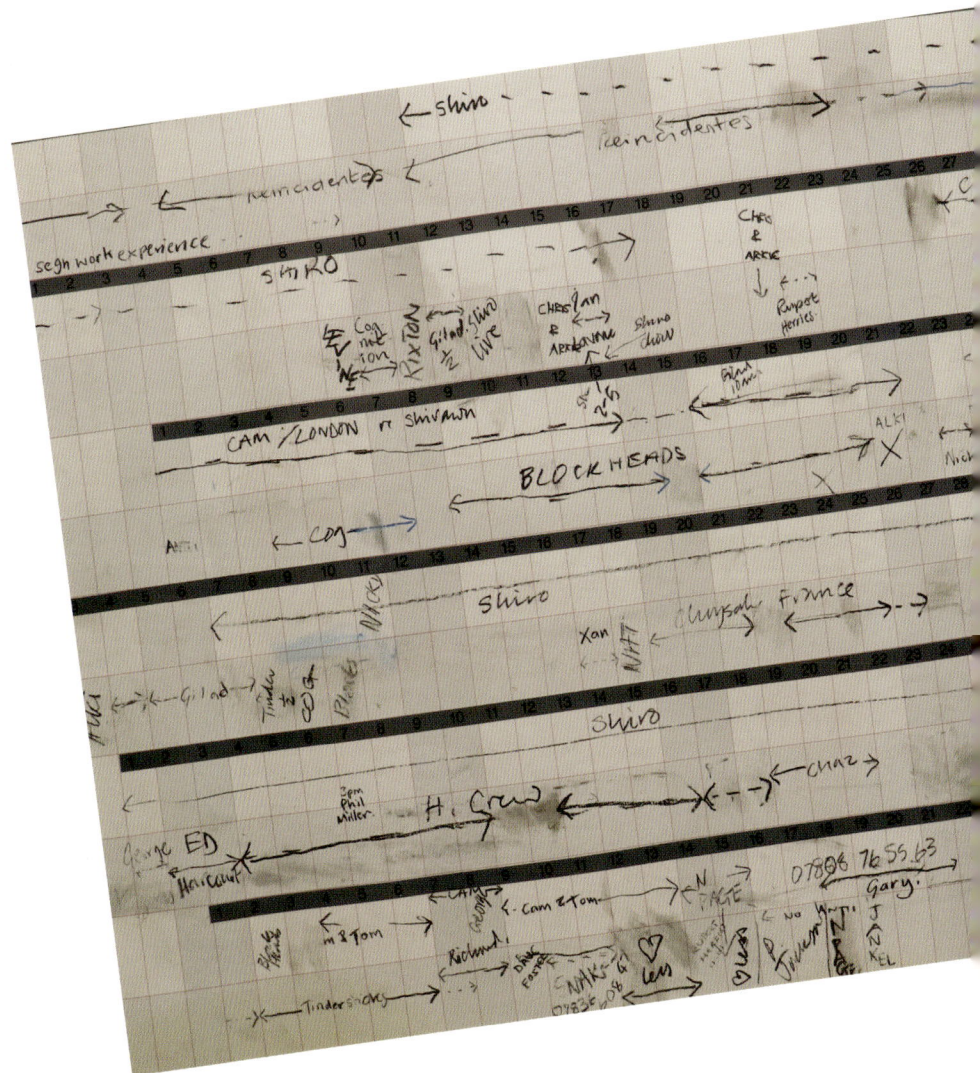

called *Cruelty Without Beauty* and is a return to form for the duo. The lyrics are darker than the synth-pop backings behind them and for me the album title sums up a rather forgettable year in British music. Britpop has fallen off the charts which are now fully invaded by boy and girl bands as well as *Pop Idol* contestants. But as we've seen in this chapter, the resistance is alive and well at Eastcote and most likely in other studios around town too. And as always, from the wealth of talented artists in this country would emerge a band that would inspire a new generation with infectious riffs and anthemic choruses. Across the road from Eastcote this year I was working on *Cobblestone Runway*, my first full album collaboration with Ron Sexsmith. I'd seen Coldplay live at Irving Plaza in New York the previous year, and when Ron said that Chris Martin had called to say he was a fan and asked if they should do something together, I suggested we invite him to play piano on a song called 'Gold In Them Hills'. It came together that summer when I was in Los Angeles and Chris came by the studio in Malibu where I was working. Coldplay were playing a show at the El Rey Theatre and we made plans to meet up and record afterwards. It was in David Foster's studio and he had rented a grand piano that was ready and tuned, but on arriving Chris said 'I like the piano track that Ron played the way it is. But I do have an idea for a vocal part!' We recorded it and it sounded amazing but, typically, he had sung the verse that Ron liked the most on his original version. We ended up putting both versions on the album. Six days after that Malibu session, *A Rush Of Blood To The Head* was released and Coldplay's music became the soundtrack of the early 2000s. ∎

Neil Fraser and Al Macaulay of The Tindersticks recording at Eastcote.

2002

FROM HAVANA. CON CALOR

It's June 2003. I'm recording at EGREM (Areito Estudio 101) in Centro Habana in Cuba. It's an unbelievable recording studio built in the 1940s that, despite having had to sell off most of the more expensive equipment to keep it going, still makes amazing sounds. Me and the musicians I brought over from London are trying to figure out how to best use the limited equipment available, an Amek console, a 2-inch Studer 24-track machine and a reasonable collection of good microphones, quite a few cheap dynamic ones, and also at least a dozen Neumann Fet 47s. There are some great instruments, amps and even a Mini-Moog, but no compressors or outboard gear. There's no need to worry though, the engineer has already set up the microphones, and Alex Cuba and his band of around 10 musicians have arrived. Percussionists, piano, horns, guitar and bass all in the live room and the drum kit in a quite small but good-sounding booth. The size and feel of the main recording space are a bit similar to Abbey Road Studio 2. It sounds more controlled than you'd imagine for a room that size, and when everyone begins to play the wooden panels and floors start vibrating from warm and beautiful tones and fiery rhythms. I'm in the control and can't believe how good it sounds. The engineer Jose-Raul Varonay has pulled all the faders up pretty much in a straight line, but it all sounds mixed already. There's a great young pianist called Rolando Luna about to take a solo and I want to hear just a little bit more of him and I pull up the faders marked Steinway on the console. For 30 seconds or so the piano gets louder but then falls back to where it was before. I try it again with Emilio del Monte Jr's congas and the same thing happens. I ask, are their headphone mixes all the same? 'Of course, it's the same as what we're hearing in here too.' And I realize. The musicians are mixing themselves. They play together and listen to each other, and if someone wants to come up in the mix, they move closer to the mic or play their instrument louder, and if they want to fall back, they move away. It's incredible to watch. They don't need any compressors, the light saturation from the tape is enough to limit things a bit and some of the roughs we run down there and then sound pretty much like what ended up on the final album. It helps that the engineer is a master of subtle balancing.

It's the middle of summer and it's very hot. Thirty-five degrees centigrade and almost 100% humidity. Tia is six months pregnant with our daughter, Hanna, and after the sessions we all get in a minibus to go back to the house we're staying together with the artist, his mum, some of the musicians and kids. This memory makes me think of when Philip had his preconceived ideas of recording shattered by a young engineer at Compass Point in the Bahamas in the early '80s. In Estudio 101, for the first time, I question my long-standing mental 'pre-set' to always compress everything as much as technically possible. I didn't dismiss it, I just realized that what Richard Dodd taught me about compression in Nashville in 1993 was right, but so was the lesson I was learning from the young engineer Jose-Raul at EGREM and the musicians in Havana. You don't need great equipment or

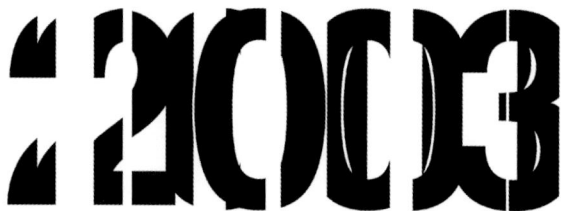

2003

a particular space to make a great record. Just a brilliant idea, skills and an open mind. I loved Egrem and the unbelievable Cuban musicians so much that I came back there to record more music a few years later. The legendary pianist Chucho Valdes played on the Alex Cuba album in 2003 on a duet with Ron Sexsmith. In 2007, I came back both with Ron for his album *Exit Strategy of the Soul*, and also to record horns and percussion with Craig David for his album *Trust Me.*

Recording studios all have their own character. Some are big spaces in amazing buildings. Some a tiny room in some basement in Soho. There are those that thrive on the idea of high-end, always upgrading to the newest equipment, so soundproofed that you can hear a needle drop and with acoustic engineers having tuned the control room at great expense for a flat response down to near 20Hz. And at least one is a constant work in progress built in the old stables of a North Kensington manufacturing plant, where the equipment is both vintage and brand new, and has been lovingly collected over the years by its owner(s).

There's no right or wrong. Depends on who you are and what you want. But if you are a musician, and whatever your instrument, you'll probably enjoy a studio where you can hear yourself well in the headphones and where there's a creative atmosphere. Maybe a bunch of instruments lying around to play with, and where you can see the other musicians you're working with. Few artists I know love having managers and A&R men in the studio, and not many would say no to a quality homecooked meal when they get tired. I come to think of a recent conversation with Nick Whitecross from KTP about their time at Eastcote in the early '80s where he explains:

One of the things about working with Philip was, you never had any A&R men in the studio. His whole ethos was, we are here, we are the musicians and we are going to make the music. You guys are not allowed in the building. And if they came by, they were made to feel so uncomfortable that they had to leave very quickly. Basically, the message was, get out. And don't come back.

Back home in London, my (soon to be) new studio Kensaltown, across the courtyard from Eastcote, should have been finished by now. But the three-storey complex was being built from the ground up and construction is slow. There was a record-breaking heatwave that summer in London too, and I remember me and Tia trying anything to cool down, including going to the Serpentine Lido in Hyde Park, only to discover there were hundreds of people in the small enclosure to the side of the pond and the water felt like a hot bath.

It was an unusual year at Eastcote. Very few rock bands and not many of the regular family are in either of the studios. One that was is Cameron McVey, who is back in Studio 2 with Siobhan Donaghy, who has now left the Sugababes and is recording a solo album. Amongst the tracks they recorded at Eastcote was the single 'Overrated', but it really isn't. It's a brilliant piece of quirky pop and in the credits I notice Cameron's son Marlon Roudette. He is a great musician and artist who I had the pleasure of working with once. Marlon had his own project, Mattafix, together with Preetesh Hirji, another of Philip's protégés. He started as assistant engineer and found his way to production at Eastcote. He features all over Siobhan's self-penned album both as producer and co-writer together with father and son McVey.

As we already know, when the world turns right, Philip keeps straight on. Or maybe takes a sharp one to the left. 2003 has some quirky bookings by the jazzers. There's one album apparently made with Ronnie Carroll. Can that be right? Carroll is a '50s crooner who represented the UK in the 1962 Eurovision Song Contest and came in fourth with the song 'Ring-

Natacha Atlas from Transglobal Underground at work in Studio 1.

Listening to the mix.

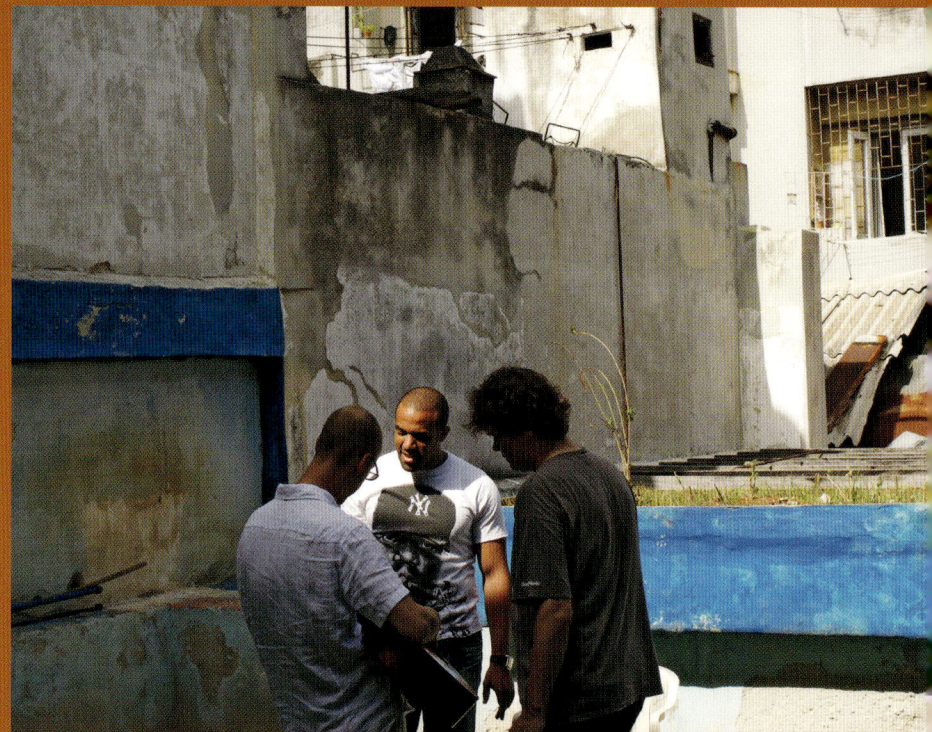

128

LEFT PAGE Top left: Outside Egrem in Centro Habana, 2003 **(left to right)** Alex Cuba, Emilio Del Monte Sr., Chucho Valdes, Ramces Rodriguez Baralt, Martin Terefe, Andreas Olsson and Emilio Del Monte Jr. **Bottom left:** Chucho Valdes, Martin Terefe and Alex Cuba in Egrem Estudio 101. **Top right:** Jose Raul-Varonay **(left)** with

assistant in the Estudio 101 control room. **Centre right (left to right):** Alexander Abreu, Amaury Perez and Jose Luis 'Chewy' Hernandez. **Bottom right:** Martin Terefe, Craig David and Ron Sexsmith working out chords at Egrem, 2007. **RIGHT PAGE Top left:** Playing the Bata drums **(left to right)** Ramces Rodriguez Baralt, Emilio

Del Monte Jr. and Emilio Del Monte Sr. **Middle:** Ron Sexsmith, Martin Terefe and arranger Joaquin Betancourt. **Top right:** Tia Terefe taking a photo in the rearview mirror on the way to the studio **(left to right)** Driver, Tia, Martin, Alex Cuba and Ron Sexsmith. **Bottom:** The big recording room at Estudio 101. Various musicians and film crew.

A-Ding-Girl'. He released a bunch of singles in the late '50s and early '60s, but then nothing until, according to an entry on Discogs, an album called *Valentine Days* produced by Philip Bagenal at Eastcote. It features Lebab, or basically Gilad Atzmon's quartet that apart from Gilad also includes Yaron Stavi, Asaf Sirkis and Frank Harrison. I can't find the music anywhere online. But on the big bad buy-deliver-everything-to-your-house-in-less-than-24-hours company website I find another album, *Back on Song*, that has the same tracks and is released in 2005 as his 'comeback album'. I figure it's the same one and click 'Buy'. Reading about his later life, I discover he had a political career running for various seats in different constituencies with a small anti-parliamentarianism party that he was the leader of called Make Politicians History. The story gets full of controversy if you follow the threads far enough, but to sum up the bizarreness of it all I shall quote from a BBC news report in 2008, covering that year's by-election in Haltemprice and Howden. Two of the three big parties were sitting the election out. The BBC anticipated one of the lowest turnouts in by-election history:

A closely fought category this one, with 14 candidates polling fewer than 100 votes each. Independents Tony Farnon and Norman Scarth came joint bottom with eight votes each – but they did not beat the existing by-election record of five votes set by road safety campaigner Bill Boaks in 1982. Former Eurovision singer Ronnie Carroll, of the Make Politicians History Party, failed spectacularly in his mission to get no votes, gaining an almost respectable 29.

I envision Philip and Ronnie Carroll at Eastcote recording romantic jazz standards, and think to myself that I really have to get myself out of this rabbit hole. I decide in favour of a break to go and make myself another coffee.

There are some great ones in the 'side roads' category as well this year. Phil Miller's band In Cahoots recorded a furious jazz rock album called *All That*. In the band were some great players, including saxophonist Elton Dean of Soft Machine fame. Also in the studio was Egyptian-British singer Natacha Atlas, known for her work with Transglobal Underground.

She's in the studio to work with Philip on the very ambitious album *Something Dangerous* and listening to the opening track 'Adam's Lullaby' featuring the Prague Symphony Orchestra is a great segue to what I think is the brightest-shining gem of 2003.

Last fall *The Guardian* made a list of the 25 best classical recordings of the century so far. On it is Max Richter's *The Blue Notebooks*, recorded by Philip at Eastcote, of which John Lewis writes:

Written in the run-up to the 2003 invasion of Iraq, The Blue Notebooks is Max Richter's meditation on violence and war, one that was recorded in three hours. The song cycle is linked by narration from Tilda Swinton, but the most compelling pieces don't require words. 'Organum' is a funereal organ solo, 'Shadow Journal' a piece of ambient house, but the centrepiece is 'On the Nature Of Daylight' (since used on countless films and TV soundtracks), where ever-expanding layers of strings are used to heart-tugging effect.

It really is a masterpiece and I highly recommend it. Those wanting to dive deeper can read Richter's own words about the album and how it came about in 'Millions of us knew the Iraq war would be a disaster. Why didn't Tony Blair?' (*The Guardian*, 8th July 2016). Even in a world suffering from collective ADD, you only have to scratch the surface to find a well full of hope. Young musicians everywhere are looking around and finding ways to express themselves and

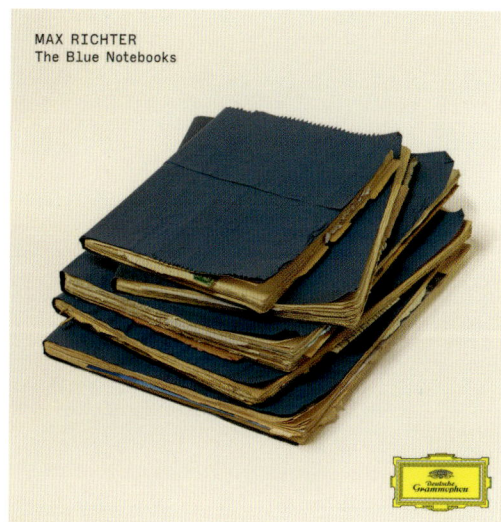

make sense of it all. Often at variance with those paths followed by previous generations. Whether intentionally or not, music connects deeper to the human psyche than most, if not all, other art forms. Yet politicians have told us that culture is not 'essential work' and that perhaps in the face of the economic fallout from the Covid pandemic 'it's best to think of changing careers'. To them I would like to say, May small glue-producing worms move into your mouths and shut them forever.

In October 2003, our daughter Hanna was born. A few months later in the spring of the following year she came with me to work at Kensaltown Recording Studios that had now finally opened. I was recording a solo album with Magne Furuholmen together with Guy Berryman and Will Champion. She loved to crawl into the bass drum when no one was there. She's 17 now and when she comes by to see me at Eastcote she tells me about her world and plays me music I've never heard of. And I know the future is bright. ∎

British composer and producer Max Richter recorded the award-winning album *The Blue Notebooks* at Eastcote in 2003 in reaction to the invasion of Iraq.

2003

Two years after Napster started its free file-sharing platform, in 2001, it was shut down. The music business had been lost for solutions apart from legal action, and along came iTunes, setting a precedent for a new and much lower valuation of recorded music. Along with a fantastic user interface that worked seamlessly with the iPod, Apple revolutionized music distribution. But it couldn't deliver the revenue labels had become accustomed to, and as CD sales dwindled, cost-cutting orders were delivered across the industry. Recording studios were closing down left, right and centre. And in New York and London, with their sky-high property prices, things were looking particularly bad. Dozens of famous studios closed their doors forever during the first decade of the 2000s, the majority to be redeveloped for residential use.

I had gone in the opposite direction and already committed to take on two whole floors of empty space in a new three-storey building at Walters Workshops, and in January 2004 we opened Kensaltown Recording Studios. There was no going back. Like a few times before, I'd put every penny I had on the table and was hoping the cards would fall my way. I mean, I really needed it to work this time as things were different now. Tia and I had young kids, so I was going to have to make ends meet somehow. So I worked. A lot.

Kensaltown wasn't a commercial studio, it was my personal one and I had designed it with a lot of help from a brilliant American engineer and friend, Kelly Pribble, and my long-time collaborator Andreas Olsson. The main room was an amazing open space, built for making records with live musicians, but we also had quite a few smaller studios and writing rooms. I hired a small staff of engineers and a back-office to whom I had to pay salaries, so I was saying yes to most every job I was offered. After a few tough years and falling quite badly behind on rent, I found myself with way more work than I could handle

IF SOMETHING'S COMING, IT'S COMING

Maximo Park in Paris in 2005. The previous year they recorded *A Certain Trigger* at Eastcote.

22 CD04

on my own. So together with my then manager, Michael Dixon, we filled the house with even more songwriters and producers and pushed on. It was a rollercoaster, we made records, had our own football team with everyone in the building, and there was a fair bit of partying too. We had some hits, most of them in America, and the travelling became crazy for a while. But I refused to see the mess I often left around me. I was finally next door to Eastcote but further than ever from the kind of studio and atmosphere Philip had created. Although I was loving both the music and the artists I got to work with – and the attention too, truth be told – every success put the pressure on to find the next one and I kept hustling. No time really to investigate what was happening across the courtyard or in the local neighbourhood. At that time Eastcote, like other commercial studios, was struggling. Philip explains:

It was a time when people were doing whatever they needed to, because budgets came down, and relatively studio prices also came down. We managed to survive partly because, well, simply put, I did everything. I did all the maintenance or most of it, I was engineering and was doing the books. I've never employed more than one proper engineer, and maximum two assistants. But most of this time I only had one assistant. I had engineers who would work freelance for me and they would quite consistently come in and do a job or people would ask for them. I think for somebody who hasn't done any work in a studio before, Eastcote had the look and the feel of what people would imagine studios to be like. A lot of modern studios don't look like that.

We got a lot of jazz bookings, which was helpful although it was sometimes a problem because somebody would want to book three weeks to make an album, and I already had a three-day jazz session marked in the diary which would've been booked six months in advance. But it was very useful having two studios, where you could do a deal, like doing a week in Studio 1 and a week in Studio 2, and that way I kept finding solutions. I mean, there was some creative accounting involved. I did feel I got away with quite a lot. People also liked the idea of it being a personal place. That it was a place created by a person, rather than a firm of consultancy, and that it had my stamp on it.

133

Young Hanna loved to crawl into the bass drum in the Kensaltown drum booth.

But Philip had enough reasons to be cheerful that year and one session that he particularly enjoyed was with the force of nature that is Grace Jones. Philip says: *It was a short session. She was fun, I liked her a lot*. Someone who remembers the session as if it was yesterday is Philip's engineer at that time, Al O'Connell. He tells me:

Grace came to Studio 2 for three or four days. She wore the biggest necklace I've ever seen in my life, with three large fist-size precious stone rocks attached from a thick piece of rope hanging from her neck. The room was full of producers and engineers with hundreds of years of experience between them. Grace was talking to all of them but mostly they were not that interested, but she really enjoyed talking at me as I was in awe and hanging on her every word. One of my main achievements assisting and engineering sessions at Eastcote was having Grace Jones and Brian Eno (separately) tell me that I made one of the best cups of tea they had ever had in their life. It was my plan to make sure I made the best cup of tea possible so people would remember me and it seemed to be working.

Ivor Guest was the producer of the session and if you recall we got to know him back in our 1995 chapter. He's at Eastcote again this year and here is what he says:

It was only a few days we were at Eastcote with Grace. Probably around '04/'05. What happened was, we wanted to make a record together, and Grace was keen to have Chris Blackwell involved. Chris suggested we record this particular song. Grace hadn't done anything for 19 years, but one thing she had been doing was accumulating songs. Like some of those songs on Hurricane. *She'd been making demos at random over the years, and the consequence was that we had some pretty good songs to work with. But there was one song that had been written by the guy who wrote 'Slave to the Rhythm' – Bruce Woolley. It was this kind of Brazilian song and I wasn't up for it at all but Grace said 'Oh, Chris said it's a good idea', so we tried to record it but it never sounded any good. After that, I said to Grace, 'Come on, if we're going to make a record, we just have to make it and not listen to Chris Blackwell or anybody else'.*

I tell Ivor that in doing the research for this book I've discovered that I'm most interested in what was going on between the really big albums that we've all heard about. Those stories always seem to lead to some unexpected and interesting places. Ivor continues:

Well that's always the way, isn't it? It's like I was trying to say, there was a bubble-y scene going on. There was this sort of experimental group – and I think you're absolutely right. That stuff is the most interesting in a way, and out of those scenes various things could have happened. Barry [Adamson] for instance was way ahead of the game. He had done The Man with the Golden Arm *and that just laid the groundwork for that whole idea of mixing cinematic music from the '50s/'60s/'70s with hip hop. Barry was miles ahead. But as you say, often those people aren't the ones that break through and make it big. I'm not sure how Barry felt about that, whether it bothered him or not. I agree with you though, It's all that sort of bubbling away, like we're trying something with Grace, it's not working. We do something else. All those kinds of things. If you only follow the big success stories you don't get the full richness of the creativity that was going on. I'm a great believer in that if something's coming, it's coming. I think, in a way, everybody who is experimenting are contributing to the successes too. You don't have to look back too far at the studios and the history to realize that that is normally the case.*

Someone who had been experimenting a lot with new sounds was a young engineer and

Philip and Grace at the Conlan Street entrance to Eastcote.

Philip Bagenal, Ed Baden-Powell and Grace Jones in the studio in 2004.

in the building, at the back of Studio 1. In The Shed. With his love of guitars, interesting sounds and circuit-bended toy synthesizers alike, along with a deep musicality and great engineering skills, he created his own unique sound and has since become one of the most successful music producers of his generation. We will hear more about Paul in the chapters to come, and whilst talking about celebrated music producers, this was also the year that Sir George Martin came by the studio. Philip was making an album with classical singer Hayley Westenra. Sir George had done some of the arrangements and his son, Giles Martin, was producing the album. Philip tells me a Beatles-related story:

I've had some very good engineers over the years and George Murphy, who sort of took over from me and is now the chief engineer, is very involved in getting the studios together for its new owners. He has a fairly wide knowledge and has worked in quite a few big studios. It's very hard to know, in this world of streaming and digital delivery – you know the story I always tell, when I was at school in Dorset in the '60s, one of my best friends' dad ran a publicity company who got the contract to do the publicity for Sergeant Pepper. *As a result of this, he had been given an album a week before the launch, and he allowed his son (much against the rules) to bring it back to school. It was the beginning of the term time, and we opened this thing, and we were like, what is this? What's happening here?*

I mean the artwork, and we put the record on... and it was this sense of amazement somehow, that this was a whole new world opening up. I just think with the formats and delivery we have now, you can't really do that. It's not the same, somehow. But then there are advantages in the way music is made now, it's a much more democratic thing, you know. More people can do it and try it,

producer called Paul Epworth. He got in touch with Philip in early 2004. He needed a studio to do one of his first sessions as a producer and had done a Google search for a West London studio with great analogue recording gear. So it was a good thing that Philip had spent some time to make a functional website. Paul decided to try out Eastcote for a session with

The Futureheads and a few months later he was back with Maximo Park to work on their album *A Certain Trigger*. Both projects did really well and through the years that followed Paul worked at Eastcote a lot, became a close friend of Philip's and an important part of the next chapter in Eastcote's story. He worked in both Studio 1 and Studio 2 and eventually took on his own space

The Magic Numbers photographed at Hanwell railway station in West London in 2005.

everybody can make music. I did meet George Martin, he came to the studio. He came to Eastcote. His son, Giles was recording some singing with Haley Westenra, and Sir George came down to check some arrangements. I don't think many people recognized him to be honest.

One quite funny thing, I used to say to everybody: 'Anybody is welcome to work in the studio except for one person, Rod Stewart'. I wasn't going to have him. I don't know what it was about Rod Stewart that I didn't like, but I just didn't like him._

I can't help smiling and ponder whether I should tell Philip that a Christmas song I've written is being released this winter with Robbie Williams and... Rod Stewart. Luckily the record isn't recorded at Eastcote, so I'll leave that one to percolate.

The Hayley Westenra album Philip engineered that year is called *Pure* and another departure from the traditional fare at Eastcote. She has a beautiful classically trained voice and is backed up here by big choirs and the Royal Philharmonic Orchestra, conducted by George Martin at AIR Studios' Lyndhurst Hall. It's very unprovocative, kind of a descendant of the 'popera' style that had become very popular after David Foster's production of 'The Prayer' with Andrea Bocelli and Celine Dion. Whilst I have a hard time envisioning Philip encouraging that sort of technically immaculate sound, it's clear that his skills were deep enough for any kind of recording situation. During my own times at Eastcote, I mainly knew Philip in the capacity of host and studio owner. I wish I could time-travel into one of his early '80s sessions, observing a maestro in the making and pick up some of his skills as an engineer. Or to Abbey Road in the '60s to sit in with Sir George Martin himself.

Despite the general woes at the time and shrinking budgets, Eastcote fared pretty well in 2004. Apart from Epworth, Westenra and

the jazzers there were a lot of other acts too working at Eastcote for the first time that year. The Magic Numbers were in for a good month, presumably writing for their Mercury Prize-winning debut album that was recorded the following year at Metropolis. *The Magic Numbers* is a brilliant album produced by my friend Craig Silvey who moved in to the building a few years later. The Kooks are in the calendar too, and by coincidence I've just bumped into Luke Pritchard on the courtyard and reminisce about a session I did with them at Kensaltown. It makes me realize that despite not really paying attention to what was happening at Eastcote around that time, in reality there was very little separation.

The Iraq war and Tony Blair's famous fairytale about weapons of mass destruction were on everybody's mind at that time. And in early 2004 a young singer called Nerina Pallot came to Eastcote to record a song that she'd written called 'Everybody's Gone To War'. Apart from being quite a brilliant song with poignant lyrics and a very catchy chorus, it's an interesting story for another reason too. It was released as a single in 2005 with moderate success and included on the album *Fires* the same year which flopped. After extensive touring she was signed to a new record label and both album and single re-released in 2006. This time it became a big hit in the UK, complete with a performance on *Top of the Pops*. Which is another thing about music: it often takes its own path to reach its audience. Predicting a hit is guesswork at the best of times, and it's really not over till it's over. ∎

Maximo Park with producer Paul Epworth and engineer Al O'Connell (right).

22 004

I first became aware of Eastcote Studios in the '80s when I was A&R co-ordinator at A&M Records and, if memory serves me correct, I booked a few sessions in with Zeus B Held. Moving to studio management in the '90s for Metropolis Studios, the '00s at Townhouse Studios (now sadly flats) and then at Trevor Horn's Sarm West (also now flats).

Studios were closing all around town and I went on to work at Elton John's management company Rocket Music. Fast forward to May 2015 working for Martin Terefe at Kensaltown Studios. Walking through the courtyard on a sunny May morning, with Kensaltown at one end and Eastcote at the other, felt like coming home! I realized how much I'd missed the studio environment. I soon started helping Philip out with the bookings for Eastcote and fell straight back into my comfort zone, and since then I've been pleasantly surprised to see so many old and new faces coming through the doors.

Julie Bateman. Studio Manager, Eastcote Studios

In 2005 a luxury property development in an old Victorian church hall in North London was completed and saw its first residents move in. In the *Evening Standard* supplement 'Homes and Property' it was awarded the title 'Best New Conversion' and was applauded for an abundance of 'history'. A re-write with a slightly different narrative would be:

The musical heritage of Wessex Studios has finally been put to rest as its conversion to nine luxury apartments is complete and ready for the market. The home to British recording artists like The Sex Pistols, The Clash, The Rolling Stones, Queen and U2 couldn't avoid its fate once the shimmer of property coins found its way into the right pockets.

Of course, the only thing that is certain is change, and many other studios were destined to face the same bitter end. You have to be slightly mad to try to keep a recording studio alive in a central area of any major city, but I

THINGS TO DO WHEN THE BOSS IS ASLEEP ON THE SOFA

View toward Trellick Tower, the iconic high-rise built by Ernö Goldfinger as social housing in the early '70s. By the mid-'00s the area was increasingly being turned into luxury apartments by property developers.

2005

can't help feeling sad for each one that closes its doors. Philip had managed to find a balance that worked though. Every couple of years a new artist or producer would fall in love with the quirky vibe and great sound of Eastcote. And that would help to keep it alive. It was all systems go in Philip's house this year.

There was some explosive young punk jazz made with Acoustic Ladyland. Estelle was in the house with her amazing voice taking in some last-minute Eastcote vibrations before heading out to make hit records with Will I Am and Kanye West in rather more fancy establishments. Another young producer, Dimitri Tikovoi, started recording at Eastcote and brought both garage rock with The Horrors and some guitar-driven indie pop with a band called Kill The Young. Max Richter was back. And there was even a bit of English metal from DAM. I could go on, it was a busy year. But I'd like to go back to Paul Epworth and two albums he worked on at Eastcote in

2005. Plan B's *Who Needs Actions When You Got Words* and White Rose Movement's *Kick*. Paul was quickly becoming in demand as a producer and was in need of a good Pro Tools engineer. And so it was that Eliot James arrived at the studio and wouldn't leave. An amazing producer himself, he is still at Eastcote in Studio 3 that Philip built in time for it to become Eliot's base camp. Eliot tells me:

I first came to Eastcote about 2004 whilst working as an engineer/Pro Tools operator for Paul Epworth. Initially I was involved in recording sessions where Paul would record stuff there on 2-inch tape and I would take it away and do Pro Tools editing work in my own studio then send stuff back to him... mail order Pro Tools edits I suppose...

I think the first long session I did there was some stuff for Plan B's first album on 679 recordings, followed by a band called White Rose Movement who were signed to

Eliot James in Studio 1.

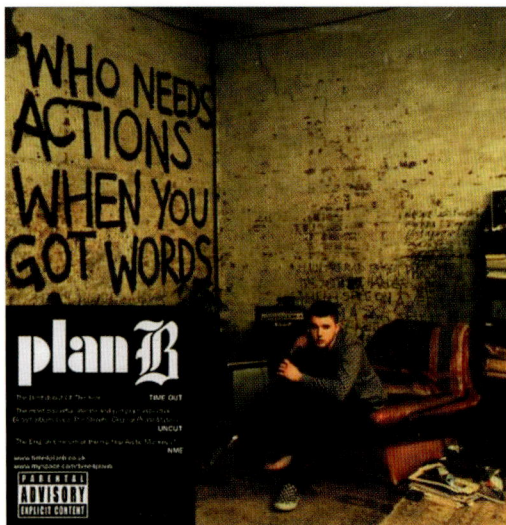

Independiente. I've pretty much lived there ever since.

First few sessions are all a bit hazy to be honest. Those were very long days which tended to blur into very long nights and occasionally even the next day too. At the time I had just been traipsing around a number of studios with Paul and I was also coming away from doing a lot of Pro Tools tech work for FX Rentals, so I had become familiar with a lot of the London studios, large and small. A lot of the studios, particularly the bigger ones, had a slightly self-important vibe going on. There would be an assistant who thought they were really cool because they worked with someone famous last week, but they were actually the bottom of this awful hierarchal ladder and everyone seemed to take themselves terribly seriously.

Eastcote seemed to be the antithesis of this. Philip had completely torn up the rule book on how to do things and had created this wonderfully homely and cosy, slightly DIY atmosphere which appeared to be as much his living room as a studio. He was very anti-establishment I suppose. Both in terms of his technical approach – he was always modifying stuff and methods – but particularly in the way he dealt with clients and conducted business. He didn't seem to be pander to anybody and would treat everybody the same whether they were a major label artist or some kid that had just knocked on the door with a CV looking for work. Total breath of fresh air to me at the time and I completely fell in love with the place and Philip.

I ask Eliot about what he remembers of those first sessions with Paul and he tells me that he got an accidental first break as a producer during the Plan B session:

Paul was asleep on the sofa after a long session and I sat down by the piano with Ben [Plan B] and started writing a song called 'Everyday'. It might not have been my first producer credit because it took a few months. But Ben called me up one day and wanted us to finish the song for his album and we did.

I also remember Philip's new assistant Anna Tjan turning up for her first day of work to find a die-hard White Rose Movement night out/studio session from the day before still happening… all looked a bit seedy I think… I don't think she liked the look of her new job.

Eliot was not only a part of a new chapter, but also a player in all subsequent chapters at Eastcote. Still based in Studio 3 and making brilliant records. And Anna very soon saw a more appealing side of Eastcote as Philip trained her to become another of our great engineers and she kept working in the studio for years.

Philip was busy engineering, hosting, teaching, intervening at the right times and mixing records. In December that year, long-time client and Eastcote friend Stuart A Staples was back in the studio. Having a break from

Plan B, *Who Needs Action When You Got Words*, 679, 2006.

Top left: Anna Tjan in session. **Top right:** Acoustic Ladyland keyboardist Tom Cawley in Studio 1. **Bottom left:** Acoustic Ladyland drummer Seb Rochford in Studio 1. **Bottom right:** Philip and Stuart A Staples.

OUT

OUT

nord electro

SYNTHES

Tindersticks, he had been recording a second solo album at his own studio that Philip had helped him set up. Stuart describes it as *virtually a mini Eastcote, keeping all the bits I loved, especially the MCI 500.* But when it was time for mixing, it was back to Studio 1 with Philip. Stuart continues explaining his relation to Eastcote like this:

We first visited Eastcote in early '93 when we were looking for the right place to record our first album. We had spent the previous year meticulously making the demos in our kitchen in Queen's Park, and London and its studios were still an exciting mystery to us then. Philip briefly said hello as he was in the middle of a mixing session with Moonshake, which we were very impressed by. We eventually chose Townhouse 3 for the recording – we were seduced by the wealth of timpanis and marimbas – but it wouldn't be long before we were returning to Eastcote to make our first soundtrack, Claire Denis' Nénette et Boni. From there on Eastcote became our place to record in London and it still feels this way today.

For me Eastcote is the embodiment of Philip, his life's work, full of his personality traits. But above all generous and warm and easy [to] play and explore music in. A great testament is the long line of assistants he has taken on and trained over the years, always giving them space to find their own voice, all progressing and moving on to greater things, not only with that wealth of experience behind them but an insight into how to relate to music. I feel Philip is a unique engineer in the way he is able to listen to music in an emotional way. In my experience this is rare and I have always sought his opinions on our work. And those opinions are always good value: 'This music is like staring deep into someone's arsehole' was how he described our score for White Material. At that moment it gave me a great sense of pride. ∎

Post-punk band White Rose Movement playing at the 100 Club.

Philip setting up the RCA microphone.

KT Tunstall performs at the Brit Awards in 2006.

HE F***ING BUILT HIMSELF A STUDIO HE DOESN'T FIT IN

One of my favourite singers and a dear friend recorded at Eastcote in 2006. And at the time of writing this, in November 2020, KT Tunstall and I are in the process of making a new album there. Well, kind of. I'm in Studio 2 and she is at her home studio in Topanga Canyon. Lockdown made it impossible to be in the studio together this year, so we decided to try a long-distance album recording. It's kind of funny because the first song we wrote together nearly 20 years ago in the early 2000s, was called 'Other Side Of The World', and was about a long-distance relationship. It's the opening track on KT's first album, *Eye to the Telescope*, and we've continued to write songs together ever since. I knew that she had recorded at Eastcote around

that time, but I have no clear recollection of stopping in during the sessions or the order of events. I get on the Zoom video machine to have a chat with KT and see what she remembers from her time at Eastcote. She tells me:

My first experience of recording in London was at Eastcote. You know the story well. Must have been around '00–'01? We had both been signed to Sony ATV and were writing together at your place on Kensal Road, at Gaia. I had the track listing for an album all done, except for 'Black Horse and the Cherry Tree'. Me and my manager Simon Banks were trying to find a record deal to go and start making the album, and we couldn't get one. We just couldn't get one. Eventually we were offered a deal with Columbia in the US, and we were about to sign it. It was in December 2002. And then just after the holidays in January the head of the label Tommy Mottola was fired, and the entire thing just went down the toilet. And not only did the deal offer go away, I was now also damaged goods. I'd had a big record deal offer that didn't happen, and from there it got even harder. Relentless had their offices on Kensal Road too and had a small imprint label for Asian beats and through them they had offered me a tiny

Alex Turner of Artic Monkeys photographed by Julian Broad (National Portrait Gallery).

KT Tunstall playing the old pump organ.

deal that we had sat on and didn't really want to sign. My publisher had said they could put up some money so we could make the record and they would put it out themselves, so that's what we set out to do and ended up at Eastcote. But we really didn't know what we were doing, and I remember, two weeks into the recording, having this horrendous conversation with Simon, just outside the studio in the sun, on the bench in the courtyard. He said that Relentless had made the terms slightly better and asked me: 'How is it going in there?' And I had to tell him it wasn't working. It just wasn't sounding good.

And you know, it's just this terrible feeling in the pit of your stomach when you know that you're making something that isn't right.

KT ended up signing to Relentless and finishing the album with Steve Osborne somewhere else. I remember Steve calling me for files to the demo version of 'Other Side Of The World' which ended up a hybrid of our respective versions, but apart from that I didn't hear much of what they were working on during the process, until KT played me the album at my new studio Kensaltown on the afternoon before our grand opening party in early 2004. It sounded fantastic.

I had asked her to play a few of the songs we'd written for the opening and she said: 'I've just bought a loop pedal, and I've written this song that I really like. Is it okay if I play that one?' That evening when she was banging the guitar and chanting backing vocals into the loop pedal, and then started singing 'Black Horse and the Cherry Tree', the guests at the party went mad. It was so good. A few weeks later there was a cancellation on *Later with Jools Holland* and she was asked to perform, and although the song wasn't on the album she was about to release, she had no doubt about what she was going to

play. It was one of those TV moments that only happened before the social media days, and the live performance was quickly stripped on to the album before its release.

Steve and KT then recorded a studio version that eventually replaced the Jools performance on the second print run of the album. *Eye to the Telescope* was nominated for the Mercury Prize and went on to win awards and sell a whole lot of copies in the coming years.

KT and Steve Osborne came back to Eastcote in 2006 to work on the follow-up album *Drastic Fantastic* and KT continues:

Despite my first session at Eastcote not going as planned, it immediately became my favourite studio. It's a bit like duckling attachment syndrome, that the first thing they see, they think is its mum, you know. It was the first experience I had of recording in London. I found it difficult moving to the city. I still don't really like being in cities. And I still don't massively enjoy being in high-end studios. There's just a sterility to them. It's like music that's been overproduced. The studio itself can be overproduced. And then feel homogenous, like you could be anywhere. Now that I've got so much experience of recording, I don't feel intimidated anymore going to big studios. I love recording at Sunset Sound, and The Village Recorder in LA. And I once went to Paisley Park and got to check out Prince's studio. And these are all high-end studios, but they're Eastcote high-end. Do you know what I mean? They are so full of character. Eastcote really taught me the importance of not necessarily creating a vibe that's so strong that you have to step into its personality to make music. You can still take your wishes and emotions… and headspace into that studio and make it your own.

Tracey Thorn at work in Studio 1.

Alex Turner in Studio 1.

When I ask KT about Philip she talks for a long time and it's beautiful to hear the love and respect she has for him and that she shares with so many others I've spoken to in the past couple of months. In particular, she confirms Philip's clear boundaries when it comes to letting label people into the studio. She describes how she felt safe at Eastcote and could allow herself to get into that creative space. And that even if an A&R man, friend, or manager would arrive to listen to something, he would read the situation in the studio and if necessary stall, delay or outright tell the person to leave:

I really liked Philip. We got to know each other a bit during my first round at Eastcote. As soon I met Philip, I knew he was a totally extraordinary character. First of all, he's two feet too big for the studio. I mean, he f***ing built himself a studio he doesn't fit in. Like a six-foot-five man deciding to buy a '70s Fiat 500 to drive. The thing with Philip was, you can just smell it, if someone knows musicianship. And knows the life of a musician. And there is an automatic unspoken kinship when you meet someone that knows what you're talking about, and what you're going through making a record. What you need and don't need when making a record. He was just a very legit, creative, knowledgeable... a wise dude and trustworthy ally. And it's great that he's a big motherfucker. Because he was a buffer to anyone trying to muscle in on the process.

With every new chapter I think, is this going to be a slower year? Well not yet. There was the usual random mix of music being recorded in the studio that year including the all-girl hard-rockers McQueen, Tracey Horn from Everything But The Girl. The brilliant Kim Richey is there to work with Giles Martin and the eccentric and one-of-a-kind Patrick Wolff.

There's a remarkable amount of top-level jazz again this year. Eastcote really has become one of the important London jazz studios by now

and Philip is behind the console for most of it. Some fantastic music from Soft Machine Legacy, Jon Opstad, Louis Vause and a new album with Acoustic Ladyland called *Skinny Grin* that starts off with a mellow piano-and-bass duet that creates an illusion that this is a gentler affair than last year's album. But you won't be disappointed: an explosion of angry rhythm erupts a few minutes later on 'New Me' and then we're away.

Paul Epworth is working this year at Eastcote on more Plan B and also on a rather brilliant album with the New York band The Rapture. I'm trying to think of a way to describe it but it's such a conglomeration of styles and influences, blended into its own unique sound.

When I hear the fat analogue synth bass and tight drums it's easy to see where Paul was heading sonically. Punky-emo-disco comes to mind as some kind of description, but really it's about Luke Jenner's wide range and engaging voice over some rather brilliant and funky tracks. The album is recorded between New York, London and LA and next to Eastcote in the studio credits is Sear Sound. That's another amazing studio founded by sound pioneer Walter Sear in the mid-'60s. I see my friend Tony Maserati in the mixing credits and still remember when he told me about Sear Sound, around that time actually, and that he thought I'd like it. I never recorded there but hope that it's still open

The Rapture on The Bowery, New York. Their album *Pieces of the People We Love* was partly recorded at Eastcote.

and hasn't been turned into apartments. I decide if it is, I'm going to do my next New York project there.

Eliot James was doing his first full album project in Studio 1 that year with indie band Vatican DC. After finishing recording their only full-length album, *Make It Ride*, it was perfect timing for Eliot to move into Studio 3, Philip's newly built room upstairs. Eliot explains:

In about 2006 I got my first production gigs and at about that time Philip had started building a third studio room upstairs. I think I was quite lucky because at the exact time I finished recording my first full album project in Studio 1 I had to move out of my studio in Shepherd's Bush (the building was being developed I think), so he suggested I use Studio 3 as a base to finish up all the edits and mixing etc. So upstairs I went, and it's been my production base ever since. One thing I remember from upstairs that year was hearing Laura Marling doing her first demos in the Studio 2 booth with Philip... 15 years old at the time and sounding like a megastar in the making.

At the end of that year another megastar in the making came to record an album at Eastcote along with producers James Ford and Mark Crossey. Well, truth be told they had already taken the UK by storm earlier that same year when their debut album *Whatever People Say I Am, That's What I'm Not* was released. Either way, a young Alex Turner pitched up with his band Arctic Monkeys in December to record their second album, *Favourite Worst Nightmare*. The Arctics were truly a burst of energy into a British rock scene that needed it. And just when everybody thought you had to have synthesizers, programmed beats or an acoustic guitar to get famous. ∎

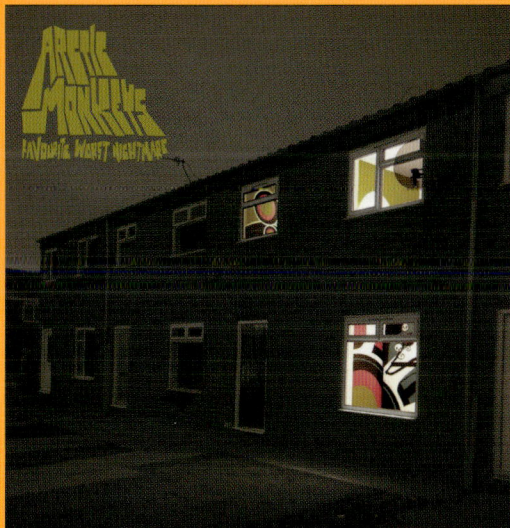

Arctic Monkeys, *Favourite Worst Nightmare*, Domino/ Warner Bros., 2007.

Arctic Monkeys in Studio 1 lounge.

CAN YOU SEND THIS BACK TO THEM PLEASE?

Philip had recorded a song with Laura Marling, and it was about to be released as a single or EP. The record label had sent through a producer contract they wanted Philip to sign, despite him having said there was no need for that. He read through the contract and made it all the way to the part with some wording like 'Territory – the universe, and any other territory yet undiscovered etc'. Then he stopped and said 'Bollocks', took out his pocket knife and cut his finger to smear a drop of blood on the signature page. Can you send this back to them please?

George Murphy

For the past three decades, my day job has been making records. And writing this book makes it impossible not to reflect on that time, and one thought I've had recently is, who were the people along the way who really taught me the ropes? And often it's not the ones who align entirely with your own ideas or taste. I vividly recall a session at Sunset Sound on one of my early trips to Los Angeles. I was in my late twenties and David Foster had invited me to come by the studio to help put 'some of those weird sounds you make' on a record he was producing with a developing artist for his label 143. At that time, and to this day, David is one of the world's most successful record producers and songwriters, and I met him because I had been doing a quirky electronic project in London with his daughter Amy. She is also a songwriter, but back then she was a spoken-word artist and was living in a flat with the Sneaker Pimps. Long story, but I pitched up at the studio with an ARP Odyssey and a Roland Space Echo ready to make some noise. On drums was Vinnie Colaiuta and in the live room with him a great bass player I didn't recognize. In the control room, and a little bit intimidated by the level of the musicians, I set up my gear next to Steve Lukather who was playing guitar. David, who had his 88-key weighted digital piano set up in front of the window to the live room, was directing and playing simultaneously. It was sounding very slick, they were working on a ballad with David's trademark 'piano and strings' sound. At one point he asked me if I had any ideas, and after some quick decision-making I decided to speak my mind. David is an incredible pianist and I suggested that, instead of the digital piano,

The south courtyard at Walters seen from Studio 2 stairs.

Top: Guitar bowing in Studio 1 **(left to right)** Laura Taylor, Pete Roe and Laura Marling. **Bottom left:** Marcus Mumford by the console in Studio 1 with Laura Marling, engineer Sam Navel and Philip Bagenal. **Bottom right:** Outside Studio 1 **(left to right)** Laura Rose (cellist), Ted Lovett (Mumford & Sons), Marcus Mumford and Laura Marling.

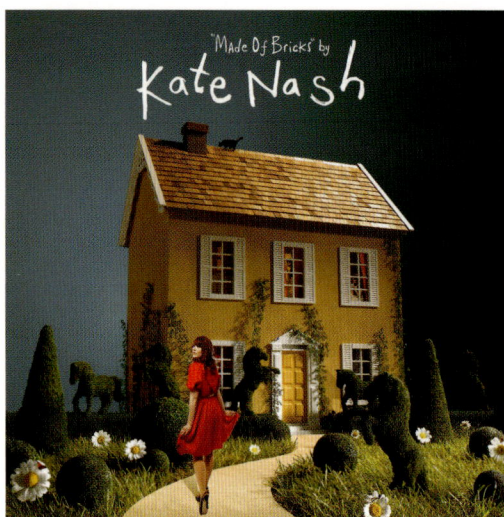

he should record on the Bösendorfer grand standing tuned and ready in the live room. He thought about it for a while and then said 'No, I don't need to do that'. I went back to making sounds with my space echo and synth, and in the break David said to me something like 'Everybody has their own taste. And my piano sound works for me'. And then the line that stuck with me: 'Compromise breeds mediocracy'. At the time I didn't get it at all. And I still feel somewhat uneasy about how it sounds. It makes me think of Ayn Rand and the very elitist philosophy she called 'Objectivism'. I mean, don't get me wrong, *Atlas Shrugged* is a great book, but in my opinion there's no objective way of deciding who is talented and who isn't. It's just a matter of context, taste and culture. And music specifically is so often about openness and collaboration. Through the years I've come to better understand what David meant though. Some producers are amazing because of the

personality they bring, you can hear them in the recordings as much as you can the lead artist. Others are nearly invisible, like a secret support mechanism, gently holding and supporting the effort of the artist. But whatever style a producer has, and there are many, they all have something in common: they've been hired to be the person to steer the ship.

And David had another vision that day and another end goal. He was collaborating, but his collaborative partner was the artist. And my opinion wasn't important in that context.

I had no idea about any conversations between producer and artist, or any fragilities or even what kind of record the artist was hoping to make. I was invited to share my ideas amongst the other musicians and I did, based on my taste. And I don't much enjoy how digital pianos sound. But someone had to make the calls in the room: yes, that's a great idea, or no, I don't need to do that. And that was David's responsibility. He was the producer.

Most record producers I know who come from a musician or aspiring artist background, including myself, start out being the type that want to get their personality onto the record. Others only want to work with a certain kind of artist, maybe because they're part of a certain scene or movement. Philip never considered producers with the same high regard as he did the artists, musicians and songwriters. He saw them sometimes as an extension of the business side of music and was also very aware that the producers who came to the studio would change over the years. In Philip's words, 'their stock goes up and down'.

I will hold my hands up and say that I'm not very good at practising the advice I'm about to give here. So it's really for myself as much as anybody else. But things really do get interesting when your curiosity takes over and you start listening and observing more than you act and talk. And maybe, if you are a producer in the truest sense of the word, you just want to hold space for the artists who are willing to do the most difficult thing of all. Baring their soul and turning their life and vulnerabilities into art. And if that's a definition of a certain kind of record producer, Philip Bagenal should most definitely have had many more producer credits.

In 2007, Paul Epworth was in Studio 1 for quite a few weeks working on a pretty quirky album with the urban-folk-pop-storyteller that is Kate Nash. And talking about evolution. *Made of Bricks* seems a very different kind of album for Paul, and it sounds great. Kate's personality is subtly enhanced by imaginative production, but it never takes over. It's all about her. It's 3 am and I'm still writing. Some sleep would be good, but I just want to check out one more album made this year before wrapping. It's Blackstrobe's *Burn Your Own Church*, another Epworth production. It is wonderfully twisted and definitely quite different from *Made of Bricks*. Don't know if it's the Cognac, but I can see how Paul and Philip would have got along just fine back then at the studio.

The extended Eastcote family kept growing in 2007. Bear with me through the next paragraph and you'll see how. Eliot James was producing tracks for Noah and The Whale's debut album *Peaceful, the World Lays Me Down* that year. Backing vocals on that album featured

Kate Nash, *Made of Bricks*, Fiction/Cherrytree/Universal Music, 2007.

'2007'

a young singer songwriter called Laura Marling. She released two EPs that year, both leading with tracks that Philip had recorded, and she also made her debut album, *Alas, I Cannot Swim*, at Eastcote this same year. Her album was produced by... Charlie Fink from Noah and the Whale. Laura's album also featured Marcus Mumford, who during a break from recording in Studio 1 sat down by the piano and wrote a song that would be the first one for his new band. But we're still a year or so away from that story.

This was also a year when Daniel Miller came back to Eastcote, not only as the record label boss but as co-producer with Simon Fisher Turner for Polly Scattergood's self-titled debut album. Polly had recently graduated from the Brit School and this really was a year for a new young generation of artists at Eastcote.

At this point in the story you might be thinking this: where did the reggae go?

Well actually, despite Aswad not having been in for a while, there were some reggae vibes at Eastcote this year. Or really more of a reggae, soul, singer-songwriter mix that turned into the album *Man Like I*. Natty was an artist with his own unique style and the first single, 'July', was produced by Jonny Dollar. It was Dollar's first project at Eastcote in a while, and tragically it would be the last before he passed away.

I'd like to end the chapter with another thought about making records. By far the most time booked for any one artist in Studio 1 this year is for a band called Clocks who had just been signed to Island Records. They were formed in 2000 and had already been touring and put out a few singles independently. But

it took signing a major label deal to end their career before it had even got off the ground. It's not an uncommon story and a tough one, especially for the artist, but also for the others who are part of making the records and spending their time doing it. Eliot James was the producer for Clocks and the album would have been called *Miniskirts & Cigarettes* had it been released. I sometimes wish there was a special record label that put out all the records that are made by major and independent record labels but never released. I'm sure there'd be quite a few gems in that catalogue. ∎

Polly Scattergood with her producer Simon Fisher Turner (second from left) and their team in Studio 2. And below playing a set of tubular bells.

Natty performing at the Shepherd's Bush Empire, London, on February 26, 2009.

In February 2008, Laura Marling releases *Alas, I Cannot Swim*. It's such a brilliant album and her songwriting is really something else. *Alas* is leading a tone-setting time at Eastcote. Many of the records made between '07 and '10 have a more earnest feel. Some amazing poetry, and a lot is acoustic and reflective. It's a new generation of thoughtful and skilled musicians who are making records in a back-to-basics way. The threads that bind together the second half of the '00s decade at Eastcote are an expanding group of not only producers and artists, but also a handful of great engineers who have been trained by Philip as assistants and are now recording, mixing and some producing their own records.

This was an explosive time in the building, both at Eastcote and in my studio Kensaltown. There was music everywhere. The courtyard was full of artists from around the world, our large kitchen table had each of the 20 chairs occupied every day at 2 pm with artists and musicians eating lunch together. And whether listening to something coming out of Eastcote, from Sacha Skarbek's room at Ktown or from The Shed, it

was likely you'd hear it again on the radio within a few months. I remember standing on the balcony of my studio on the third floor hearing '21st Century Life' being played from Paul's room in the courtyard. That summer me and the family were on holiday in Spain, and the Sam Sparro album was on repeat in the car. The kids were only five and seven and we all sang that song together at full throat at least a hundred times. At Kensaltown I had been working for months on a new album with Jason Mraz and the first single had just been released in the US and this was my first real holiday for a while. It had been an amazing session. Almost all live with some great musicians and Jason's inspiring voice and positive spirit. Around Thanksgiving 2007 we delivered roughs to the label of what I thought was pretty much the finished album. Shortly afterwards I received a call from the A&R guy. He asked me how I felt about what we'd done and I showered him with excitement. There was silence. And then 'I'm not sure this is going in the right direction. There are a few moments but it's pretty far off'. Fuck. I thought it was sounding great! It was funky and had some insane horn parts. Inventive lyrics, quirky synths and a couple of 'Little hippy songs' (as Jason called them) on acoustic guitar. 'I'm Yours' and 'Lucky' were two of them. For a while I thought that was it, game over. But despite the doubts from the label, Jason also loved the records we'd made and wanted to come back and finish the album. He did, and we wrote a couple of songs with Sacha Skarbek that we recorded very roughly, just the three of us in the studio, playing together. One of them was called 'Love for A Child', and when we sent the new songs to the label everything

DID YOU SEE THE FLASH?

2008

Mark Ronson playing the grand in Studio 1.

changed and it was all systems go again. We went to New York to mix the album with Tony Maserati and 'I'm Yours' started to take on a life of its own. And such are the margins of error. That album could easily have been one of the ones that needed the special label for unreleased records. And 'I'm Yours' was never a given. Jason had written it years before we made the album and, in fact, an acoustic version was already out as a bonus track on his previous album. And in the UK the worry from the marketing experts was that it didn't have drums until late in the song. 'It would be impossible to get in on radio.' A year after the song was a hit pretty much all over the world except in the UK, the label gave up the remix and additional production attempts and released the original version that was already out everywhere else. And it connected here as well.

I wish it could be said that really great music always finds its way to an audience. But that's far from the truth. The good news is that sometimes it does. That year Paul Epworth and Eliot James are booking long blocks of time in Studio 1. Eliot had teamed up with Mark Ronson to produce a new Kaiser Chiefs album, and Ronson too would end up spending a lot of time at Eastcote in the years to follow, *Off With Their Heads* was released this same year and reached number 2 on the UK charts.

Eliot was making some fantastic records during this whole period: varied, quirky and some breathtakingly beautiful. Apart from Noah and The Whale, there's a brilliant album made with Two Door Cinema Club. The trio from Northern Ireland recorded their debut, *Tourist History*, upstairs in Studio 2 and it's an ambitious

Laura Marling in Studio 1.

gem of a funky pop album with some great rhythms. Broadcast 2000, ever heard of them? Me neither, but their self-titled album produced by Eliot, mainly in the smaller Studio 3, is a gentle and great listen. Does it Offend You, Yeah?'s album *You Have No Idea What You're Getting Yourself Into* is the opposite: a restless late '00s dance record. And another brilliant one is I Am Arrows' *Sun Comes Up Again*. The solo project from Razorlight's drummer Andy Burrows is a turn back to quirky indie pop, and if I was making a solo indie record at that time I'm pretty sure my producer of choice would have been Eliot James.

One of my favourite English singers is Tracey Thorn and she made a beautiful album at Eastcote during this time called *Love and Its Opposite* which was released in 2010. She also worked on her 2007 album *Out of the Woods* in Studio 1, but it turns out that her history with Eastcote goes even further, almost to the very beginning. By a crazy coincidence I'm listening to one of Tracey's albums when I get a call from my friend Colin Lester. I had wanted to speak with him about his memories of Eastcote as he was a partner with Ian McAndrew in Wildlife Management, who manage Arctic Monkeys. He says:

Yes, we did Favourite Worst Nightmare *there, but it was mainly Ian and Jeff who were in the studio with the band. I'll tell you the best memory I have from Eastcote though. It was an amazing all-girl band called Marine Girls that we all thought would go very far. They were amazing and I remember Zeus [B Held] producing and Philip was engineering. It sounded fantastic and such a pity the world never got to hear it. We loved Eastcote.*

Marine Girls was originally a duo with Tracey and her sixth-form friend Gina Hartman. There are some very early recordings of the two of

Nick Hodgson and Ricky Wilson of Kaiser Chiefs with producer Eliot James on the steps at Eastcote during recording of *Off With Their Heads*.

Nick Hodgson with Eliot James in the studio and relaxing at Eastcote.

them and by the time they were in the studio with Zeus they had been joined by Jane and Alice Fox on bass and percussion. And whatever they recorded is another album we'll most probably never hear. Another one perhaps for the label that puts out all the unreleased records. I'm starting to think it actually might be a viable idea.

'We're being watched by experts, and what will happen next?', sings Jack Barnett of These New Puritans on their 2008 single 'Elvis' and it seems a pretty timely question in our current Covid times, when hard-fought-for laws to

protect citizens' rights are being dismantled a little bit more each week by parliaments and governments around the world to rush through new surveillance legislation designed to protect us from the coronavirus. Will the new regimes be reversed when the pandemic is under control? We will have to see. I'm not a politician so I embark on research into the making of this brilliant track instead, and it turns out it's actually the B-side 'fff' that was recorded at Eastcote. It's a cool track too, but the band definitely chose the right song for the A-side.

There are too many threads to be able to follow each one, but I should mention Bryn Christopher's soulful single 'The Quest', recorded at Eastcote this year. Hotel Persona was a kind of Euro-pop project with Stefan Olfsdal from Placebo and his partner David Amen. They had been able to recruit guest singers as diverse as Spanish troubadour/crooner Miguel Bose, '80s pin-up girl Samantha Fox and Brian Molko.

But perhaps the most unexpected booking in the calendar from these years is for the early hip hop pioneer, Grandmaster Flash. Philip engineered a vocal recording with Natacha Atlas (from Transglobal Underground) for Flash's 'Oh Man'. It was released as a bonus track on the album *The Bridge (Concept of a Culture)*. I wonder if the Grandmaster himself was there with Philip. Either way, I love music for this very reason. It brings entirely different worlds together and creates dialogue. Here's to two legends:

Grandmaster Flash and Philip Bagenal. ∎

Peanut from Kaiser Chiefs in Studio 1 lounge.

Andy Burrows playing the harpsichord in Studio 1.

2008

Eastcote Studio 2.

Just last year, Marcus Mumford spent a couple of months in Studio 2 working on his first score for a movie. Since then I've managed, together with a new partner in the studios, to acquire the freehold of the building Eastcote is in, and we've spent most of the lockdown refurbishing both parts of the building and the studios. I've set up for my Zoom call with Marcus in the updated Studio 2 so he can see how it's changed. Same room, different gear and actually, layoutwise, converted back to where it was when Philip opened the new second studio in the mid-'80s. I ask Marcus how far his relationship with Eastcote goes:

It was the first studio we ever recorded in and at that time we'd been playing in all the bars around West London. Mostly places like Bosuns Locker on King's Road. Then we moved a bit north and did the Nambucca and Frog. We were just on the surface and mostly playing as session players and I got asked to join Laura Marling's band and to go on tour with her. Then to record for her first record, Alas, I Cannot Swim, *which was all done at Eastcote with Charlie Fink from Noah and the Whale, who was producing it. So, we went in there knowing that the Arctic Monkeys had been in there, and Adele, and the sort of group and community of musicians that we all knew, and that that was their first place to record. It was appropriate in that narrative that Laura's first record was done there. While we were recording in there, her and Charlie went off to do some promo one afternoon and in that little drum room, in Studio 1, I wrote, 'White Blank Page' which was the first Mumford and Sons song. I took it to the three other lads and we're sort of moonlighting with them whilst playing for Laura.*

I remember seeing Mumfords play at Hoxton Bar and Grill around that time, or maybe a little earlier. I went to see them with Colin Barlow who was then the head of Polydor and who I'd just done a couple of albums with, including James Morrison's debut *Undiscovered*. The

PEOPLE THE MUSIC INDUSTRY'S ROMANCE IS BUILT ON

place was totally packed. Two or three labels were there, and it was pretty clear they would get signed. The gig was amazing, Marcus was all-commanding and loud in the right way. I'm surprised to hear they hadn't been doing gigs for longer at that point. I ask Marcus about what role Philip had in the studio after nearly 30 years at Eastcote:

So, Philip at that time was the host, but he was also the only person that knew how the desk worked. Plus being the only person to fix it when the gremlins came calling, which they did quite often. It was an amazing-sounding desk but just needed a lot of TLC and Philip was the only person to administer that. So he was there a lot, even in the evenings where he would sleep on the sofa and it sort of became clear to me about how much love and personal attention that the studio demanded of him. Without it, it wouldn't have been a great studio, I don't think. Mostly because of the bones of it, there were quirks to it, which made it romantic as long as someone like Philip was giving it the time and attention that it needed. And that went beyond maintenance, like he would cook for us. He was an amazing chef. He would cook these unbelievable meals, French, rich buttery meals. Like pears with a butter sauce after a long day of recording. He would eat with us a lot and we'd hear his stories. He was just a unique and wonderfully gifted character. He was one of those kinds of people that the music industry's romance is built on. A lot of us got attached to not just the studio but also to Philip and the people he employed to help run it which tended to be French people. I remember at that time he had two great engineers, Anna and Sam.

Marcus and the band really did become part of the Eastcote family and came back time after time to work both in Studio 1 and upstairs in 2. He's not sure he's getting the chronology right, but essentially his work includes a lot of what happened at the studio in those years:

A young Marcus Mumford in front of the RCA microphone in Studio 1.

We did Laura's first album there, and then Noah and the Whale recorded their album there with Eliot James. We did our first album there with Marcus Dravs. Smashed it out in six weeks, and then when it came to doing the second album, we did it there again. I then produced King Charles' second record starting at my place and then we did all the band recordings at Eastcote. Second record I produced there was with a guy called Christian Letts who's a guitarist from Magnetic Zeros. Similarly, did a bit here and then did all the band stuff tracking at Eastcote. And we did Laura's second record, some at Real World and then I remember Ethan Johns, who was producing, getting his hands on that MCI desk [at Eastcote] and some completely magical recordings happening – all live in that space. I remember him fiddling especially with the H3000 that Marcus Dravs loved. Stringing double basses through it, which I completely nicked for the Christian Letts record.

Upstairs, we wrote all of Babel. We did a lot of the rough tracks from Babel up there and then we also wrote our collaborative songs with Baaba Maal up there. We did some writing for Delta upstairs too, and then took that to Paul Epworth's place, up at The Church. And most recently, as you know, I did all that Ted Lasso score which was my first scoring job, in that room that you're talking to me from.

So that's my history with it. It was the first-stop shop for early musicians from that era to go. People like Arctic Monkeys, Adele, Frank Turner, Beans and Toast, the Maccabees, so it was completely the place for us, and you know, it's one of those rooms that you go into that have a special energy. Electric Lady has it in New York, and any room that T Bone Burnett has worked in too. But Eastcote just has magic in the walls which has been passed down, I think through lots of hands. I always get excited when I show up there because there's always cool people around making cool music.

We talk for a while and hear again, like I have from so many others, about how Philip always put the musicians and artists first and would go to some lengths to make sure that they knew that when they were at Eastcote, it was their home. No one else's. And about his way of giving the sessions a gentle nudge forward from time to time:

I got a real excitement when he walked in the room if we were tracking. And his presence – I think great producers have that kind of impact on the recording space where he walks in the room and everyone ups their game. I remember a couple of specific things both during Laura's first record and ours too. He would never come in the room unless he was invited, which is rare for a studio owner. He would come in when invited, and only give opinions when invited to as well. I remember him being pretty withering about one idea on Laura's first record but staying on and seeing through the idea with us and when he thought it was good, we knew it was good. The same thing happened on our first record. He came into the room when I was playing drums on a track and he thought my timing was a bit off and of course he was completely right. But he's got such a musical ear and then to be able to do something magical with the gear that no one else would be able to do, which would produce some awesome results. Not only have I really admired his way of creating the right environment for people to thrive creatively, but also he's a proper musician. And he's got great taste. Those are the things it takes to be good at your job. So, I love that man.

We've spent some time on the screen now and Marcus's kids think that it's quite enough. Before we hang up Marcus says when I ask him if there's anything else he remembers:

The harmonium. That little pump organ is particularly awesome, I've often tried to buy it off him, but he won't let me.

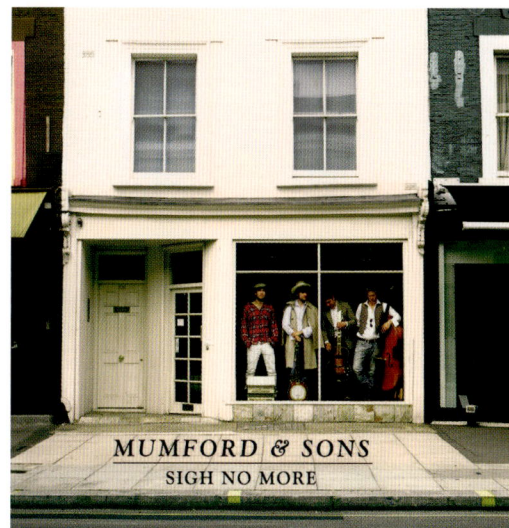

I'm glad Philip didn't sell the harmonium. The old ship organ from the late 19th century was used for playing psalms aboard an unknown vessel. It's probably around the same age as the building Eastcote is in, anno 1880. I've used it so many times, most recently both with Yungblud, and I even took it with me to a gig at Wembley with A-ha. I crated it up properly and took all precautions, but thinking about it now, that will be its last outing. It clearly belongs in the building.

On 2nd October 2009, Sigh No More was released. It was produced by Markus Dravs and in the spirit of the three humble maestros who are Marcus, Markus and Philip, there won't be any summary here of its extraordinary success. Instead, suffice to say, it is a fantastic album. ■

The Eastcote pump organ on a rare outing to Wembley Arena.

Mumford & Sons, Sigh No More, Island/Glassnote, 2009.

3 MILLION SYNTHESIZERS DEEP

That track '3 Million Synths' is an absolute classic. The amount of people I meet who are kind of cratediggers, I always have money on these conversations, and if it goes on long enough someone always says: 'Oh, have you heard that Chaz Jankel tune?', and I'm like, 'I know the man who made it'.

Paul Epworth

It's another sunny lockdown day at Philip's place in Oxford. Paul Epworth, Charlie Seaward, Philip and I are sitting outdoors in the garden, talking about the early days at Eastcote. Was Chaz difficult to work with? Who isn't? We talk about partnerships. In a studio there are many. Between members of a band. Between two writers. Between artist and producer. Engineers and studio owners. I've known Paul for quite a long time, but his history with Philip and Eastcote goes back further.

Philip: *You know you got Lennon-McCartney, you got Ian and Chaz, the list goes on forever. When there's that sort of competition and conflict between two artists, it generates a sound of electricity, and they're at each other's throats, but they love each other at the same time. You know if one pisses off, it's very hard to recreate that.*

Paul: *That's really interesting, the duality of music.*

Philip: *The excitement for me was being in the room while these musicians were playing the fuck out of each other, that was my buzz.*

Paul: *The thing is, I come from a background of working in corporate studios. Well, first I worked at a little demo studio in Harlow, but then worked at AIR as a tape op and that was a bit of a shock. I had to relearn everything I thought I knew, even though I had been engineering for two and a half years and made records with bands and demos that got them signed. I just remember being an aspiring musician, and there was nothing about studios that felt musical. You know there was a piano and there was a Hammond organ and that was it. When I think about the people I used to work with back in the day, I mean, I used to cart shit around, a boxed-up drum kit and there was an MPC and a tambourine and a case of floppy discs. Did you know, I found Eastcote totally by chance?*

2210110

Some of the extensive synth collection at Eastcote.

I'd never worked in West London before, and with short notice I needed a place to record something with the Futureheads. I'd done live sound for them and I remember I googled 'best analogue recording studios' and there it was. I went through the gear list and thought that's it. My first experience going into Eastcote was, I had a lifetime of ideas musically and a belief that if I just had an opportunity to use the gear, the time and someone to help fill in the blanks, then I could do it, and I did it! It was that place, at that time, and that moment. It was a combination of all those factors, and there was that serendipity.

Philip: *It's funny because I always used to think you were one of these jumped up DJs.*

Paul: *I know, and I knew that but what was amazing, I could feel that sort of dynamic from you, but in all honesty it drove me. I also knew when I was on to something good because you would come in, and I could see that you would engage with it, and I knew if it met your critical approval, it was working. If you work in music long enough, you have that psychic ability, humans are telepathic, we are, we just don't know how to use it.*

Charlie: *If it resonates with somebody, you pick it up.*

Me: *And if it doesn't, too. Sometimes you feel it even before you played anything. And then you don't want to play it, but you have to sit there and listen through, although you already know.*

Paul: *100%, that's what I'm saying. It's an amazing thing to hear, because it clarifies my trust in my music.*

Me: *I didn't know you [Paul] came from a studio/ engineer background. When I came to Eastcote,*

Adele in front of the RCA mic in Studio 1.

163

22.0h

it was as a songwriter and the first studio I worked in was Studio 2, upstairs. Must have been mid-'90s. When you started playing, was it mostly keys?

Paul: *No, I started playing guitar when I was about five or six, but I stopped having lessons because I wasn't really into classical guitar. I was such a shit little kid, I should've been a bit more humble and paid attention instead of thinking 'I'll find my own way to do things'. But then I just sort of made my own thing work, and I wanted to go to a studio, so I had my own control over everything and could do it all myself. I spent so much time in the studio and doing other things that I never kept up my musical ability until I started writing for people and then I was like 'Fuck, I need to sort of know what I'm doing!' So I started learning the musicality side of it, and I had to take theory lessons just so I could understand.*

I think most of us would agree that it was a good thing that Paul didn't focus too much on mastering the classical guitar. He had a bigger picture to work on. Just like Philip. And this year is a special one in the Eastcote calendar. The making of 'Rolling in the Deep' is one of those stories that prove that, when the intention is right and the stars align, you can actually reach beyond the sky. Adele had already had some success with her first album, *19*, and was on and off at Walters, both at Kensaltown and in Paul's studio, the one we still call The Shed, to write for a new album. Adele and Paul wrote and demoed 'Rolling in the Deep' there, and for the album version it was sent off to another producer but it fell short of expectations. Everyone was in love with Paul's demo. He decided to keep the parts he liked, including the recording of Adele stomping on the wooden box by the door that serves as a step down from the courtyard. They took the session into Studio 1 and finished the final version there.

Paul: *I remember explicitly when we recorded 'Rolling in the Deep'. You came in [Philip] and went 'This is going to be fucking massive'.*
Philip: *And I've only said that twice.*
Paul: *We did everything in the small room, we did the demo and the wooden step that she would stomp on, and then she went 'Can I just put the demo out?' and I was like 'No'.*
Charlie: *So you reworked it in Studio 1?*
Paul: *We basically just exported the logic stuff into Studio 1 and we got Neil Cowley to come and play the piano. We had Leo play the drums, and it just came together that way.*
Philip: *But it had a wonderful freshness about it.*
Paul: *Yeah, well it's kind of the sound of that board and then tracking it to the 2-inch. It sounded amazing to the point at which apparently Prince rang her up! She was breast-feeding but answered and said 'Hello?', and Prince went 'Did you record that whole track to tape?', she said 'I dunno, you'll have to give Paul a shout'.*
Philip: *There's this sort of myth with recording studios, it was those mythical places that you weren't allowed in, unless you were a famous musician. I think there could be a film about Eastcote, what it needs is somebody to do the research to find out how much stuff is there and then tell it like it really is.*

Philip and Paul have worked exceptionally hard to achieve what they have. Their legacies and musicality speak for themselves, no need to count the wins. But they both remember the day they laid down the live instruments for 'Rolling in the Deep'. And I think they both felt that the song had a chance to connect far and wide. This was the day when Philip's words and spirit broke down my bravado and my 'I'll just put a book together, shouldn't be too hard' attitude. It's fucking hard, I had no idea how much research would be involved, or how many days and nights it takes a suburban Swede to put the sentences together clearly enough to do this story justice. Paul didn't know how to make records when he first came to Eastcote. But he had decided he could learn, given the chance. He was right about that. ∎

Adele photographed by Julian Broad (National Portrait Gallery).

Patrick Wolf performing at the *Time Out* Lovebox London Weekender Festival. In 2011 he released his album *Lupercalia* which was recorded at Eastcote.

2010

Keyboard player Jon Lord of Deep Purple performing
on stage during the band's US tour in 1974.

> I've had the pleasure of working with a man called Jon Lord. He had an orchestra in his fingertips. An orchestra!
>
> **David Coverdale**

I was a big Deep Purple fan in my mid-teens. I remember being 16 years old and spending the night in a sleeping bag on the pavement outside a record store in central Stockholm to get the best possible tickets to a show with the reunited Mark II line-up, including Ian Gillan and Jon Lord. I got goose bumps standing a few rows from the stage, when the distorted organ set the tone for a long intro, swirling through the Leslie and from left to right in the PA. It was gloriously loud, long before the days of automatic level cut-offs during live shows. So although it was only a one-day booking, I have to mention that maestro Jon Lord was in the house on 8th February 2011. And I guess, by sheer coincidence as always, another artist I hail as a true icon, PJ Harvey, was there the following day. Both in Studio 1. It feels like this is going to be a good decade at Eastcote.

A month later, Duran Duran released their album *All You Need Is Now*. Simon Le Bon, Nick Rhodes and the rest of Duran Duran set up in Studio 1 in the summer of 2010 to work with their new producer, Mark Ronson. He was intent on helping them make 'the imaginary follow-up to "Rio"', and almost three decades after the release of 'Girls on Film' they did make an album that is largely regarded as a return to form for the '80s pop stars. And there were no expenses spared in the Jonas Åkerlund-directed music video for 'Girl Panic'. Naomi Campbell, Eva Herzigova, Helena Christensen and Cindy Crawford are playing the band in the 9-minute-long clip. At the time, Eastcote Studio 1 had not changed significantly since its opening in 1980, and from the well-sat sofa and old carpet in the studio lounge it must have been quite a contrast to the glossy interiors at The Savoy, where the video was shot, shortly after its grand reopening

FACTS, FUN AND FUSION

2011

following a £220 million renovation. And that's the beauty of pop'n'roll. It's all in the illusion. This is a great-sounding album and a fun, tongue-in-cheek reminder of the glory days of the MTV era.

Mumford & Sons are back with Markus Dravs in the studio and for a few months they have booked both Studio 1 and Studio 2 to work on their second album together, *Babel*. There is a story at the studio about Markus not letting the bass player into the studio and on a call he tells me what happened:

Well, the bass player turned up at Eastcote and he didn't have an instrument, and so I asked him what does he play? I asked him to introduce himself, because everybody was carrying their instruments in and he didn't have anything. I was like ''Ey, what do you play?' 'Bass' but he was like, 'I haven't got one'. Well fuck off then... Ted is the bass player. I kicked him out of the studio because he didn't have his instrument. It seemed appropriate at the time, so he had to go and get it, and then he came back.

Markus continues to tell me that most of the album was done during a few months at Eastcote:

We did a lot of pre-production in Studio 2, and then we recorded the album downstairs. Apart from a couple of drum overdubs which we did at AIR studios, we did everything at Eastcote. Laura Marling was there a lot to hang out, she cooked us food, which was nice.

The beginning of a new decade also holds a promise of more of the usual Eastcote magic,

Beth Ditto and Brace Paine of Gossip at Coachella Valley Music & Arts Festival in 2010. In 2011 they started recording an album at Eastcote with Mark Ronson but it was never finished.

PJ Harvey performing at the Troxy, London, in 2011.

with jazzers and indie bands booking any free time between the blocked-out months for more established artists. Smoke Fairies, To Kill A King and Brite Futures are in the studio. On the jazz front, drummer Gary Husband is making *Dirty and Beautiful Vol 2*. The list of jazz-rock royalty to accompany him is long and includes guitarists Mike Stern, Alan Holdsworth and John McLaughlin. Jan Hammer on keys and bassists like Jimmy Johnson and Mark King. If there was a sonic dictionary to describe the music genre 'Fusion', it could be this record.

Dickon Hinchliffe is back in Studio 1 with Philip working on the soundtrack for James Marsh's film *Shadow Dancer*, a brilliant spy drama starring Gillian Anderson. And to make sure all aspects of what is familiar at Eastcote are covered, there's another record for the never-released catalogue. Mark Ronson is back at Eastcote for a couple of projects this year, but the one we'll never get to hear is his work with American indie-rockers Gossip. They were a few months into making an album and the chemistry wasn't quite right in the studio. On top of that, Mark's close friend and collaborator Amy Winehouse passed away in July and left him in grief. In an oft-quoted interview with MTV about the Gossip collaboration he says about the recording:

It was really strange. It was almost like a turning-point. When I found out that Amy passed, I was in disbelief. I walked out of the session and I never fully came back. I think the main thing, the chemistry of what we had going on with the Gossip album wasn't really amazing and being reminded about how good it is when it's good, maybe I thought I was forcing something.

The new decade at Eastcote also continues the line of great engineers Philip trained. George Murphy was only in his early twenties when he started working at the studio this year, and one of his first sessions was the Gossip recording with Ronson. It was a big project for a new assistant with a successful band and a famous producer:

I think Mark Ronson was the first person to catch me off guard, it's only because he looks so consistently famous all the time. I can't even picture him in jeans and a T-shirt.

He was a real regular for about a year or so. He did an album here with Gossip which took forever and never came out, so that was my first kind of major label album experience with a dysfunctional band who had a famous producer. And a seemingly infinite budget, the ability to hire everything that your heart desires for a session. And then all the complications that come along with that and partying all the time.

Like many of the assistants Philip trained, George was thrown in the deep end because there really wasn't much of the shallows at Eastcote. Since 1980 the studio has been part of some era-defining movements, bustling with music of all kinds. The kind where culture aligns with artists and producers and the sum becomes bigger than its parts. George started at a time when Philip had started to do less engineering himself and also at the height of another time at Eastcote, when everyone seemed to pass through the studios.

But he learned quickly, and I think Philip soon realized that he had found an extraordinary talent. George wrote down a few lines about his experience of working with Philip and I think they are a great way to end this chapter and to begin the fourth decade at Eastcote Studios:

Eastcote Studios has been a huge part of my life for longer than I ever dreamed of when Philip first asked me to fill in for a session as his assistant back in 2011 (give or take). I was a wide-eyed beginner sound engineer who was

Photoshoot for the album cover of *Babel*.

Mumford & Sons, *Babel*, Island, 2012.

largely unaware of how much I had to learn. Luckily, Philip usually managed to maintain a fine balance between throwing me in at the deep end and maintaining a guiding hand over what I was doing.

When I started working at Eastcote, I must confess a certain amount of ignorance about the studio's history and importance within the music world. But as the months went by and I worked with a revolving cast of clients that varied from the uber-famous to complete unknowns, I found they all came here for the same reason: they felt comfortable recording their music in Eastcote, and a lot of them had done their best work here. The fact that we had such an amazing collection of vintage instruments, microphones and outboard gear was only a small factor for most of them – there are loads of studios with

this stuff. What brought them back again and again was an atmosphere that was the opposite of most large studios, that made them feel at home, and this was all down to Philip.

Philip was able to maintain an informality within the studio that could take anyone's nerves away. His occasional interjections shouted from the control room doorway – 'Turn that fucking snare UP! IT'S GREAT!' – could puncture the tension in any inter-band discussion and make people laugh enough to be able to see the bigger picture in their music again.

Whilst there are some nerdy tips I've gained from Philip that will always be used as a starting-point for any recordings I do – RCA44 always goes behind the drummer's head, Rhodes needs a bit of 4KHz, use the Dimension D whenever you can – it's his approach to

recording in general that has been the most special to witness: are the band all engaged? Are the energy levels dropping? Are everyone's headphones the perfect balance? Are there too many awkward silences? Do we need a round of coffees/mad fx returns fired up/off-colour anecdote to spark the session back up again?

Whilst I fear I may have missed out on some of the true glory days by starting in the music industry a decade or so too late – Philip often bemoaned the relative sensibleness of modern musicians when compared to years gone by – 'The Klaxons only wanted to drink fucking FIZZY WATER!' – I'm very fortunate to have ended up where I did, working for and learning from Philip.

George Murphy

George Murphy with Dickon Hinchliffe by the console in Studio 1, 2011.

George Murphy at the Studio 1 console in 2020.

2011

When I was in my late teens and it was clear that music was where it was all heading, I made myself a promise. That there was one thing that I would never do: participate in any capacity whatsoever in the Eurovision Song Contest. For someone in the UK, it's probably hard to understand how important it is considered to be in my native country. We have regional competitions leading to a series of finals where eventually someone wins the big prize: to represent Sweden in the competition. No sarcastic comments à la Terry Wogan or Graham Norton are allowed on Swedish television during the broadcast of the big European final. This is dead serious. Everyone is watching as the nation holds its breath. And quite regularly Sweden will win the glitz and glam extravaganza with a ridiculously catchy pop tune and a new domestic star is born. Which then means that we get to host the event the following year to great excitement, and the cycle continues.

Let's fast-forward to 2012 and here is a story that relates to Eastcote through three bananas. I had been working on a very ambitious project, recording a duets album with the crooner legend Engelbert Humperdinck. He was 75 at the time and, after a 45-year career and 150 million albums sold, he had decided to ask his friends and artists he admired to sing with him. We recorded over 20 tracks with, among others, Elton John, Olivia Newton-John, Willie Nelson, Smokey Robinson, Kenny Rogers, Dionne Warwick, Lulu and even Gene Simmons from Kiss. It was a weird and wonderful project with so many great stories attached, but the one we're focusing on here is about the Eurovision Song Contest.

One day the head of Engelbert's record label, Graham Stokes, came into the studio and said: 'I know this is a curve ball. But the BBC has asked Engelbert to represent England in Eurovision. Can you write him a song?' Well, can you break a promise to yourself? Of course

A DECAPITATED AWARD. AND THREE BANANAS

The Glass Animals with Philip Bagenal and Paul Epworth (centre) at The Church Studios, North London.

Engelbert Humperdinck singing the UK entry for the Eurovision Song Contest, 'Love Will Set You Free', in Baku, Azerbaijan, in 2012.

2012

you can. This was getting so absurd that I most definitely had to follow through and see where it would lead. I called Sacha Skarbek and after some convincing he agreed to join in, and we wrote a song called 'Love Will Set You Free'. It was decided by the BBC that this was the one. Two months later Sacha and I are on an empty (apart from us) tour bus being driven with police escort from the airport in Baku, Azerbaijan, to a hotel bar were we are about to have drinks with Engelbert, Graham Norton and the rest of the British delegation that had arrived a few days earlier. This could be a long story too, but let's narrow it down to the Eastcote part again.

Before we all left for Baku we were recording the single version of the song to be ready for release in time for the competition. I had another project going on at Kensaltown and we were in a rush to cut the vocals, so I decided to talk to Philip and he said Studio 2 was free on 12th March. But someone (I would assume Eliot) was using the upstairs live room. It's worth mentioning at this point in the story that Engelbert, like Philip, is a tall man. At the time there was a very small vocal booth/amp room in Studio 2 and it would have to do. Sacha and I are in the studio when Engelbert arrives that day, and we all love the vibe in that room. It was always special, and we spend a while talking about the song, and the competition and how random this all is. And then, time for vocals. Engelbert squeezes in to the booth and he is having some problems with the listening. Sacha recalls;

Engelbert asked if we could bring him three bananas. I wasn't sure if he was joking, but we got some from the fruit plate and he proceeded to put one of them behind one ear and another one behind the other – 'so I can hear myself better'. He was ok with the listening now, and I remember wondering what the third banana was for. Well, since the booth was so small, he couldn't really move around the hanging condenser microphone the way he wanted to. So the third banana became a prop. His handheld pretend microphone.

We laughed a lot that day and Engelbert ended up singing the song like only someone with his experience can. It sounded great. And it feels like a day that could only have happened at Eastcote. If there's a problem to solve, you use what's available.

Bananas will do.

There were a few other things happening that year at Eastcote as well you might imagine.

Eliot, who maybe was the reason Engelbert had to record in the tiny booth, could well have been doing something for an album with Gabriella Cilmi that day in March. They recorded at Eastcote throughout the year and the album, *The Sting*, was released in 2013. The '90s dance act Leftfield were in for much of November and December, starting work on a new album for the

Studio 2 in 2012.

Gabriella Cilmi with Eliot, his son Leland and wife Aitzi in Studio 1. To the left a young George Murphy.

first time since 1999. The work would continue over a couple a years before they finally released *Alternative Light Source* in 2015.

Glass Animals are a brilliant electronic indie-pop band from Oxford and have done really well, especially in the US, since they started recording their first tracks at Eastcote in 2011. This year, in 2012, they signed a deal with Paul Epworth's label Wolf Tone, and worked on their third EP. And here's the best part of the story: in 2014 they released their debut album, *ZABA*, exactly 30 years after Charlie Seaward and Philip Bagenal were working together on the first Man Jumping album at Eastcote. Which was around the time Philip suggested to Charlie that they'd buy a house together in Oxford. And that's the house where Charlie's son Joe Seaward grew up. And he is in the band... Glass Animals.

The Music Producers Guild's award ceremony that takes place each year in London hands out awards for best producer, song,

engineer, album, etc. The awards are made of a gold-coloured Shure replica microphone on a table stand with a little winner's plaque attached.

In 2012, Eastcote won the Studio of the Year award, and in the toilet, on a shelf under the Ultra gold record that's on the wall, there is the bottom half of the award but the microphone is missing. I ask George what happened to the decapitated award, thinking it might have fallen to the ground or something, and that maybe we could order a replacement. George says:

Oh, Philip and I took it apart to see if the mic worked. It didn't. ∎

173

Top left: Joe Seaward, Drew MacFarlane and Sid Leaman. **Top middle:** Dave Bayley; **bottom middle:** Drew MacFarlane; **right:** Joe Seaward.

In 2012 Eastcote won the Studio of the Year award.

I REALLY DON'T LIKE THAT GUITAR SOLO

It's definitely contemporary times in this story now. I think about what the response would have been if I had told a band I was working with back in 2013 that within a few years Donald Trump would be President of the United States, journalism as we knew it then would have been largely assigned to the history books, along with any universal definitions used to explain the word 'truth', and that we would also be engulfed in a global pandemic that would slow down the world to a near standstill. That the airlines we flew with every other week to go somewhere, would have so few passengers that most of them would be struggling to survive. I think such statements would have been received either with a good laugh or 'I'm not in the mood for conspiracy theories'. Yet here we are.

Like me, many of the artists and producers working at Eastcote and Kensaltown in the past decade still are. Researching and getting hold of people who 'were there' during these years isn't difficult. But sorting through the sheer amount of sessions and information is. From a studio perspective, there are fewer and fewer of the months-long bookings where bands or artists set up camp for an entire album project. Instead they come to track some live parts before heading back to their own studios or home set-ups to do the bulk of the work that doesn't require live rooms, drum kits or a grand piano. At Eastcote there are also the many jazz sessions, several every month, where a whole album is recorded and mixed in a couple of days. Philip's house is also truly the jazzers' house and we shall delve deeper into that in a coming chapter. But the point is, there are many more artists coming through than ever, although not for quite as long. We are also now in the days where a further combination of factors makes it very difficult to pinpoint exactly what has been done at any one studio on any one record. In part because, in the digital world of music distribution, crediting the creators involved has gone out of fashion except for the headline ones. You'd think that with the ease of collecting and storing data nowadays it would be the other way around, but it isn't. And one reason might be the sheer amount of credits involved. Looking at songs where labels have submitted correct metadata to sites like Discogs or AllMusic makes you realize that perhaps just listing the artist and producer is the only way. Some songs have dozens of contributors. It's not unusual to see eight writers and five producers on a track, and if you spread the net wide enough to include engineers, assistants, mixers, studios, etc, you might well end with a booklet for a track and a bible to summarize an album. So I decide that from now on I'll focus on who was in the studio in any given year, and where I have enough information, we'll go a bit deeper. Sound okay?

For me it was a time of little reflection and a lot of doing. And of an almost Jekyll-and-Hyde-like separation between my day job, which was writing and producing music with different artists, and submersing myself in Apparatjik, the art collective I founded together with Magne

La Roux photographed by Julian Broad (National Portrait Gallery).

2013

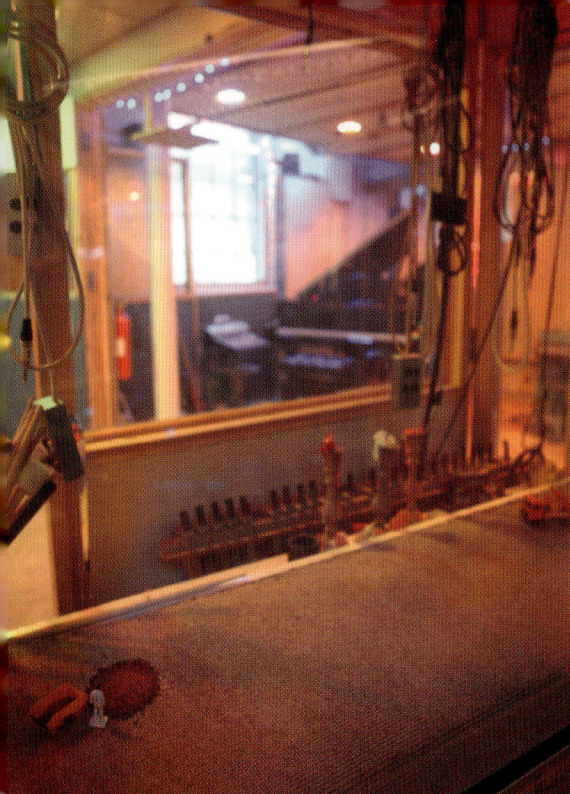

Furuholmen, Jonas Bjerre and Guy Berryman. We had been spending a couple of years on fairly ambitious projects that were a combination of curious inquiry and unhinged child's play. Some were performance art and collaborative recording projects, as well as experimenting with composition that had no parts directly written by humans. Instead we collected data from CCTV cameras and GPS units in cars and found various algorithm-driven ways to edit data into musical pieces we could perform with orchestras and choirs. All whilst dressing up in glittery combat gear and military helmets with antlers attached.

Not quite as separated were the worlds of Kensaltown and Eastcote now. Artists, songwriters and producers who were on one side of the courtyard one week would be on the other side the week after. In 2013 I recorded with Scouting For Girls, and Jesse and Joy, in both studios. I remember being in Eastcote Studio 1 recording a song called 'Dueles' with Jesse & Joy and our co-writer Cass Lowe. George was engineering and there was a moment when I looked around the studio with a strong feeling of wanting to give the room some TLC. Studio 1 had been a non-stop recording session for 33 years at that point. My place, Kensaltown, was coming up to its 10th anniversary and obviously looked a bit newer that Eastcote, but there too, from the day we'd opened, there hadn't been a longer natural break. And most things that were left unfinished on opening day had remained unfinished after constant back-to-back sessions. Perhaps it was a premonition of sorts. Or maybe

Studio 1 before the 2020 renovations.

Roy Stride of Scouting for Girls at BBC Radio's Big Weekend in 2008. In 2013 they were at Eastcote recording.

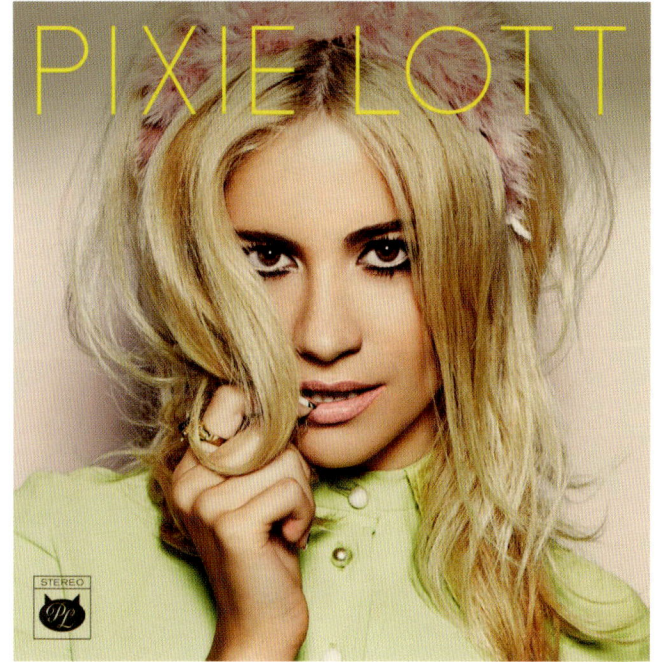

PIXIE LOTT

it was prem(u)nition. Changing just one letter describes something wholly different and it relates to immunology, which is a science I'm sure most have heard of in these corona times. Premunition is a state of balance between a host and an infectious agent. For example, if someone has been infected by an agent such as bacteria or a virus. And has a strong enough immune system to resist further infection, but not sufficiently strong to destroy the agent. Chaz's filmic description of Zeus looking around Studio 1 like an animal ready to pounce floats through my mind and I decide that I prefer to remember it as a premonition.

2013 saw the first sessions at Eastcote for some amazing young women who would continue to record at the studio for years. Elly Jackson (La Roux), Pixie Lott and Birdy were all there cooking up beautiful tones in generous servings. Birdy's first session at the studio was with Ben Lovett from Mumford & Sons. They were writing in Studio 1 because Ben wanted a grand piano and the result was 'No Angel', a fantastic piano ballad that was produced by Jim Abiss for the album *Fire Within*.

Pixie recorded a couple of songs with George Murphy engineering and Gary Abbott as producer. George tells me that Gary and Pixie had written a song called 'Ocean' together and also cut a cover of Andrew Wyatt's 'If I Ain't Got You' during that session:

It was a perfect Eastcote session. We recorded a full band, strings and horns. Pixie is a fantastic singer, especially on a song like 'If

La Roux, *Trouble in Paradise*, Polydor, 2014.

Pixie Lott, *Pixie Lott*, Virgin EMI, 2014.

I Ain't Got You'. That session is why there's a cup in the kitchen saying 'Tonemeister George'. She got that for me so she must have thought it sounded all right.

He continues to talk about another album I love from that time. It's the fantastically funky and original *Trouble In Paradise* from La Roux:

Elly first came here to work with Mark [Ronson]. He's like an encyclopaedia of music and always comes up with great references, but she wasn't into that at all. She said, I just want to sound like me, and Mark went: 'Come on, no one sounds like themselves'. They didn't see things quite the same way, and when she came back it was with Ian Sherwin. He was part of the first session too but had now been upgraded to co-producer.

George explains that Elly did a lot of the guitars and vocals during that session. And that she struggles with latency when recording, despite there 'not being supposed to be any' with the newer Pro Tools systems. Something I personally can really relate to. I strongly dislike latency in the headphones and it drives me crazy when an engineer says 'But there isn't any, it's impossible! I've set it to the lowest setting'. George continues:

She's a great guitarist and was doing all these Nile Rodgers-style funky guitars. I fed her cue directly through the desk instead of through Tools as it's easy to do that with our set-up. She was amazed that there was no latency and said she'd never recorded like that. She loved it and that's how aware of time she was.

As usual, there was a lot of jazz recorded, some quirky indie bands and some new singer-songwriters. One who could fit in several of those categories is Sarah Gillespie, but the same categories are also a much too simplistic description of an artist so unique. Sarah is an extraordinary lyricist. A seriously skilled acoustic guitar player. And putting music to the side altogether, a razor-sharp commentator on current affairs and the relationship between politics and art. About her latest album, *Wishbones*, the *Financial Times* concluded in the 4 out of 5 review: 'Like Dylan on amphetamines'.

But she started recording at Eastcote much earlier and is deeply connected to the jazz scene that has flourished at Eastcote in the 2000s. As accompaniment to her sometimes quite intricate guitar playing she has always used jazz musicians, and in 2013 she recorded her album *Glory Days* at Eastcote with Gilad Atzmon, Ben Bastin and Enzo Zirilli in the band. We're having a chat about that time and her friendship with Philip. Sarah says:

He's such an intellectual and there's such a poetic aspect about him. And when I first came to Eastcote, a young girl, kind of insecure, having impostor syndrome and all that, it was reassuring to meet Philip. He loved my lyrics and one thing that made me feel really safe around him was I totally trusted his aesthetics. He would have quite strong gut reactions, and I remember once Gilad brought in a guitar player who played a very wanky guitar solo over a track that was essentially a mixture of hip hop and folk. It had a weird rhythm and Philip said 'I really don't like that guitar solo, I don't want the solo!' And he got so angry about it that he stood up and pushed the chair over, and then stormed out. And I felt that this guy really cares, even though in a way he was criticizing the session. Philip had a view, he's not a people-pleaser. And when everyone else had enough and I wanted to layer more vocals, he'd stay and light candles and pour my wine and be really patient while I let rip on endless vocal takes. He got out of me things I think no one else could have. He co-produced my records and recently, when I did my last album Wishbones, I just wanted him there as an extra set of ears that I trusted. I knew he had stopped doing studio work then, but he came down and was there with us. Sometimes he'd have an opinion and others he'd fall asleep on the sofa. I guess there's only so many ballads you can take.

If there's one thing Philip wasn't, it was a people-pleaser. And thank the universe for that. ∎

Gilad Atzmon and Sarah Gillespie performing at Pizza Express, Dean Street, London, in 2009.

I fell in love with Philip being so anti-establishment.

Eliot James

A BIT OF GRAVITAS AND NO BULLSHIT

It would be hard to decide on any one year at Eastcote that would best illustrate the studio's deep connection with the indie rock scene. There have been generations of indie bands recording there through the years. Some remained signed to independent labels throughout their careers. Many went on to sign with majors. And then there are the ones whose defiance and refusal to be involved with any kind of establishment become as important as the music they make. Philip welcomed all of them, but of course cheered extra-enthusiastically for the underdogs. And as an example, 2014 is as good a year as any.

Eliot James pretty much moved in to Studio 1 from the beginning of the year until Easter,

working on consecutive productions with Coasts, The Carnabys and The Coronas. The Irish indie rockers released three albums on their own 3u Records label before they recorded their first and only album for Island Records, *The Long Way*, at Eastcote in 2014. Later in the year, Eliot and Jon Green started work on a new project for Daniel Glass's Glassnote Records with Brooklyn-born Tor Miller. It's a beautiful and quirky indie pop album, *American English*. Jon Green is a brilliant writer and producer who has spent a lot of time at both Eastcote and Kensaltown, most recently working on his and Eliot's joint project 'Reuniøn'. Jon says:

The first time I got to work at Eastcote was actually playing some piano on a session for Pixie Lott. She'd written a ballad with two guys who actually went on to be Beats and MC Grindah from the hit BBC series People Just

Danny O'Reilly of The Coronas playing at La Cigale in Paris.

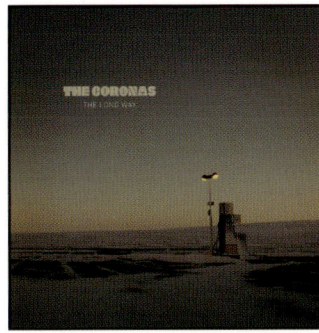

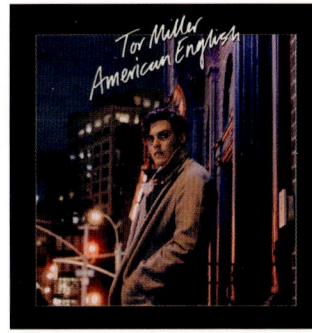

Do Nothing... I recall watching the show and thinking, I know these guys?! After that there was a little gap before I was lucky enough to get to co-write and produce the debut album by American artist Tor Miller, alongside Eliot James.

Following on from that, I was always keen to revisit the studios there. I spent many writing sessions in The Shed. I knew many great songs had been written in that room before me... and loved how unassuming and homely it was. In that room I wrote and did most of the production with James Bay for his song 'Wild Love' as well lots of other ideas that went on to become his second album, Electric Light. I wrote with Kylie Minogue in there too. On our first ever day together we wrote a tune called 'Lost Without You'... the finished production was pretty much as we left it on that day.

I've been there a lot recently, working with my now dear pal Eliot James on our own project called Reuniøn. We do all the writing and recording there in his room. Eastcote and the whole of Kensaltown has that special something that is very hard to recreate, lots of people try to and it can slightly miss the mark... It's got a warmth and familiarity to it all that makes you feel comfortable to create, whilst knowing some legendary things have taken place in all those rooms too.

Some bands that were in this year are really indie, like Police Dog Hogan, who come back regularly, timing their recording sessions between their day jobs. And there's a booking for 'Kuki and The Bard' and after some digging I find it's a young brother-and-sister duo that are so indie that they are now operating off the electrical grid entirely. They live a fully

alternative lifestyle with their family in Devon, teaching off-grid power generation, cooking and blacksmithery. As well as running a small solar-powered recording studio.

Back again this year were also Mumford & Sons, now to work on their third album, Wilder Mind. James Ford was the producer this time and the recordings were done between Eastcote and AIR Studios (Lyndhurst Hall). And Philip was there again as usual, 'stirring things up a bit' both in the studio and in the kitchen.

Most will know Johnny Borrell as the frontman of Razorlight, but he was at Eastcote throughout this year and in 2013 too, working on another project with his band Zazou. Out of the sessions came the 'The Artificial Night' EP and his album The Atlantic Culture. It's a great listen and inspiring to hear the sound of the room and the joy of playing in the recordings. I've just got

The Coronas, The Long Way, 3u Records, 2014.

Tor Miller, American English, Glassnote, 2016.

Marcus Mumford and Christian Letts in Studio 1.

Johnny Borrell on the step to Studio 1.

Following pages: Johnny Borrell and his band Zazou working on their album The Atlantic Culture in Studio 1.

hold of Johnny who is in the Basque country with no Internet. On a Stone-Age device called a phone I tell him that no Internet sounds nice, and I feel great excitement about not having to log on to Zoom. Johnny tells me:

I made an album called The Atlantic Culture *and that was when I first got into Eastcote, and then whenever I was playing with those musicians or doing any project that wasn't Razorlight, I always did it at Eastcote. I just loved the studio. It was perfect for us and what we were doing on* Atlantic Culture. *Part of it was George. Pretty much every track on that album was George just catching it as soon as we were all plugged in. There's that thing with musicians that as soon as you're plugged in, you're excited. You want to play. I always thought, if you play for the first 10 minutes, and the guy is just getting sounds and then he says 'All right, now play'... well, we've already played. You can't tell us to play, that game's boring now, we want to do something else. I remember the first thing we recorded there was a track called 'The Artificial Night'. It was literally just the first time we ran through it, and I had that horrible sinking feeling when you know you've put down a great take and you're not sure if the engineer has got it or not, and I said, 'Oh George, did you get that one?', and he was like 'Yeah yeah, it's in the box'. I thought, brilliant, we can work here. One of the other things about George is he is very quick, which is good because it's all about capturing the vibe, but his board mixes are fucking brilliant as well.*

Philip was there and would sort of come in now and then, and I really liked him. He would just come in and sort of go, 'Oh yeah that's a great triplet feel you got there' and I'd be thinking, I never really knew what a triplet is... but, you know, great. Philip was one of those instantly liked people, it was always a pleasure when he was around, he's got a measure of gravitas to him which I think people of his generation always seem to have. You always get the feeling that they know their stuff because they worked in an era when you could only make records with musicians. That is a really crazy concept now that we think about it all these years later, but there was a time when you could only make records with musicians. There was a bit of gravitas and no bullshit about it.

I always felt there was a bit of a vibe in Eastcote. With things like that, I never really search out the details, I like to just go and see. Especially with a studio, I personally never want to get too overburdened with thinking, 'Oh you know, this is where Ray Charles laid his head'. I'll get freaked out. I always felt that Eastcote is such a cosy studio, you just kind of slot into it. Because of the small little bit when you first come in, as soon as you brought in two flight cases, you feel like you own it. It's never that feeling like AIR Studios, where you are really aware that you're just renting a bit of space for a moment. It's such a lovely feeling and it's kind of what we miss in a few places.

Independent labels, indie rock, indie pop. indie: words that can mean many different things. In my teenage kid's world, indie as a genre is very different from the pop and rock indie bands I think of. Maybe the most independent scene of all at the moment is in the hip hop world. And the importance of that has so many historical layers that it's another conversation altogether. In this context, let's narrow 'Independent' down to meaning an artist or label that is not owned by, signed to, or partners with any of the major label groups. I come to think of a conversation I had with Daniel Glass in New York a few years ago when we spoke about culture, and specifically the impact of black culture on literally all current mainstream art, music, film and fashion. In youth and corporate culture alike, in the United States and all around, the heavily US-influenced, Western world. He said: 'You can't create culture. Culture creates itself under certain circumstances'. And by definition a large corporation can't be part of creating culture. Regardless of how many young people they hire to have endless meetings about just that. And no matter how 'part of the scene' any new executive that gets hired is, the system is too slow. At best, record labels, both major and independent, can magnify culture once it already exists. Some truly independent labels might even become part of it. That's all. In the world of recording studios, Eastcote is definitely independent. It can't create culture, but it is a part of circumstances where creativity can flourish. And creating such a space takes time and trust. And Philip had time for people. And patience. And didn't give a flying fuck about the establishment. A bit of gravitas, and no bullshit. ■

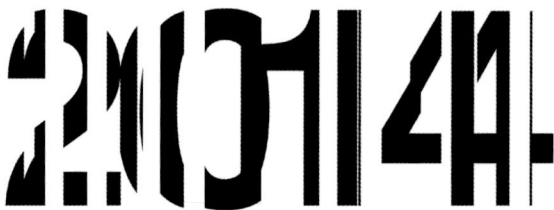

James Bay performing at the 2016 American Music Awards in Los Angeles, California.

THE NEIGHBOURHOOD ISN'T EXACTLY THE CHAMPS-ÉLYSÉES

I've tried to find the right place to write a little bit about the jazz and improvised music that have been recorded over the years at Eastcote, and I've realized there is really no chapter better than another because so much has been recorded at Eastcote. Year after year. So I'll do it here. It's also not fair to set a specific time when it all started. It was always a part of the studio from the day Chaz first started recording there. His and Philip's curiosity about all kinds of music and Chaz's own musicianship led the way. And in The Blockheads of course was Gilad Atzmon on saxophone.

There is a period from the late '90s to the early 2000s when the one- or two-day jazz sessions really start becoming an increasingly regular event in the calendars. Gilad brought in his projects to the studio and, because improvised music is by definition about exploring and experimenting, many of the musicians involved came in with other groups in different settings. Word spread across town about a good place to record in Ladbroke Grove. Studio 1 is a great sounding room for small groups of every genre, but recording improvised music is particularly dependent on a few things that Eastcote can offer. A good sounding cue and headphone system so the musicians hear each other well and enjoy the sound. Good visual communication so it's easy to improvise together and see any cues from the band leader. And possibilities to sonically control and get some separation between instruments, despite the musicians wanting to record close to each other. The latter two are sometimes not easy to achieve at once. But the way Eastcote is built around the control room is perfect. It feels open-plan, like you're in the same room, but you can actually choose to be quite separated sonically.

I'm on a call with two of Philip's engineers, Anna Dourado (Tjan) and Sam Navel. Anna was there first, from around the same time as Eliot James and Paul Epworth, in 2005. She

187

Asaf Sirkis has played drums on many great jazz albums recorded at Eastcote.

Left page: **Top left:** Liam Noble. **Bottom left:** Justin Quinn. **Top right:** Hugh Hopper. **Middle:** Jon Opstad. **Bottom right:** Simon Cosgrove.

This page: **Top left:** James Opstad. **Top middle:** Tom Herbert. **Top right:** Ernesto Simpson and Anselmo Netto. **Middle:** Andy Hamill and Glen Scott. **Bottom left:** James Allsopp. **Bottom right:** Ernesto Simpson.

was there as an engineer for a couple of years but had other plans and started a label for improvised music that Philip supported with studio time. Sam started right after and was there until around 2011 when George Murphy took over. When I show Anna the layout of the book she asks me: 'Where are all the pictures of the jazzers?' I explain that I need some help with identifying many of the photos. There's such a depth in the story of improvised music at Eastcote that it would be a great read on its own. Let's start with checking the calendars between 2013 and 2015 to find a good jumping-off point.

The Jim Mullen Organ Trio is in the studio in September 2013. Like many of the jazz bookings it's for a few days only and to record their album *Catch My Drift*. Apart from Jim, the trio consists of Mike Gorman on Hammond organ and Matt Skelton on drums. It's a brilliant listen from one of the UK's true masters of the guitar. From the opening track, 'Deep In A Dream', his guitar-playing is warm and effortless, a bit like Chet Baker when he sings. Track 8 is a version of my favourite Donald Fagen song, 'Maxine', and it brings back memories. I saw Jim play live once at Pizza Express, and I remember that warm tone and also that I was very impressed to find out that he had played with The Average White Band. His legacy of course goes back way further, having worked with greats like Mose Alison, Gene Harris and Georgie Fame. His first time recording at Eastcote was in 1983 with Dick Crouch and his fusion band Paz recording their album *Making Smiles*, also well worth a listen.

Just following the threads around Jim illustrates the interconnectedness between the musicians who are part of the Eastcote jazz scene. Between Ronnie Scott's, Pizza Express, The 606 Club and The Jazz Café, and in studios like Eastcote, these musicians played together in various constellations. Later line-up Soft Machine members have been part of several projects

Gary Husband in Studio 1 while recording an album for Antoine Fafard. He also recorded with John McLaughlin's band 4th Dimension.

Philip keeping an eye on the session set-up.

Steve Hackett – the lead guitarist for Genesis in the 1970s – recording in Studio 1.

Philip with the band Gary Husband's Drive: Julian Siegel, Philip, Michael Janisch, Gary Husband, Richard Turner.

over the years. And of course many musicians work across genres as well. Like Gilad with Sarah Gillespie. The amazing bass player Tom Herbert was part of the young jazzers who recorded at Eastcote. He was a member of Acoustic Ladyland, but also plays on many other great records recorded here, including Adele's. He tells me about how with the help of Philip as their co-producer his band took a journey from acoustic jazz on their first album to something quite different on *Last Chance Disco*:

We'd recorded an album of Jimi Hendrix songs that Pete Wareham (saxophone) had arranged for acoustic jazz quartet (hence the name of the band). That was Pete's way into trying to find a way to incorporate some of the non-jazz influences that had helped shape him as a musician. Camouflage *was still very much a jazz record, but* Last Chance Disco *was the result of us taking it further and allowing more of the feeling and energy of the punk music Pete had grown up listening to to seep in. We gradually started using electric instruments and by the time we recorded that album the double bass and piano were long gone. Philip helped us realize that vision by encouraging us to do things like recording the tenor sax through a massive amp, using delays and fuzzes and for me to really drive the studio's Ampeg amp to make it sound as dirty as possible.*

Saxophonist Tim Garland is in the booking calendar during this period as well, and in 2014 he released an album called *Songs to the North Sky* that features Asaf Sirkis on drums and percussion and the legendary John Patitucci on bass. Asaf is a long-time friend of Eastcote, having recorded in Studio 1 consistently over

192

Legendary Swedish noise artist and saxophonist Mats Gustafson in Studio 1.

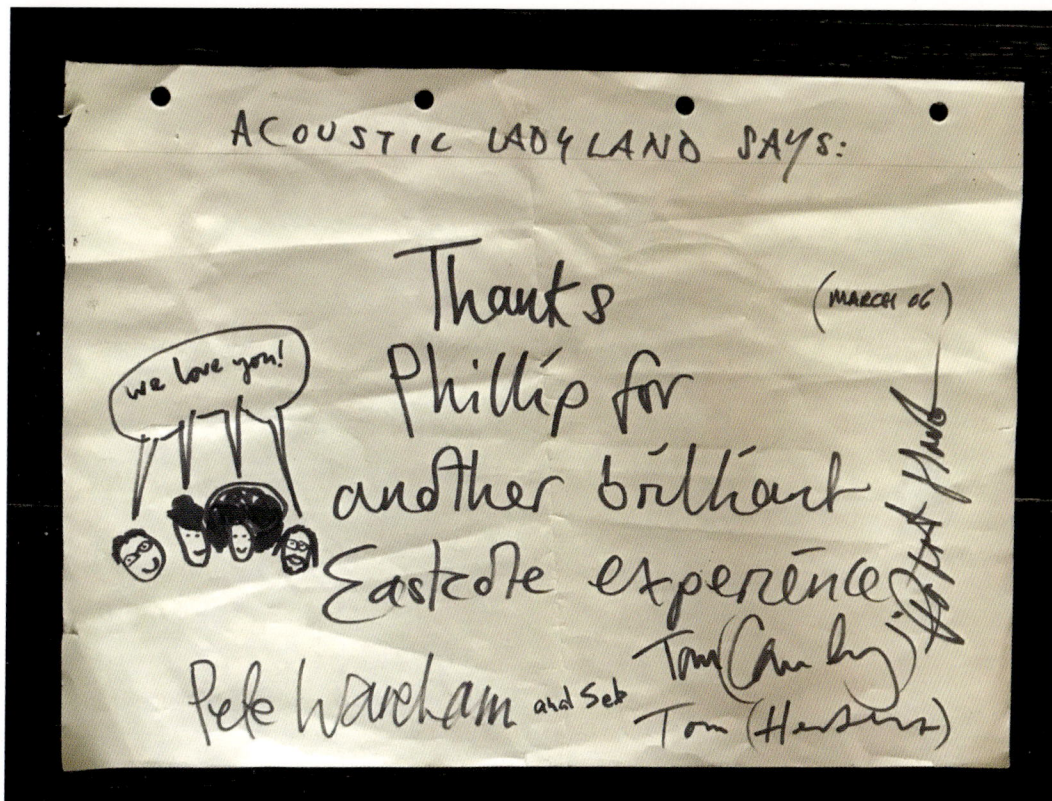

Thank-you note from Acoustic Ladyland to their
co-producer Philip Bagenal.

the years, and connects back to Gilad as
well. Garland himself is a celebrated musician
and arranger who has collaborated with
contemporary jazz greats such as Bill Bruford
and Chick Corea. In 2009 he won a Grammy with
his orchestrations on Corea and Gary Burton's
The New Crystal Silence.

Philip was very fond of all the jazz, improv
and experimental sessions. Anna tells me:

*When we got those big, blocked-out, four-
to-six-weeks-long band sessions, Philip used to
say he was happy for the business. But he felt
bad for all the smaller jazz and Improv groups
that had made Eastcote their home and came
regularly for a day or two. It meant they couldn't
get in the studio for a long while and he was
worried about that.*

Sam Navel adds:

*We used to have so many of those
recordings. Two to three jazz albums every
month around that time.*

Sam also tells me that one of the reasons
Philip could manage all the sessions that were
going on was that he empowered the assistants
and engineers to quickly learn the ropes and
take responsibility in a way that was quite
unusual in more corporate studios:

*I came to London from Paris in 2007. I was
looking for a job opportunity in a studio and had
sent out my CV everywhere. And one day Philip
called and said okay, come over. My English was
very bad at the time, so all I remembered from
the interview was to come back the next Monday
to make some coffee. I was there helping out
for a while, and then Philip said that Anna was
going to leave in a few months and that he'd
like me to stay. He offered me a job. A few
weeks after Anna left there was a session with
a band and Philip told me, you do the session!
So he did put a lot of trust in us, and because of
that freedom and also knowing he was always
there to support us if we needed help, it made
you feel empowered. In some studios I know,
assistants have to wait years to even touch the
console.*

Anna Dourado's (then Tjan) label is called
Dancing Wayang Records and was most active
between 2006 and 2011. All the releases on DWR
were recorded at Eastcote and released only on
limited edition vinyl with beautiful screen-printed
sleeves. Anna explains:

*This is a very avantgarde music scene
and our releases included Alex Neilson, Chris
Corsano and Borbetomagus, who are legends
in their own right, having played 'noise' since
1970, long before it was an actual genre, and are
the subject of a documentary called A Pollock
of Sound. All of our releases were recorded at*

193

'2D

Eastcote, which was the whole point. You're Swedish right?

I confirm that that is the case, and Anna tells me about her sessions with my fellow Swede and one-of-a-kind noise, reeds and breath explorer Mats Gustafsson:

He's a real giant of this art form, we made the album Needs! *together in 2010 and was a contributing factor to Mats being awarded the Nordic Music Prize a year later.*

It's great to listen to Anna and hear about her passion for the most explorative forms of making music. She recorded, produced and released these records and created a whole little alternative scene of her own at the studios.

Another jazz session in 2015, is with one of the true greats, John McLaughlin. He was back in the studio making a new album with his band The 4th Dimension, who apart from John consists of Gary Husband, Ranjit Barot and Etienne Mbappe. The album was called *Black Light* and McLaughlin says about recording at Eastcote:

It's been quite a few years since I entered the hallowed ground of Eastcote studios and met Philip. My career goes back many years and during the course of that time I've been in more studios than I can remember, some very impressive especially during the 1970s in the US. The famous CBS 'Church' Studio on W 34th St. and the equally famous 52nd St studios where I recorded a number of times with Miles Davis. The very impressive RCA Studio in Manhattan, Electric Ladyland with Jimi Hendrix, The Powerstation, etc, etc all gone I believe… I'm not counting European studios, that's enough

194

George Murphy and John McLaughlin at work in Studio 1.

other studios... In any event, when seeing the exterior of Eastcote, I really wondered... already the neighbourhood isn't exactly the Champs-Élysées. On entering I was not impressed either. Then I met 'the' Philip Bagenal, who truly impressed me with his expertise and knowledge.

I was impressed enough to want to record there, and lo and behold, there was George Murphy at the wheel and from that point I was hooked. Since then I consider Eastcote to be 'my' studio in the sense that I want to make all my recordings there with George.

Till now I've made at least three albums there and one movie score (still waiting to be released thanks to Covid). I could go on but I think I've made my case.

Enough to say, each time I arrive at Eastcote, I'm happy.

John has been back several times in the last few years, and the jazz recording scene is as alive as ever at Eastcote, spanning three generations of musicians who regularly visit. The list of projects I would love to write about is too long. I decide instead to gather together a collage of images taken of the amazing musicians in action at Eastcote through the years.

There was of course a lot of other music recorded in 2015 at Eastcote, and some you will hear about in adjoining chapters. But I'd like to conclude this one by sharing (with kind permission from Dancing Wayang Records) the liner notes for Mats Gustafsson's *Needs!* They are written by the brilliant American musician and record producer Jim O'Rourke, who apart from having been a member of Sonic Youth was a staple of the Chicago improv scene. I think he sums up the spirit of experimental music in a brilliant way: ∎

now, this guy, he's been my friend for half of my life, something that didn't quite sink in til i sat down to write these notes. mats has a couple of years on me, but the poor guy has known me almost half of his life as well, sorry about that mats. i still have a strong impression of the first day i saw him, although not the first moment, again, sorry about that mats. he and kjell were playing duo, and mats had a stance that i had never quite seen before, it was, frankly, like i was watching rambo. he didn't have the relaxed shoulders of brotzmann, or the furrowed brow of parker, or the hair of barbieri, but there was this incredible explosive tension in his forearms which made me think his horn must weigh a damn ton or something. kjell had these fluted bells, hung upside down, three or four of them in a row, and i really thought any moment they would start dispensing soft serve. it was 1990, london, and all three of us were there as the 'young upstarts' at derek bailey's company week. derek was like a dad to us all, and he has always been to mats and me. we even got to show our appreciation (and privately be freaked-the-fuck-out) when derek later asked us to make a duo for him. i haven't heard it since we made it (again, sorry, mats) but i know it had little to do with what went on that week in 1990, which was starting to be a foregone conclusion with both of us, seperately, and definitely together. for example, the first time mats hit chicago, we hit the studio, and as i was in my accordion phase, i showed up with a case that most definitely didn't bode well for most in attendance. only one person was non-plussed, mats. all the more surprising since we hadn't played together in maybe 3 or so years, and the last time i had a strat lying on the floor. if i remember correctly, mats had a whole bunch of other doo dads himself, so made sense to me. over the years i can honestly say i don't know if we've actually played the same combination of instruments more than twice. i can't keep track of what he's using. i don't think i need to, 'cause when that sound comes, that rattle from the deep, and the krakon awakes, there's mats. one note is all it takes. (and usually a few more before i decide to get off my ass and start playing) again, here's a record from mats, another missive from the field, keeping us on top of what detours, retraces, cul-de-sacs and breadcrumb paths he is treading through, leaving destruction in his path. he really should think about a headband though. i still think the rambo look was good.

Jim O'Rourke

196

Baaba Maal on the Pyramid Stage at Glastonbury
Festival 2016. That same year he collaborated with
Mumford & Sons on their EP 'Johannesburg'.

2015

IF YOU TAKE SOMEONE'S HEART OUT, THEY DIE

2016 is an odd year. I'm looking through the calendars and I keep getting stuck. This was the year I took over from Philip, but the transition wasn't completed until early 2017. In a way it didn't feel like a transition at that time. After all, I wasn't planning on using Eastcote any more than before. I have always loved Eastcote, but I had Kensaltown, I had my writing studio in New York and, actually, the longer Eastcote could continue as it had, the better for me. Because to start with it was a rescue mission more than a business decision. I didn't think it over very much. I had seen Philip get increasingly worried that he had no concrete plan for someone to take over, and on top of that it was looking like it would be a pretty slow year. The options seemed unappealing to both of us. Would someone take it over to be a private studio, a rehearsal room? Would the landlord convert It back to offices if Philip didn't find a successor? One thing I felt deeply was that if Philip and Eastcote shut shop, Kensaltown's days were numbered too. Not only because of all the residential development going on around us, or the general gentrification of North Kensington. But because for 40 years Eastcote had been the heart of the community around the courtyard at Walters Workshops. Even physically, the Eastcote building is at the centre of the site. And if you take someone's heart out, they die. So this was a rescue mission.

And it was both Kensaltown and Eastcote that needed saving.

I wanted Eastcote to keep operating as before. We agreed that Philip would stay on as tech and general support a day or so a week. But it wasn't the same. I saw in Philip what I know about myself: I can't do something just a little bit, and it made me sad to see Philip at Eastcote without being the puppet master. There is something about the sessions that year that in retrospect look almost like a simultaneous farewell and celebration. The studios got as busy as ever before the year was over. Long-time and new-found friends of Philip were there for weeks at a time. The jazzers, as usual in a myriad of constellations. Dickon from Tindersticks to score another film. Shiro Sigasu, who has been recording at Eastcote for long periods through almost three decades. Sarah Gillespie and Gilad Atzmon. The indie bands class of '16, a few for the first time in a professional studio. And also some beautiful and unusual sessions, like the one with Stephen Horne, who is internationally known as one of the best accompanists and composers for silent films.

Mumford & Sons were back in the studio to finish their brilliant collaborative EP 'Johannesburg' with Baaba Maal. It had started with a meeting and initial jam in the studio in 2015 before the majority of the EP was recorded whilst on tour in South Africa. Eliot James tells me a great story about when he accidentally met Baaba:

One of the best moments for me at Eastcote was a few years back. There was a ring at the door. I answered but didn't quite catch who was there so I buzzed them in anyway. A moment later the very famous Senegali artist Baaba Maal walked into my studio, announced he was here for Winston, and sat down on my couch. Now, I was a big Baaba Maal fan when I was a teenager in the '90s – I had his early records on vinyl, so this was something like Bono walking into the room for me! Turns out he had been sent to the wrong studio by his management and he was supposed to be somewhere else. The Winston he was looking for was of course Winston Marshall from Mumford & Sons as they were doing a collaboration at the time.

Peter Tosh, Jimmy Cliff, The Cult and Joan Jett would make a proud CV for most producers and engineers. But then you add his involvement as co-producer and/or engineer on albums like *Sticky Fingers*, *Some Girls*, *Emotional Rescue*, *Tattoo You*, *Undercover* and *Steel Wheels*. And now you think, this guy knows how to make records. Chris Kimsey is most known for his work with The Rolling Stones. He is a true master of recording music and, oddly, a recent, new friend of Philip's. They met in 2015 and this year, 2016, he practically moved in at Eastcote, working on various projects with young and unsigned bands and more established artists alike. Which makes me think two things. That some legends remain legends because they never stop, they just keep starting. And also that Chris likes Eastcote and enjoyed being around Philip. Chris has written me a letter and asked that I pass it on to Philip. In it he writes:

Being a South London lad, to go north of the river to record and produce an album was always a pain. It was Friday 21st August 2015, and I was just starting to produce an album with a great singer songwriter, Noah Johnson. I had a vision of a sound for the album, especially the drum and bass sound. I recorded a lot in New York and Memphis and I wanted a tight, funky drum sound. I've recorded in most studios in South London, a lot that have now closed. I knew I couldn't get that drum 'n' bass sound in those studios so I started looking just north of the river and I discovered the Eastcote website. I looked at the photos and I saw the drum booth and booked the studio. I didn't even go there to check the sound, I just had a feeling that that room would be the killer sound I was

looking for. The best studios are those that make you feel like you're in someone's house, not in a recording studio. It's all about the artist and the music and the chilled environment of the room. Not a lot of flash gear. Naturally you need good equipment and a good engineer and that's what Philip built. Not only did he have a good ear for music, but he picked a brilliant engineer, one of the best that I've ever worked with, George Murphy, who studied at Guildford and is a Tonmeister. With the legendary Julie Bateman as studio manager and booker keeping an eye on Phillip, this was the A-Team. It still stands today virtually the same as it was 40 years ago, although I think there is hot running water now. And the smell from the bass booth has been irradiated after discovering it was rat urine! Eastcote has all the things in the right place, a pleasant courtyard, sunlight, a great community, the school next door, the laughter of children at playground time. And the church with the church bell that's another nice sound to hear when you are outside for a break. But the best sound is inside, with musicians playing live together and hearing each other with the best sound you can imagine. I only discovered Eastcote five years ago and I've been nowhere else since.

Noah Francis Johnson, who was the first artist Chris recorded with at Eastcote, also sent a note, talking about his experience at the studio and with Philip. There's a part where he says:

Philip would sit with me late into the night, and together with George he would lend an ear, and his views, positive and negative, on my recordings. I know I was blessed to share that time with a man who got accepted for an architecture degree at Cambridge University because he made a suit of armour out of pots and pans he'd taken from his family kitchen. Eastcote studio was built by a genius who just so happened to love music more than academia. He fixed the place up, somewhere between a

college dorm and a spiritual home, a place for weary musicians, troubadours just like myself, to bare their soul.

In the calendar there is also one session in particular that appears to say 'Hey! I'm the future'. Well actually it was said better than that when the Recording Academy nominated Wolf Alice's 'Moaning Lisa Smile' for a Grammy. It was the one track on their album *My Love Is Cool* that Catherine Marks produced, and the nomination was for Best Rock Performance. A few months later, The Music Producers Guild gave Catherine the 2016 Breakthrough Producer of The Year award. I worked with Catherine on her very first session when she was Flood's assistant and he was mixing an album I had produced with A-ha. Fifteen years later she told me when we ended up being jointly interviewed in front of a dozen music students:

It was my first session in the studio after I had moved here from Australia, and I remember it being really intimidating. With you and Flood and the band. A lot of pressure.

I do remember it was quite a stressful session and I'm glad she continued working in the studio because she has become an amazing record producer. At Eastcote that year she made an album with Big Moon called *Love in the 4th Dimension* which is unruly and dark, with some great guitars. I've got hold of Catherine while she is in a cab on the way to a South London studio to record with a young band from Atlanta called Lower Town. She says:

I first recorded at Eastcote in 2016 with Big Moon. We basically recorded an album in eight days. It feels like a lifetime ago. I should've kept a journal or something. I just remember the exhaustion and all the things people have reminded me that I've said – dumb stuff. Like the girls would be talking about cheese or something, and apparently to everyone else I was engaged in the cheese conversation but actually I was thinking about something else.

Then mid-sentence, I would say: 'Actually I think the faster tempo feels better'. Then that would be the end of the cheese conversation, and everyone was like 'What has she been thinking about for the past 20 minutes?'

There weren't many women engineering back then, but I vaguely remember around 2008 or something someone said 'Oh there's another girl, an assistant engineer working', and I remember there was one at Rak called Helen, and another girl called Anna that worked at Eastcote, but I never met her. I was definitely told that there weren't a lot of girls who engineered, which I always saw as an opportunity to stand out. It was really competitive, and all the assistants were really mean to each other. Especially if you were a runner, which essentially I was when you were doing the A-ha album. It was pretty brutal. I remember it so clearly because I was so foolish and had never had any studio experience before. It was intimidating because I didn't know what was expected of me, and no one really told me when I did anything wrong. I was enjoying it in some ways and I knew there was an end goal, but I wasn't enjoying those 16-hour days, and I remember the first day coming in early and it got to 10 pm and I thought, 'Do we do this every day?' I just didn't know but I caught on very quickly. I wanted to learn everything but obviously, like you said, you were really stressed out and it's not until you're in that position that you start to understand the dynamic of what it means to be in a studio. If you're a runner and you want to be a producer, you're forgetting that a lot of people are under pressure and it has nothing to do with you. You learn though, and that's why I like working in studios, you learn how to manage people and the psychology. Essentially dealing with artists or producers or engineers and trying to get the best out of everyone and learning how to do that. I was going to say manipulate.

2016

I agree and tell Catherine that Philip calls it 'to stir things up a bit'. It certainly is a bit like some sort of group therapy, being in a recording session. And the more open you can be with acknowledging all the pressure and emotions flying around the room, the more likely you are to come out on the other side with something everyone feels good about. And of course there is a hierarchy of whose emotions need to be considered most when you're making a record. And as Philip tells us over and over, at the top of that hierarchy are the artists and the musicians, because they are the ones in the most vulnerable position. But producers are not far behind. They are the ones who have to navigate expectations on all sides and try to please labels and artists and, in between that, be able to bring their own creativity and vulnerability to the table. And sometimes that's a challenge. Catherine continues:

I started to learn when I was engineering or assisting for other producers that often all they needed was support. As in moral support. You know that classic thing when producers turn around and say, 'What do you think?' And there's that idiot who tells them what they really think, and then it sends the producer or engineer into a downward spiral because they are experiencing self-doubt. Actually all you need to say is 'It sounds fucking amazing' because they are the ones who are ultimately going to know when it sounds right. I remember watching those situations and thinking that's the worst thing to say right now, especially if you're under a lot of pressure. How does that snare sound to you? After you've been working on it for three hours and some smart ass in the back goes 'Oh I think it could still have a bit more body'. Nowadays, when someone does that I'm like, 'Get out, get out of the room!'

I think about the A-ha session which was an eight-month rollercoaster of emotions. Up to that point I had mainly made records with friends and bands I knew really well. Working with a really famous and experienced band who had their own issues and with a new record label that had huge expectations, that was my real baptism of fire as a record producer. One of the guys in the band said in an interview after the album was released: 'Our producer's shrink thanks us from the bottom of her purse'. It was funny, but also true. During the mix sessions with Flood, I was as unexperienced in the situation I was in as Catherine was being an assistant engineer. I tell her, you must have thought we were all insane? She replies:

Well, I was too nervous to think that anyone was insane. I just wanted someone to notice me, but that's the whole point. In the role I was in, you're supposed to just be there for everyone else. That's part of the learning process, I think. It was a bit of a shock because the week before, I worked for an architectural firm and I had people working for me. Suddenly I'm making tea and vacuuming.

I shouldn't be surprised, but I ask Catherine if she's an architect:

Yes, I have a masters degree in Architecture.

I tell Catherine that Philip too was an architect, and a few hours later I find myself pondering whether budding engineers and producers should study architecture instead of going to music technology college. The truth is, you pick up the technical side of recording

whether you like it or not once you start working in a recording studio. It's much harder to learn how to keep focused on the bigger picture of making records. Catherine had that skill coming into it, and she's also very good at talking about the emotions that are attached to the creative process. That's probably why she keeps making such great records and is able get the best out of the bands and artists she works with. ∎

199

Martin Terefe and Catherine Marks interviewed by Jack Horner for The Rhythm Studio's Local Legends event in 2017.

Legendary engineer and producer with The Rolling Stones, Chris Kimsey, with Philip Bagenal in Studio 1.

WE'RE ABOUT TO BLOW UP THE BEST STUDIO OF ALL TIME

2017 was my second year as the owner of Eastcote Studios. I was still mainly recording at Kensaltown then, or in New York, and business at Eastcote had continued largely as usual, with Julie Bateman managing the studio and George Murphy at the helm by the console in Studio 1. Many artists now booked the room specifically asking could they have George to record which sometimes wasn't possible as his mix and production work was also getting increasingly in demand. I found out why during a session that year when I was trying to finish a new acoustic recording of 'Take On Me' with A-ha. I made an arrangement that had quite a dark and sombre tone, and had recorded it with Magne, Paul and Morten at Kensaltown. Everyone seemed happy with the version, but before the final mix Morten wanted to make some small changes to the vocal that I already loved. I can be quite resistant to changing things once I like something, and I was worried we would lose the thread along the

Yungblud in the courtyard at Eastcote.

way. So I decided to do it with George down in Eastcote to get some fresh ears on it as a back-up. He was quick and super-communicative, and let Morten try out a bunch of different ideas without losing track of the line through the vocal I had told him I already loved. It didn't take long before we were all happy, and by the time I got out to the car George had sent us all a brilliant-sounding rough.

At the time, Philip was still coming in a day or so a week, doing tech work and making sure things ran smoothly. But his Parkinson's was getting worse and he would get tired and easily worried about things. He engineered his last session at Eastcote that year with John McLaughlin, 46 years after his first gig as a sound engineer, which was also with John and his Mahavishnu Orchestra at a club in New York City.

One thing Philip never gets tired of is having a dig at the ruling classes, and it's not only the Etonians in charge of our British Isles he has an issue with now. We were one year into Trump's Presidency and I remember him saying: 'The whole world has gone mad'. We did call Trump all kinds of things in the courtyard at Walters but never the President of the United States. And looking back, this was the year, accidentally perhaps, I joined Philip and la résistance. I was tired of making records, of doing meetings at record labels and listening to their new signings. I was probably just exhausted, but I heard nothing interesting. I was pushing through. I enjoyed recording with old friends and worked on a couple of rock projects that were a bit outside my comfort zone which got me excited. We had a Thursday night live music club at a venue close to the studio, and I was slowly letting my guard down. Some years ago, after several unsuccessful attempts to start a label of my own, I had decided that making records was what I was good at and to not bother myself with the business side of things again. And when fatigue

2017

Paloma Faith at the V Festival at Hylands Park, Chelmsford, England, in 2015.

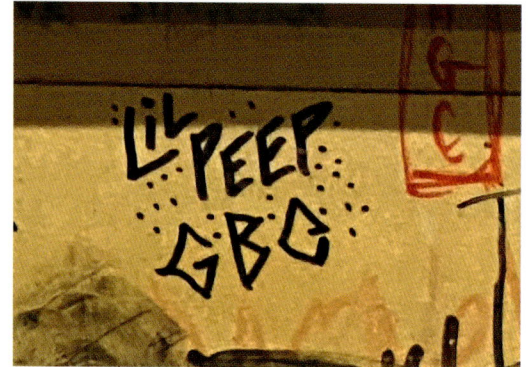

set in, my gut reaction had always been to do more of the same. But Philip's words were true. The world had gone mad and I was going mad too. With a little help from my friends and family and my Gonzo therapist Mr Hyde, I started to question everything. And it felt great.

I had been talking on and off to my long-time friend and publisher Declan Morell who wanted me to get involved with a new music company he and a Danish friend of his, Tommas Arnby, had started. I was slow out of the starting-blocks, as with most things, but on a miserable and rainy night that year I went with them to see a young punk from Doncaster they had just signed. He was playing in the basement of a pub in East London, called himself Yungblud and I liked the name. There were 10 people in the room at the most and out on stage steps this force of nature, acting like he was at Wembley Arena and shouting, 'This song is about northern England', and I was in. I hadn't

seen or heard anything like it in quite some time. I forgot all about not getting too involved in the business side of things and became a partner with Tommas and Declan in Locomotion Music. I was managed by Neil Jacobson at the time who was also the head of Geffen Records in the US and after a few no's and some healthy competition from another label he agreed to take a meeting with Dom (Yungblud). We got the whole Locomotion crew and Dom over to LA for a show at Chris Douridas's 'School Nights', and it was only yes from there on, from everyone who came out to see the show that night. We partnered with Geffen/Interscope and got to work on his debut album, *21st Century Liability*. We worked at Kensaltown, in my studio in New York and at Eastcote.

It was another very busy year at Eastcote and other sessions included Aluna George, George Ezra, Kat Cunning, Cat Stevens, Birdy, Ward Thomas, The Coronas and Tindersticks.

Lil Peep recording at Eastcote in September 2017.

2017

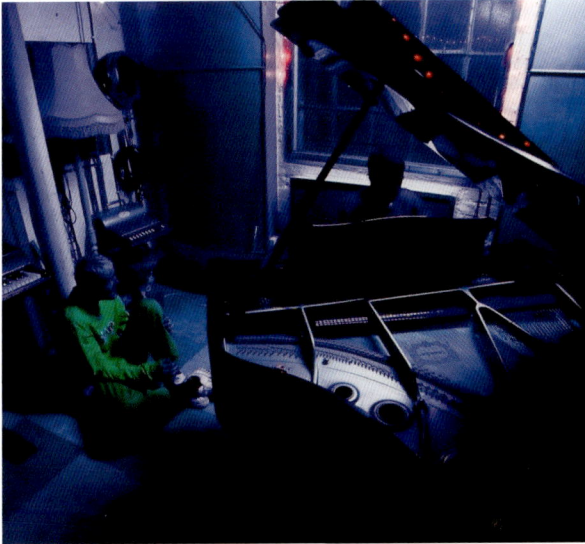

Paloma Faith spent a lot of time in Studio 2 this year, mainly with producer Starsmith, working on her album *The Architect* that was released later in the year. It saw the throwing in the deep end of another young engineer and musician who is now part of the core Eastcote team. Clem Cherry had spent only a month or so assisting me and my then main collaborator, Oskar Winborg, over at Kensaltown. When Eastcote got the Paloma booking that looked like it could go on for a while, we decided that Clem would move across the courtyard and take charge of Studio 2. He tells me:

It was one of my first sessions where I had to take responsibility and make things happen. It was all very new to me, and Paloma had a big personality and I hadn't assisted on a high-profile project before then. I assisted through the sessions and did some engineering. And also ended up playing guitar on a track. We worked on the album The Architect *first, and Paloma loved the studio and had just become a mother, so she liked that it wasn't too far from where she lived at the time.*

Luckily Clem was prepared. He had been to university studying sound engineering for three years but says this about learning the ropes:

The other thing I did when I came to the studios, apart from assisting you and Oskar, was that very soon after I started I was asked to help Philip and Rob to wire up the Studer console in Studio 2. I remember Philip handing me the soldering iron, and I learned more from working with Philip for a week than I had during two or three years at university.

It was also an unusually sad year for the studio. In late August Lil Peep spent two weeks in Studio 1 to finish up his debut album *Come Over When You're Sober, Pt 1*. The young emo rapper from Long Island, New York, had become increasingly influential after he started to release mix tapes in 2015 with lyrics that dealt openly with difficult themes such as his sexuality, mental health and drug use. Only a few months after his sessions in London, on 15th November, he was tragically found dead from a drug overdose whilst on his first major tour of the US.

I'm with Dom in Studio 2. It's a few weeks after we finished refurbishing it and all the equipment from what used to be Kensaltown Studio A is in there now, including my all-discrete 1973 Trident B-range that I had been pretty sure was too wide to fit in the room. I had just made an impulse buy from a US audio dealer during one night of psychedelic lockdown dreams when I woke up and couldn't go back to sleep. It's a monster broadcast compressor, a '70s UREI called the Modulator and it's essentially an LA3A and 1176 in one box with three(!) VU meters. It was used for vocals on Green Day's *American Idiot* and I've just recorded a song with Dom where we tested it out, and the sound is incredible. I adjusted the name on the front to

DOMULATOR with some creative cutting and sellotaping before he came in today and, after a bit of laughing, the conversation turns a bit more serious as we talk about the challenges he feels his generation are facing. We soon end up talking about Peep:

Me: *He was here in August 2017 and so were you. Did you meet?*

Yungblud: *What's so crazy to me is we knew about each other and we were in the same building, we probably crossed, but just didn't ever meet. I love his music so much and I love what he did for rock, he had the same ideologies that I do and if we had met and done something together it would've been crazy. We were in the same building, literally about 20 meters apart, and we never even met and to me that blows my mind. I think it's a real tragedy to our scene, that he went so soon. I respect him. I would've loved to have met him.*

Me: *What did you feel was different in Eastcote when you first came into the building?*

Yungblud: *Dude, it's just in the walls. It's this unexplainable thing. Do you know what I mean, you walk in there and so many great songs have been made here, and that isn't a fucking fluke. I always think, songs are flying above my head and one day it'll just come to you because when you're in the booth, in that moment, that split second before you get that melody, there's something in the room, there's something in the walls and that place has buckets of it. Like 'Waiting On The Weekend', I remember when we did that with Crossey, and it was all live. It's just fucking live. You don't know exactly what you're going to find in the studio, there's fucking writing on the walls, and there's an old Leslie that hasn't been used for a while and Mike Crossey goes 'Let's record this live through the Leslie', you know what I mean. You just don't know what the fuck you're going to find in there. That's the same as inspiration, like I go in to*

write a ballad and I come out with a punk song, and I go in to write a punk song and I come out with a ballad. There's just something flying in the fucking air that makes you go 'Oh shit'.

I think what makes Eastcote fucking special is that when I go to LA, I get so sick of formulaic bullshit. Music is maths right now and that's so fucking boring. You're not going to go in there and try to emulate 25 hit songs that you heard on the radio and try to copy every sound. Eastcote doesn't have time for that, it's not made for that. You're can't tell me that 'Rolling in the Deep' did that or 'A Certain Romance' by Arctic Monkeys did that. No, it fucking didn't, it just did its thing. Sometimes you go into a studio that looks like a doctor's or a dentist's office and it makes you want to kill yourself. You know exactly what song you're going to come out with.

Me: *Did you ever meet Philip?*

Yungblud: *Yeah, I did, the dude in the back of the room who built Eastcote, with his cigs and coffee breath, waiting to fix the patch on number 64 that's still faulty. He just rocks.*

Inevitably what I'm noticing in music right now is live instrumentation is coming back. It's been all programming for seven years, but live music is coming back, and that's why I think Eastcote is going to have an insane next few years because it's coming back. If you want fucking magic and things blowing up and shit, capturing a moment, then come here. If you're an artist, you can handle that.

I shouldn't tell you but it's fine because it's fixed, but one time we were doing a thing, and I spilled beer on the desk, and it started smoking. I'm like, 'FUCK WE'RE ABOUT TO BLOW UP THE BEST STUDIO OF ALL TIME' and Adam is just stoned as fuck laughing, and I'm like 'NO NO', taking my t-shirt off and shoving it down the desk, luckily it still works till this day but the downstairs desk almost blew up because we were off our tits and I was just spinning around and spilt a lager down the desk.

I'm pretty sure Philip has fixed the occasional accident with the MCI before and the studio still lives on. And with a new generation of artists and producers discovering the studio and the magic that lives there, it will take more than a spilled can of lager to blow the place up.

In the walls at Eastcote there's triumph and tragedy. Certainty and mystery. The sweat of the workers in the foundry and the smell of the horses in their stalls may have evaporated but the history of the building goes back to before recording studios were invented. And the real magic might be that each new tenant, and every new artist who passes through, has been allowed to make the space theirs for a while. All contributing to a story that is still being written. ∎

RIP Gustav Elijah Åhr 1996–2017

Yungblud's debut album *21st Century Liability* (Locomotion Records/Geffen Records). Produced by Martin Terefe and Mati Schwartz.

With 2 Otari MTR 90s, an MCI JH16 and a Studer A80 8-track, Eastcote is prepared for anyone who wants to record to tape.

Terry Hall and Lynval Golding of The Specials
performing at The Roundhouse, London, in 2014.

A VERY SPECIALS YEAR

I'm at the studio having a conversation with Toby Laurent Belson, a visual community artist, activist and political campaigner in our local area of North Kensington. We've gotten to know each over the years as we've crossed paths through common friends and around the neighbourhood. We bumped into each other on Golborne Road a few days ago and decided to catch up. He tells me how after years that he and other campaigners have taken over the running of the Westway Trust. An organization that in the wake of the Grenfell tragedy has lost a lot of trust from the local community. It's an important and monumental task they've taken on, made more difficult by the historical underfunding that most likely will continue as councils and NGOs struggle more than ever financially in this year of the Corona virus pandemic.

I show him some pictures and tell him about my book project and what I've learnt about the history of Eastcote. He's amazed to hear about everything that has been going on inside Walters Workshops, despite knowing the neighbourhood so well. He says; *I have always wondered where the socially connected music was. In the late 80s, it seemed to have all but disappeared. Maybe it was all happening in Bristol then. But I had no idea they came back to Ladbroke Grove to record. To this place.* There were all kinds of music made at Eastcote, but Philip did keep a more open house than most. Not only because he cared more about music and people than he did about the money. But because he was naturally curious and at times a bit of a troublemaker. He loved artists who as he called it *would stir things up a little*, and stirring was needed. The attitudes and prejudices, then as now, and the consequence of centuries of colonialism and white privilege, are so deeply entwined in our politics, economy, education and cultural institutions.

After Toby leaves I think about how I've described our neighbourhood as a melting-pot, an exciting multicultural place, etc, in this book. I realize that is quite a simplification. It would fall short of reality to write about the history of a studio in Ladbroke Grove without addressing some more uncomfortable issues. This is a year where the one thing apart from Covid that we will hopefully remember for a long time is the global mobilization of the Black Lives movement. The moment that black communities across the Western world had once again had enough. History repeating itself, but with an undeniable force that brought a centuries-long conversation to the top of the liberal agenda anew. But how do we talk about it in a society racing to take sides? And a media environment that has fallen into its own trap by simplifying everything to bite-size jingles, relentlessly and for years. Toby, like my own children, is of mixed heritage and I decide to send him a draft of what I've written to see what he thinks. The answer I receive goes deeper than I expected and provides further education for me in a year that has forced me as a white man married to a black woman to re-think my own prejudices and laziness when it comes to actively addressing the issues of white privilege. It also relates strongly to The Specials and Lynval's decades-long call for dialogue as the way forward, despite suffering first-hand from thuggery justified by racism. Toby notes that I use the term 'mixed race' in the text and says:

Race is a dangerous word to legitimize. It is true that it is purely a concept, dreamt up many hundreds of years ago and codified once and for all in the mid-to-late 18th century by European men, who classified the world according to a number of groups - sometimes three or five and anywhere up to eight or ten I believe. The most influential appear to have been the five of Mongolian, American, Malayan, Ethiopian and Caucasian, as depicted by Johann Blumenbach in 1775. But, there were many other theories that covered hundreds of years and were seen as simply facts of nature, seemingly amongst an epistemology (the creation of knowledge) that had barely the faintest scientific grasp and is now widely acknowledged to have been steeped in prejudiced and discriminatory thought and practice - not to mention rapacious economic expansionism. To further indicate how far removed these people were from what we would consider modern scientific thought, this was a time where people still commonly believed - and scholars commonly debated amongst themselves - that black people were dark-skinned due to a biblical curse (the curse of Ham). And to be clear, there are still deeply religious people who retain this particular belief today. So, with that knowledge, what does it mean to refer to oneself as 'mixed race'?

I now refer to myself as mixed heritage or mixed heritage black. Mixed heritage because heritage is a term that denotes a particular history that is worthy of recognition. Black because I do remain a believer in the power of blackness and black culture to support our current collective journey to equality.

This is a book about a recording studio, but music and art exist in particular contexts and Toby's words feel like a good place from where to consider the particular heritage of our area in West London. For anyone interested in digging deeper, there's a wealth of information available just a few clicks away on the Internet of things. One place to start is an article on intermix.org.uk that Toby wrote in 2007, and in it he writes:

I am very proud to have been born on the 25th of March. It is a constant reminder to me that precisely 170 years previous to my birth,

Britain brought in an Act to cement a political decision to end its direct involvement in the transatlantic slave trade. I now feel that I, along with the rapidly increasing members of the mixed race community, are the living, breathing outcome of that despicable trade and that righteous decision.

If you have grown up around an area with cultural and racial diversity, as I have in West London, you may agree that the polarizing descriptions and stereotypes that follow the terms 'Black' and 'White' do not do justice to the people you know. So why do we continue to use words that are loaded by a history full of opposites and destruction to describe a people of the future, created by togetherness and common individuality?

I will keep educating myself further but Toby's words make a lot of sense to me. Why do we? I don't have the answer, but the actions shown by the ruling classes and current political establishment in Britain appear to endorse and actively work to keep the divisions alive. For example. My kids and other black and ethnic minority teenagers still have to be reminded that if they are stopped and searched by the police, they ought to keep quiet and agreeable to minimize the risk of being humiliated, beaten or worse. Because even if the older-style 'sus' laws were abandoned in the early 80s, stop and search is still commonplace on the streets of Notting Hill, and around our studio. Now they are carried out under different legislation, mainly section 60 of the Criminal Justice and Public Order Act 1994. And according to the Home Office's own internal data, published in a *Guardian* article in May 2019, you are 40 times

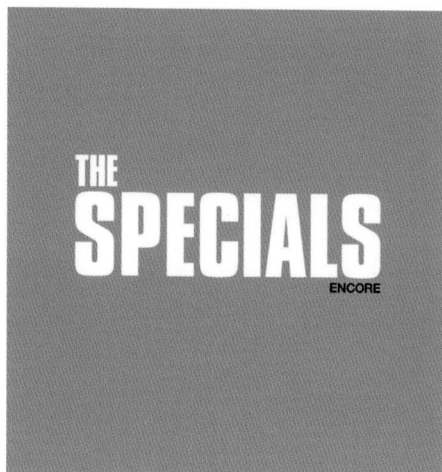

more likely to be stopped and searched if you are black as opposed to white. 50 years after the trial of the 'Mangrove 9', the streets in North Kensington are still policed by a racially biased system. That's pretty fucked up.

Someone who knows about racial conflict in British society is Lynval Golding from The Specials. The first time I heard him talk in person about his own experiences in the late '70s was a couple of years ago when we were playing a show together at Laylow, a local club close to the studio. We had just played 'Why?', a Specials' song from the 'Ghost Town' EP that Lynval wrote after having been brutally attacked and beaten outside a London club by a group of racist thugs. After the performance, Lynval was interviewed on stage by a young French/Iraqi/British beatboxer and rapper called Psi who we were recording with in the studio. She is an amazing musical talent and also a young activist, studying politics and history at Oxford University. The conversation quickly became about how and if racism in the UK had changed since the early days of The Specials. I remember Lynval saying:

Well, back then we were in danger of being attacked at every show that we played. Only because we were a mixed band.

Four years after the attack in London, Lynval was stabbed in the neck inside another club in Coventry. This time attacked again because he was black. He was certainly speaking from personal experience and probably because of

the wit, humour and connection they had on that stage, I remember the night as if it was yesterday. The Specials were also at Eastcote that year recording *Encore*, the first time in almost 30 years that Lynval and Terry Hall were back together in the studio. They had been enjoying touring together again, but the motivation to finally make another album and write new music was concern about the state of the world and the recent increase in divisions and injustice. And as the album went to number 1 on the UK charts on its release in 2019 it was clear that the conversation was welcome. And of course that we all had secretly been craving some new music from The Specials. I'm on Zoom (yes, again...) with Lynval and Nikolaj Torp, the band's keyboard player and producer of *Encore*:

Lynval: *I'll tell you, Martin, It was so strange reflecting back when I was talking to Nikolaj about our journey as The Specials. You know, it really is an incredible journey. I can sit back down with everyone and say, 'We must have dialogue, right? We must communicate. Let's have a civil discussion', and I'll tell you one thing which is so important, all that come around two years ago when we got to your studio and we started working on the Encore, that is when it all came to me. We've got to approach these subject matters. Some can be very, very difficult and quite emotionally painful to talk about. But we've got to do away with the distance, we're not going to hear each other across the street shouting at each other. We have to social distance right now, but we should really be so close to each other to have a quiet conversation.* [Lynval switches from speaking loudly to a

The Specials, *Encore*, Island/Universal, 2019.

whispering voice] *When they get rid of this social distance, we must actually talk to each other in a civil way – quietly. Listen: we've been kept so far apart from each other. We don't hear each other when we shout at each other.*

So you know, writing and recording at your place was the best and such an amazing journey. I was looking back and when we recorded our first album at TW Studio with Elvis Costello, we were young lads then. That experience was fantastic, you know why it was fantastic? Because we got drunk day and night, day and night. Do you remember that guy down at Baker Street? That wild saxophone player? He would come to your studio and I had a few sessions with him and he was out of his head – and when we were all drunk, he'd play and... wow. Because that's what it was at the time. This time around we communicate with each other. I don't know if Nikolaj told you but it was very difficult getting the band back together, you know. It took me five years to get the band back together. And the only one person that I couldn't get back in the band was Jerry. It was very difficult and that was one good thing about social media. It tells you, 'Look guys, we want you to play the music right, we don't care, just move on – don't bother, just come back with music for us', so that really encouraged us to fight and get the band back together. But you know, I would definitely stay at your studio, it was an amazing experience. The experience was being able to write and record those songs without anyone consuming any alcohol or any substance, none at all. No big bongs smoking, there were no weed smokers, it was sheer music and getting together.
Nikolaj: *And having fun.*

Lynval: *And having fun, and we did it.*
Nikolaj: *Well until the string section came.*
[Laughter]
Lynval: *Because I think when you're high you're not being able to communicate with each other, and for the first time we let the joy of music lead us. You know, we didn't lead the music, the music would lead us. And we were in this beautiful state of mind that was absolutely wonderful, you know. That's why we did what we did. One thing I can give to new young bands with my experience is this: do three years together then break up, and don't talk to each other. Because the only way it's going to work is when you come back together and reflect on where you're coming from and your past and you learn. I'll tell you, Martin, you need to live through this life to be able to reflect back on life, and that's where the journey really begins for you – when you can reflect back on the past. It's the same with history, you do learn from history. So it is important.*

But definitely, man, I will say the comeback and doing the album at your place was just... I mean, what a vibe. What a feeling. The togetherness we brought, you know it was a wonderful feeling. Amazing feeling. It's like creativity was just coming out of us. Horace has been in the band for 40 years, he was a stranger to us. We didn't even know who he was. Horace was like a shadow that would disappear, but this session really brought him out and I just thought... wow. We just love the new Horace, we literally met Horace and got to know him. After 40 years and he is definitely Sir Horace, gentleman.*
Nikolaj: *And he had a say all of a sudden. He hasn't said anything for all the years we've been touring. He hasn't raised his voice, he hasn't said anything basically and now he's here and has suggestions. He told us to stop putting so many parts on. He put a sign over the MCI saying, 'Does it need it?' He would sit behind the desk, that was his place.*
Lynval: *Then you would just see his head pop up and say, 'Guys, does it need it?'*
Nikolaj: *Yeah, and point to the sign over the desk.*
Lynval: *Then he would disappear again.*

We laugh a lot, because it's impossible to not fill up with joy when in the presence of Mr

Nikolaj Torp recording in Studio 1.

DOES IT NEED IT ?

Page left: **Top left:** Lynval Golding. **Top right:** Sleeping
Lynval Golding. **Bottom left:** Steve Cradock. **Bottom
right:** George Murphy, Kenrick Rowe.

This page: **Top:** Steve Cradock. **Bottom:** Nikolaj Torp
Larsen, Kenrick Rowe, Terry Hall, Tom Pigott-Smith,
Bruce White, Oli Langford, Ian Burdge, Lynval Golding

THE YEAR WAS 1954
SIR WINSTON CHURCHILL SHOUT
ACROSS TO THE WEST INDIAN
ISLANDS.

"COME," HE SAID
HELP US REBUILD THIS COUNTRY SO
DEVASTED BY WAR..

AND SO..
MY FATHER SET SAIL UPON THE
WINDRUSH,
BOUND FOR A NEW LIFE

HE WAS A TAILOR BY TRADE
AND THIS COULD BE THE
POSSIBILITY OF ALL POSSIBILITES.

BUT NAH,
THERE WAS NO CLOTH TO STITCH
INSTEAD
HE FOUND WORK IN A STEEL FOUNDRY,
POURING HOT METAL, DAY AND NIGHT

AND EVEN WORSE
TRYING TO FIND A ROOM TO RENT
WAS BECOMING A NIGHTMARE.

HE KNOCKED ON DOOR AFTER DOOR
BUT THE SIGNS IN THE WINDOW
KEPT SAYING THE SAME THING..

NO DOGS, NO IRISH, NO BLACKS

WELCOME TO ENGLAND..

Golding. We talk about memories, and how different they can be between people who were at the same place and the same time but have their own unique version of what happened. And what was said. How the brain works. Then we talk about Philip and record labels:

Lynval: *I don't think you know about Steve? But Steve never came to the studio because he was banned. Steve was my old manager. He couldn't come to the studio and he didn't hear anything.*
Nikolaj: *The label wasn't allowed to hear anything until it was finished.*
Lynval: *I went into Johnny's office and we shut the door and I said, 'Right Johnny, this is what we've done'. He had no idea what to expect and he was like, 'Wow'. Same with Steve, we never played Steve a demo or nothing. Nothing. With Johnny, he came down to rehearsal once to hear what we were doing, but really you can't hear what we're doing because we're just working on it, and you can only hear it when it's finished. Take it in – we don't need your input.*

The Specials' first album was released in 1979, the same year that Philip and Chaz decided to take on the old stables at Walters and build a studio. We talk about how the business has changed since then and the expectations. I tell them about something my friend Dave Robinson, who founded Stiff Records, told me as we were trying to tow my boat off the riverbed when it had gone aground at Chiswick Pier. Long story, but Dave said: 'When I started in this business, the artist made a single and then if it didn't work we'd fire the promotions department. But now, the label tells the artist how to make a single, then the artist makes the single, and if doesn't work, the label fires the artist. It's all wrong.' Lynval tells me about when they got signed:

Lynval: *We signed to Chrysalis. It's funny because for me, I do this podcast through Island, and me born in Jamaica, the music that influenced me and the roots of the music is Jamaican. So obviously home for me would be Island Records. Just natural. I remember we played in Kensington and this thing that happened when we signed to Chrysalis, because all record labels companies know what's going on, and Island came with a counter-offer for us last minute. But we'd already decided and it wouldn't have worked without Chrysalis, because we wanted to have our own identity within the label, and that was Two-Tone, that's what used to win us over. To give us the opportunity to do that and to be able to release singles with bands that we choose, like Madness, Selecta, all the records on Two-Tone. So that's why we ended up signing with Chrysalis.*

We talk about Lee Scratch Perry and the magic stones he hid behind the speakers, to the dismay of Zeus at the time. Lynval asks me if they're still there and I say I don't know.

Nikolaj: *Even if the stones aren't there, there's magic in the studio.*
Lynval: *It makes sense to me now, how we actually became creative and we locked in together. There's something about it. There's something about that place that's spiritual that got us back together. It brought us there. Terry said, 'I've been in the band with Horace for 40 years and I've never talked to him', and that is true! Until we got in that studio. I can reflect back at it now and I can ask questions like, 'How did we get back together? How did it work? What was it?' I can look back, and sometimes I'd fall asleep on the sofa, but we were so comfortable.*
Nikolaj: *Sometimes? Every day you would fall asleep on the sofa.* [More laughter]
Lynval: *I'm not a Christian guy, I don't go to church. I was brought up in a Baptist church and I have too many questions and I never get the answer. I would definitely say the Creator of All send Nikolaj with us, and with The Specials. Without him, there's no way we would complete this piece of work and everyone has major territories but we're so chill with it all. There's nothing at all that we would go re-do. I would say I give a lot of the credit to Nikolaj. We've seen miserable Terry, but this time I would see him crack a joke because his humour is so weird. But to see him smile in the studio, spiritually that was amazing and I think it brought him here and healed him.*
Nikolaj: *He's back to being miserable now.*
Lynval: *I've got to get him back again. But Martin, a person who lives in his own little world and getting into his dark place, and then to be told that you can't go out 24/7, because of lockdown. It's like a white tiger being caged. It's very difficult for him. The most important thing in my journey right now is reflecting on 40 years of where I'm coming from and it's been an amazing journey. What can I say? I've got no stories to tell. It's all real. You know, I never exaggerate at all.* [Laughter] *It's the truth and nothing but the truth. So help me God.*

I've been doing the Zoom from home, and I feel light and elevated. And I'm pretty sure there was only coffee in that last cup. These are weird times. And it's hard to keep positive sometimes when you're not allowed to see family and friends. And all these video calls, they make your head hurt and eyes twitch. I walk down to the sitting room and exclaim to the family who are sat in the sofa: 'I've just spoken to Lynval. And I feel good. So happy. It's impossible to not be blown away by his energy.' And whether Lee's magic stones are still in the speakers or not doesn't matter. Lynval, Nikolaj and The Specials have enough magic to turn any studio into a Two-Tone temple. No questions. No need for answers. ∎

The Mangrove Cafe on All Saints Road in Notting Hill in 1970. The restaurant was repeatedly raided by police that year, prompting a protest march by local residents. A group of protesters, known as the Mangrove Nine, were arrested and tried for inciting a riot. They were all acquitted of the most serious charges and the trial brought the first judicial acknowledgement of evidence of racial hatred in the Metropolitan Police.

EXPERIMENTATION AND MISTAKES

The House Gospel Choir recording at Eastcote in December 2020.

I came into this as a singer and a songwriter and I don't think I really understood about producing. I always thought the producers were the guys that had all this information and knowledge, but when I did start to understand it better I realized it was actually project management in the first instance. It's because of being in Eastcote and having that freedom to try things that I was really able to step into that as a role and a title. Especially as a woman, I was very nervous being a producer. I basically learnt how to do this sitting next to George and we really did make it our house in the weeks we were there. It's an amazing studio.

Natalie Maddox, House Gospel Choir

The beginning of 2019 feels several years long when I start thinking about it. There was so much going on personally that I'll have to dig into what went on at Eastcote as if it was a research project all over again. I had spent a lot of late 2018 working with a brilliant artist from Froglevel, VA, that we had just signed to Locomotion. Evan Barlow's story is one of hardship and survival in rural middle America, a life that he managed to turn into poignant and powerful poetry. The album was a difficult one to make and to get out into the world for a few reasons and every time there was a step forward, there soon would be two backwards. And when the pandemic closed down the world, the project ground to a halt, or at least was set on a long pause. During lockdown I worked on a podcast with Evan that I hope the world gets to hear, just like his brilliant music. Evan was and remains an enigma, but there's no mystery at all with regards to his talent.

Yungblud was selling out big shows both in Europe and the US and was in various studios, including Eastcote, working on a new album. The Locomotion offices had by now moved to Walters Workshops too, and were busy non-

2.019!

stop. With everything happening in the same place, there began to be the kind of days I thought I had assigned to the past, where I was in the building from early morning until late at night between Kensaltown, Eastcote and the Locomotion office, then home for a few hours to sleep and back again. During the first half of the year I made two albums at Kensaltown with Jesse & Joy (*Aire*) and Theory Of A Deadman (*Say Nothing*), and one at Abbey Road (Ricardo Arjona), all artists I love working with, which is probably why I managed to keep it all together. In the early summer I started working with Oskar Winberg and Alex Lacaimore on a project that would end up taking the better part of what was left of the year. Choreographer Kate Prince had created a brilliant script for a contemporary dance show with the narrative being told through the songs of Sting and The Police. We had some initial conversations with Sting about the music and then off we went to re-record, re-work or re-arrange almost 40 songs from what is an amazing catalogue of music. During the year, the last assistant that Philip had taken

on at Eastcote also had a quick promotion to the deep end. Sophie Ellis started assisting George Murphy for The Specials' sessions in Studio 1. She was finishing her sound engineering degree in Liverpool, but came down to Eastcote for work experience in between terms. Sophie started at Eastcote when she graduated, but when the scope of the Sting project became clear she started working full-time with Oskar at Kensaltown. Responsible for much of the technical and logistical work involved, she quickly became an important part of the team. We started with the Police material, and had recorded around 20 songs by the time we all took a summer break. I didn't know it then, but there would be some worrying news waiting when we got back.

At Eastcote too, the year was a rollercoaster of sessions. Philip wasn't coming in regularly any more, and although I occasionally recorded in Studio 1 my mind was mostly on my production projects. George, Julie and Clem were pretty much left to do what needed to be done and they were keeping the house jumping to say

the least. After a couple of months of recording, one of my favourite new indie bands, Husky Loops, were wrapping up 2018 in Studio 2. The New Year kicked off with a film session. I didn't know it was happening and one day in January there were trucks on the street and dozens of people running around shouting instructions and carrying camera gear. It resulted in the rather brilliant video for Wiley's 'Boasty' featuring Sean Paul, Stefflon Don and Idris Elba. In the following months Stormzy, Razorlight, Jack Savoretti, Birdy, Celeste, House Gospel Choir, Nick Cave, Yungblud, Tindersticks, Jamie Woon, John McLaughlin and Omar were all recording at the studios.

And great producers. Some with decades of experience and a couple with the producer's hat on for the first time.

Guy Chambers has been one the most successful writers and producers in the UK over the past few decades. After meeting Robbie Williams in 1997, they formed a collaborative partnership that would last until the present day, and together they've written some much-loved

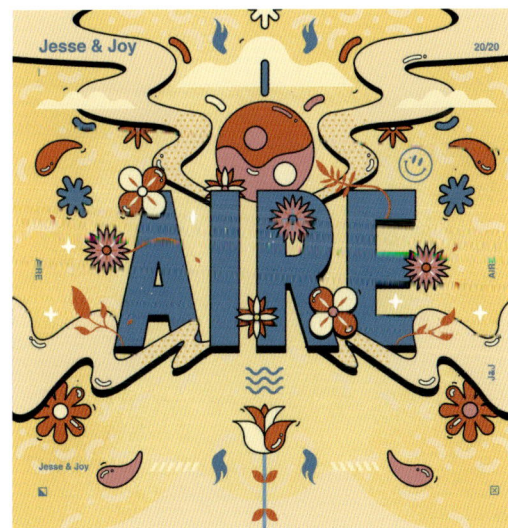

Tyler Connolly of Theory of a Deadman performing at the Fremont Street Experience in Las Vegas in 2017.

Jesse & Joy, *Aire*, Warner Music, 2020.

songs, including 'Angels' and 'Rock DJ'. This year they did a session in Studio 1, but Guy first came to Eastcote in the late '80s. He explains:

I first recorded at Eastcote around '86–'87. I remember Chaz Jankel was working in the studio upstairs. I asked if he could come and play something on the track and he very sweetly sat in and played guitar on the session. I don't know if you ever heard him play? He's a monster musician, and funky as fuck! I met Philip on a session I did shortly after that. He was hanging out by the fire escape, smoking. He was working with Transvision Vamp and Zeus B Held. Wendy James, the lead singer, was in the studio when I first turned up, and I remember what an incredible joker Philip was, very funny guy. And properly eccentric. I used to use both spaces in Eastcote. I liked downstairs because I liked the live room, there's a great piano, and the desk sounds fantastic. Then I liked upstairs because it had a lot of synths, and I'm a synth lover, I collect synths.

And while we're on the subject of synthesizers, James Blunt, whom I've worked with on a few records over the years, was at Eastcote in the early summer as a producer. And artist. As in, he was flying solo and producing one of his own records for the first time, called 'Should I Give It All Up'. It was released just a few months ago during lockdown and when I hear the pulsating synth arpeggio that opens the track I think, of course: that song had to be done at Eastcote. James says:

The only reason I knew about Eastcote was because sometimes when we were standing on the balcony of your studio [Kensaltown] you used to point at Eastcote and tell me about how much history there was there. Then I came there last year to work on 'Should I Give It All Up'. I wasn't sure if it was going on the album but I wanted to get it to a place where it sounded good and if necessary someone else could finish it off. What was quite fun, really,

was I just used a ton of people to add bits and bobs to it, and then I just locked myself in Eastcote for a week or so and picked and chose what I wanted to use. I worked with your engineer Jorge Arango and he was really patient with me while I was pottering around making various noises on different instruments. None of them particularly well played, but he recorded them very professionally. Sometimes it's the experimentation and mistakes that come along that makes it interesting, and Eastcote is great for that. With instruments lying around everywhere. We did everything in Studio 2 but we went downstairs to Studio 1 to record the grand piano. You can hear it in the end of the song.

And you really can. A big low note ringing out in the Studio 1 live room. And not to negotiate myself out of any future work, but James should produce more of his own records. It sounds great, with quirky synth sounds and like he was having a lot of fun.

Another first-time producer in the studio was Natalie Maddox from the House Gospel Choir. Their original take on mixing classic house with gospel had seen them get signed to Island Records and they were in Eastcote to work on their debut album *Re//Choired*. It's an irresistible full hour of house and gospel music and has some brilliant collaborations, including with Brooklyn-born house legend Todd Terry. I'm on a Zoom call with Natalie and her manager Laura Leon. Natalie tells me:

After my first time at Eastcote I just wanted to come back there, it just felt very West London but also very separate. So many new studios are super-cold, with hard edges. Eastcote kind of reminded me of studios I used to look at growing up, and I remember thinking that's where I'll be when I record one day. Where it was just like science, do you know what I mean? It was like watching scientists at work. Most new studios are just a computer and a mic. There's

nothing wrong with that, but all that outboard gear is really wicked to see still, and also to see George working it, it's not just for show.

Even the foldback system where you plug the headphones into, Philip built those, didn't he? They sound amazing! So, when they were wheeled out, we thought they looked a bit ancient, but they always worked so well. I think I learnt a lot about recording because of that system, and that is why I am so aware that we don't get such a good sound everywhere we go. Also, the techniques that George taught us about recording choir vocals in terms of position and mic technique. He was always willing to share what the intricacies were. I've always been quite nervous about saying 'Hi, I'm the producer', but by sitting next to him and getting that insight I learnt so much, in a very classic space, which makes it transferable and I can use it anywhere.

When I got back from the summer break, I had a message from one of siblings in the family that had owned Walters Workshops since the late 1800s. Could I call her. There was no indication to what she wanted to talk about and I immediately thought, they're going to sell the building. I'm pondering how much to go into the events that followed, and I decide for a short version. For a few months it looked like there was a 50/50 chance to come up with some ownership structure that would keep the studios going. In come some serious property developers and for a month or two it looked like our days were numbered.

Before Christmas though I had joined up with two new partners and together we thought, this building is made for making music. There were many bumps in the road along the way, but they don't make for very interesting reading. There's a Roxette greatest hits album called *Don't Bore Us, Get To The Chorus!* that springs to mind. I won't. Here's the hook:

Eastcote Studios ain't going nowhere. ∎

Top left: Martin Terefe and Alex Lacamoire in Studio 2 during the recording of *Message In A Bottle*.
Top right: In the control room. At the back (left to right): Martin Terefe, Jamie Woon and Lianne La Havas. Oskar Winberg by the console and Dan See (right).

Bottom left: (left to right) Lianne La Havas, Jamie Woon and Martin Terefe in Studio 1.
Bottom right: Kristoffer Sonne recording drums for *Message In A Bottle*.

WEIRD AND THE BIRTH OF ZOOMING

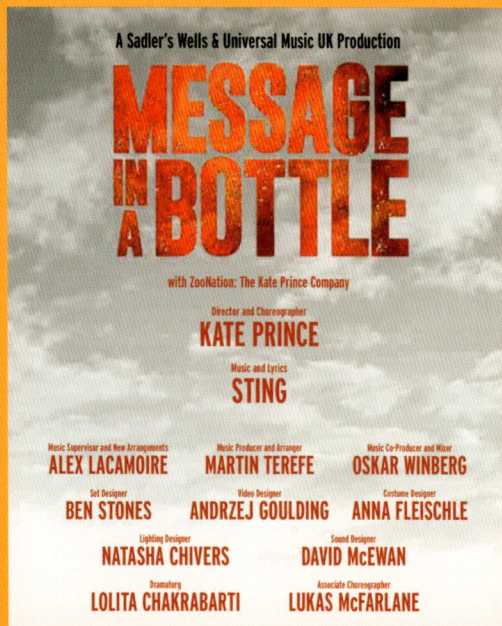

A Sadler's Wells & Universal Music UK Production

MESSAGE IN A BOTTLE

with ZooNation: The Kate Prince Company

Director and Choreographer
KATE PRINCE

Music and Lyrics
STING

Music Supervisor and New Arrangements
ALEX LACAMOIRE

Music Producer and Arranger
MARTIN TEREFE

Music Co-Producer and Mixer
OSKAR WINBERG

Set Designer
BEN STONES

Video Designer
ANDRZEJ GOULDING

Costume Designer
ANNA FLEISCHLE

Lighting Designer
NATASHA CHIVERS

Sound Designer
DAVID McEWAN

Dramaturg
LOLITA CHAKRABARTI

Associate Choreographer
LUKAS McFARLANE

Did you cast for the builders?

Julian Broad, photographer

It seems almost unreal looking in the calendars for 2020, both Eastcote's and my own. Like some antique archives of a lost world. January was full steam working on *Message In A Bottle*, the dance show we started to work on more than six months earlier. We were recording Sting's vocals and string sessions, going to rehearsals, getting feedback from Kate Prince and the producers Eliza Lumley and Sadler's Wells. More changes, more rehearsals and in my mind there would be some sort of cut-off date. But this was learning a whole new world, and in theatre you keep working until the first show and beyond. On 6th February we had our first preview at The Peacock Theatre. It was a thrill to see how well the story worked with no dialogue, just the amazing movement of the dancers and the choreography, along with the lyrics in the songs that took on a whole new meaning in their new context. A few weeks later was press night, and at that point the show about the plight of a family fleeing war looked and sounded amazing. I had some work to finish in the US, and at the end of February I flew first to LA and then New York. I was back for our Kensaltown Live show at Laylow on 7th March and, as far as I remember, things were still happening as normal. The studio was still taking bookings, plans for new recordings were being made and airplane tickets bought. I was also about to release an album I'd made with an accompanying film and was deep in planning and preparing for a live show at the Southbank Centre in connection with its release in May. Tia had said for a week or so by now that there would definitely be a lockdown, but I was still sceptical. A few days later the world as we knew it was put on pause.

It was early on 25th March and I was doing my daily lockdown run around Hyde Park. This morning I continued through Green Park past Buckingham Palace and along the Strand. It was what would usually have been the start of rush hour at 7 am, and I was practically alone. I stopped to take some pictures, it was so eerie seeing the city entirely empty on a beautiful spring morning. But the birds were happy and singing and it felt a bit as if London had been given its first holiday break for a long time and it was healing. At Eastcote we had just agreed all the details on the purchase of the building. The major change for me at the studios was that I was about to move out of Kensaltown Studio A, the studio I have built and worked in for the past 16 years. And that doesn't even describe it right. It was the room I walked into almost every single day for a decade and a half, sat down in the sofa, picked up my bass or a guitar and, along with wonderful musicians and artists, played music all day. There are mixed feelings, of course, but mostly excitement. In the next chapter for me at Walters Workshops, I will be at Eastcote. The Kensaltown world will exist around it on the south side of the site. Our partners, NH Analog, are refurbishing the old Kensaltown side for their new studios and, with luck, the community in our little oasis between Kensal Road and Conlan Street will be making music for years.

It does feel a little bit odd to write this book about Eastcote without not also telling the full story of Kensaltown, as for me it's all intertwined. There are so many people who were a big part of how it all started for me at Walters. My then musical partner and collaborator, Andreas Olsson. Kelly Pribble, who helped design and build the studios and was part of the Kensaltown project for years. Sacha Skarbek, Craig Silvey and Glen Scott, who all had their own studios there, and of course my manager back then, Michael Dixon. We worked together for more than 20 years and through most of the Kensaltown days. All the hundreds of fantastic musicians, writers and artists who passed through to work with

us. Eloisa, our amazing cook in the Kensaltown kitchen. And most recently Oskar Winberg, my brother-in-arms who for years and up until my last sessions before lockdown in March had become the engine that moved Kensaltown on. But I have to stop myself, because it is its own quite extraordinary story. Perhaps it will be told one day. But for now back to Eastcote, and the year of weird and the birth of Zooming.

The first few months it was business as usual. Marcus Mumford was back in Studio 2 working on a soundtrack for a new Apple TV show called *Ted Lasso*. New bands like Marthagunn and Stepbrother. The brilliant Jamie Cullum and Celeste. And I remember having a chat with John Newman and Paul McDonald on 12th March, when they were in for what became the last session before lockdown. And then. It was 16th March.

The streets were suddenly empty and the calendar, too.

About three weeks in to the lockdown we were all talking about what to do. Who wanted to work? Could they? There were obviously no studio bookings and no one was travelling anywhere. We had discussed renovating the studios, particularly Studio 2 as I was about upgrade the room with all the equipment coming over from Kensaltown. I called my long-time friend and collaborator on many of the albums I've made, Dyre Gormsen. He is running his mastering business, Eastcote Mastering, out of the building, and like for us with recording, there wasn't much mastering going on either. We all decided to push ahead with a bigger renovation of the entire studio, and embarked on a project that we finished just a few weeks ago. Dyre, who is from a family of architects, was the right man to spearhead the project in the spirit of the architect who built the studio. Philip. He tells me about the first time he met Philip:

The first time I stepped in to Eastcote was to mix a DVD for MEW. It was called Live in

Marcus Mumford at Studio 2 in 2020 recording acoustic version of 'Lay Your Head on Me' by Major Lazer (feat. Marcus Mumford).

2020

Copenhagen. I remember Philip meeting us and he made me feel so welcome. I always felt it was my home away from home. Glad that it has become... home.

A month later it was early summer. The builders were hard at work and they were a quirky bunch. They'd start each morning singing 'She's Got Bette Davis Eyes' and through the day I was never sure if I was at a building site or a club. It was exciting and the team of craftsmen and craftswomen Dyre had put together felt like a rock'n'roll band on tour more than it did contractors at work. But with all projects like this it always takes longer and costs more money than expected, and the last few months were tough. We had started getting bookings again but didn't even have a roof in the live room. So we all started working crazy hours, especially Dyre. Everything that didn't get finished during the day got done at night. I was there most of the time, just lugging stuff around and helping where I could. Schools were closed, so I asked my daughter Hanna if she wanted a summer job, and a few days later she started painting in Studio 2 and The Shed. George and Clem from the studio were on both building and soldering duties. Literally everyone I could rope in was helping out.

In the end we got there. We had been worried it would be slow to get going after (the first) lockdown, but there were plenty of artists waiting to get back in the studio.

My friend Julian Broad is a fantastic photographer. Three of his beautiful pictures from the National Portrait Gallery are in this book. He has his studio at Walters, and one day during the building works he joked and said:

'Who are those guys? They look fantastic. Did you cast for the builders?' And we might as well have done. Without the spirit, craft and skills from Dyre and his team, it would have been a long and boring summer. I'm going to tell you a bit about them as they are now forever part of the Eastcote story.

Constantin Groenert is a brilliant sound engineer and musician, but also tall, strong and good at building. He was the first guy Dyre brought in to help out, and he would connect us to the next one. In came blacksmith, musician and metalhead Justin Bravo. When he was done restoring the big Victorian steel window, he was straight in to the podcast studio for his new show, 'Metal on Metal'. We had the amazing carpenter and visual artist Liam Hayhow, whose dad, as it turned out, went to school with Philip. I wasn't even surprised, the coincidences along the way keep appearing like a well-spun web, stopping just short of revealing the full picture. Liam turned his art into diffusors and built what must be the best-looking and possibly heaviest dividing doors I've ever seen in a studio. The reason for the weight is that we kept the old doors that Philip built 40 years earlier inside the layers of the new doors. Lee 'Scratch' Perry would have approved and said 'to keep the studio magical'.

We wouldn't have been able to power the studio back up without Steven 'Brains' Philips, who came in every morning after his night job. Scratching his head and chasing cables, rewiring fuse boxes and cleaning up 140 years of old redundant wiring. And without ever saying 'There's a big problem'. It wasn't necessary, we all knew there was, but Brains always had

This page: **Middle:** The metal worker, Justin Bravo. **Right page: Top left:** Hanna Terefe on painting duties. **Top middle:** Constantin and Justin. **Top right:** (left to right) Martin, Liam, Roman, Justin, Dyre, George, Clem and Sara. **Middle right:** Martin Terefe in Studio 2. **Bottom left:** Thomas Cantu. **Bottom right:** Master carpenter and artist Liam Hayhow.

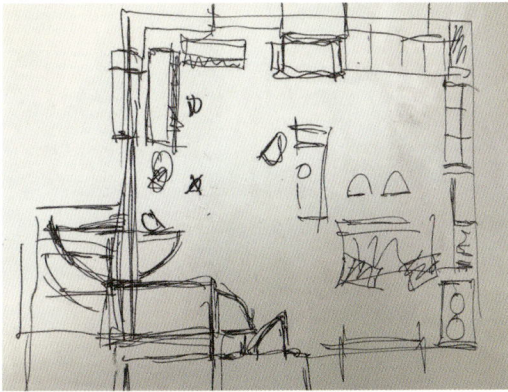

the solution and a smile to go with it. When the heavy-duty work was done, Martyn Leiper, who was the bass player for Sixto 'Sugar Man' Rodriguez, came in to do another thing he is great at. He painted and decorated the place while another artist came in to finish the remaining detail work. Thomas Cantu arrived in Sunday shoes and a suit that he folded neatly before putting on his pinstripe work overall and white gloves. So what did they actually get done?

Well highlights are: Studio 1 has gotten a full MOT and raised ceiling height in the live area, which can now be fully opened up to one big space. Or closed to become the 'old' Studio 1 with three separate spaces. And we've restored an old Victorian steel structure that held some skylights in the days of being stables. Again, don't worry if you liked the darker vibe: electric window dimmers can instantly stop the daylight from coming in. It feels amazing. Studio 2 is back to its former glory, too. After a full redesign we found pictures from when Philip first built the room in the mid-'80s, and it turns out this was more of a restoration we were doing. The small amp room/vocal booth is gone, giving access to the balcony and a more open space, as it would have looked in the days of Tim Simenon and Depeche Mode. The Shed has been renovated and the old Studer broadcast console from Studio 2 found its place in our newest studio, a multi-purpose podcast, broadcast and video-cast room that we have decided to call... Kensaltown.

As we started welcoming our first clients back, The Shed was the first room to be back up and running. After 40 years Eastcote has seen a few generational shifts, and this is reflected with

Clem Cherry by the MCI 500 console in the Studio 1 control room, December 2020.

Martin and Noah Terefe recording in Studio 1, November 2020.

great clarity both for me personally and in the calendar as new bookings start coming in.

Noah Terefe is a brilliant young producer, songwriter and musician. He is also my son.

Nineteen now, he got the music bug when he was still in primary school. It's been very exciting to have crossed over on several projects over the past two years as well as working on a few together. This year he has definitely been the busy one, and in The Shed there's an amazing community of young artists and musicians developing. A few of them, like Locomotion artists Psi and Henjila, have records coming that will most likely be released by the time this book is printed. Celeste was the first artist back in Studio 2, where TMS have also been working on and off through the fall with Anne Marie, Freya Ridings and Jess Glynne.

And since the roof was restored over Studio 1, it's all back to normal there too, with jazzers, indie bands and pop stars all back to work. Jon Opstad, Michael Chillingworth, Rita Ora, Skepta, Niall Horan, Tom Odell, JC Stewart, Amy Wadge, House Gospel Choir and The Drugstore Romeos have all been in already.

It's hard to look past the tumultuous events that shook the world in 2020. But here, around the courtyard at Walters, it's a very special year too. Maybe it's befitting Philip and what he has created at Eastcote that on its 40th anniversary the world rocked to the point where it will require years to get back in steady orbit. Maybe there's a Philip out there, somewhere in a vast universe, who thought things needed to be stirred up a little bit down on that troubled planet Earth. 'Forty years of independence – years of creativity, ingenuity and brilliance.' That's what Charlie Seaward wrote in the Foreword.

We sure could use some of that now. ■

Cathrine Classon Holst and Dyre Gormsen in Eastcote Studios' new broadcast room: Kensaltown.

Dyre Gormsen at work in the Eastcote mastering studio.

2020

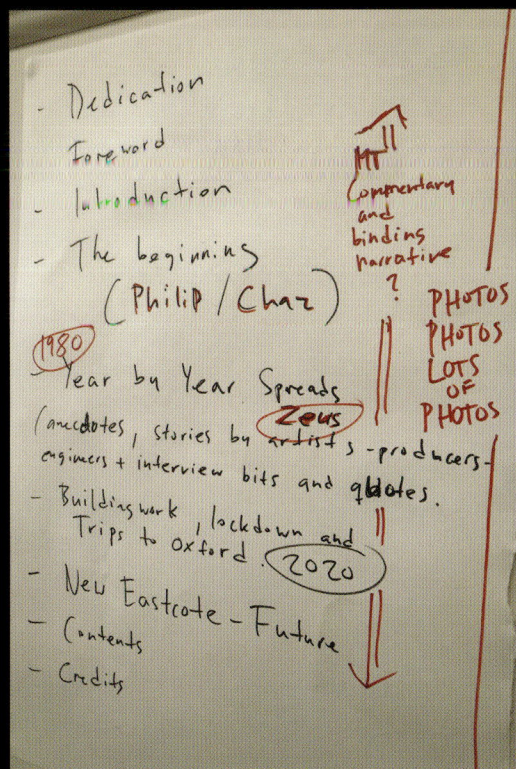

Left page: Top left: Philip, Dyre and George. **Middle left:** Eastcote mastering, the big plane tree and The Shed seen from the courtyard. **Bottom left:** Philip always kept all the components for the console and other equipment neatly organised in the studio tech shop. **Top right:** The Eastcote inspired home studio in the dolls house. **Middle right:** Philip has been renovating the rather remarkable dolls house he built for his children for the grand kids. **Bottom middle:** Philip ready to welcome new musicians to the studio. **Bottom right:** Old Eastcote note and phone book.

This page: Top left: Tools are needed for writing. And coffee. **Top right:** Calendars, notes and photos to look through. **Middle left:** Drugstore Romeos with their producer George Murphy during one of the most recent sessions in Studio 1. **Bottom left:** White-board in the writing room.

It's a mathematical certainty that somewhere among all those millions of stars there's another planet where they speak English...

- Peanuts

Anyone who has produced a record knows that the easy part is to start. And that it's another story altogether to take the responsibility to say, 'This is done'. And had I known how hard it would be to finish a book I might never have started it at all. So many threads left I'd like to follow. Artists and producers I've not been able to talk to. Have I done Philip's life work justice or do I need to keep going and how should I end this story? I've been spending a week or so thinking that I probably need some time to reflect, come up with a great conclusion or an on-point summary of Philip's philosophy on how to make records. And maybe a bit about how it relates to me and the current group of musicians and artists who are making music at Eastcote in 2020. But suddenly I get it. I'm done.

I'm not going to write a conclusion because this is not the end. In fact, I should be in the studio right now catching up on the projects I've left on the back burner whilst I've been on this wonderful and unexpected deep dive. I've learnt a lot. But I'm not done with that either. *'NO'*, said Philip. *'You can't be a caretaker'*. So while we get ready to begin a new chapter at Eastcote, let's wrap this with one last story about Philip. Going back to the beginning. Really, the beginning.

I'm walking around Queen's Park trying to get hold of Tim Bran, a friend of mine who has a lot of history both with Eastcote and the building. He tells me about when his band

Dreadzone were in the studio in the mid-'90s to record what would end up being their most successful single, 'Little Britain'. Tim says:

There is a quote at the beginning of the song that says 'Britain today is a powerhouse of ideas experiments... imagination' from the movie if... directed by Lindsay Anderson from 1969. Philip was casually tinkering with something in the corner of the studio and said quietly, 'I was in that movie...' We were like, 'WHAT?' 'Yes', he said, 'I was the young bespectacled boy in the film'. What a ridiculous coincidence; magical really.

And it was. Philip was Peanuts in Anderson's apocalyptic boarding-school drama and when I ask him how that came about, I'm given what is probably the best insight so far into the wonderous curiosity of the man and the mind that is Philip Bagenal. And maybe it explains, as much as anything else I've written, what made Eastcote Studios what it is. Philip tells me:

I made a film when I was at school with three other guys whose parents were in the film industry. It was a dreamy, rather psychedelic film shot on 16mm. It was after that, my aunt sent me a cut-out of an ad, in my gap year. I had left school, got a place at Cambridge and a job at Huntingdon Research Centre, the place now infamous for the smoking beagles. A part of me still wanted to become a scientist and I had this job chopping up dog livers, frozen dog livers, and readying them for tests. Anyways, I went up to London one day, my parents gave me a lift. I wanted to go and see a friend and we were driving down the Marylebone Road and I thought damn, I looked at my wallet and realized I didn't have any cash, so my father

NEATLY FOLDED AND IRONED

dropped me off at a bank. And in my pocket I had the cut-out that my aunt had sent that said, 'Young boys wanted to film in public schools, turn up in Marylebone Road – 28th March, 6 pm'. And I was there, on that day. I went in and the director was at the audition, and the scriptwriter, and there were about 400 people too. They took my picture and they knew the school I went to did traditional drama. I said I'd done some acting and they said, 'Don't ring us, we'll ring you'. And then one day while I was drying up a dog liver I got a message – would I ring them. Then I went for a rehearsal and I got the part of Peanuts; he was a geek. There's a wonderful bit in the film when they are being beaten by the prefect. In the script, we were required to be quiet, so we would hear the beating going on. And there's a shot of me looking down my microscope at some microbes. It was great fun, because it was a brilliant film, and the people involved loved what they were doing. They were good actors, Malcolm McDowell was great, and our set designer, Jocelyn Herbert, was a real eccentric. In order to act on a film, I had to become a member of Equity [the union] and they had to fiddle it, because strictly speaking I wasn't allowed to do it. So they got this dodgy agent. He was called Jeff and he said: 'You look after me, and I'll look after you'. He got me into the union, although I had to tell a lot of lies, like that I'd been in a band called The Peanuts. That qualified me to join Equity. Anyways it was good fun, took about three months. Quite chaotic and boring sometimes, too. They used schoolboys as extras, but some of us from the core acting team always had to be among them. Certain days, I'd come in and get given breakfast, and then I

just had to stand on set all day without saying anything. Or things would go a bit mad and they were shouting 'You're on, you're on', and someone came and whispered some instructions in your ear.

This was in 1968, the year that the students occupied the Sorbonne, and there was the Grosvenor Square riots. And there was this real feeling that there was going to be change. At least my generation thought so. We were young, and there were young teachers at Cambridge, and we all thought there would be an end to the Etonians running the country. But there wasn't. But making the film was a great way to spend your summer holiday. There was quite a lot in the movie about the school cadet corps. And shots of me teaching younger kids how to load their rifles. It was quite an experience.

I think that there's a theme after all. Philip's accidental ending up in big cultural moments throughout his life. He must have been drawn to them, or they to him. if... won the Palme d'Or at Cannes the following year, and in 1999 the British Film Institute put it on their list of the best British films of the century. Stanley Kubrick drew inspiration from both Lindsay Anderson's dark film and its lead actor alike when he made A Clockwork Orange, and cast Malcolm McDowell in his film. Philip went to Cambridge and got his degree in architecture. All whilst reading about recording and sound. Then off to New York to 'accidentally' get a job at the Gaslight at the Au Go Go, to be the house sound engineer at one of the most explosive times in American music culture. Well in both culture and politics, actually. I decide this is the wrap. The curtain call on what has been an unbelievable journey in music and a

history lesson alike. I'm ready to head back to the studio and make some music. But Philip has one more thing to tell me about the summer of '68:

After the filming, I went to Iran with the ambassador's goddaughter. The ambassador knew about it, by the way. We flew to Istanbul and hung around there for two or three days. And then we got a bus that took us four days and took us right through Turkey, to Tehran. When we arrived we were hot and sweaty. It's a terrifying drive, it's going up the big mountains and they had a thing that played 78s and it was scratching and wailing, and if you sat at the front of the bus you would literally, as it went round the corners up the hairpin bends, you were right out over the side of the mountain. We arrived at the bus station in Tehran and it was full of people carrying chickens. Off we went to the British Embassy and I remember taking off my jeans and putting on the only posh trousers I had. We went downstairs, had some sherry and a swim in the pool. It had some scary creepers in it and little statues around the edges. I went back to my bedroom after a while and there were my jeans.

They had been washed. Neatly folded and ironed. ■

PICTURE CREDITS

6 Philip Bagenal **8** © Franki Raffles Estate, all rights reserved. Image courtesy of University of St Andrews Library and Edinburgh Napier University **10** Philip Bagenal **12** Philip Bagenal **14** (top) Gary Husband **14** (bottom) David Redfern/Redferns **16–23** Philip Bagenal **24** Philip Bagenal **25** Michael Putland/Getty Images **27** Philip Bagenal **28–33** Philip Bagenal **34** Pictorial Press Ltd/Alamy Stock Photo **37** Roberta Bayley/Redferns **38** Courtesy Humphrey Ocean **39** Courtesy Paul Stolper and Peter Blake **41** © Peter Anderson **42–50** Philip Bagenal **51** Fin Costello/Redferns **53** Michael Putland/Getty Images **54** Philip Bagenal **55** David Corio/Redferns **56** Philip Bagenal **57** Dave Hogan/Getty Images **58** (top) David Corio/Redferns **58** (bottom) Sobli,Sobli/RDB/ullstein bild via Getty Images **61** Philip Bagenal **62** © Derek Ridgers/Nina Hagen & Lemmy/1986 **64–67** Philip Bagenal **68–69** © Beezer **71** Alain Benainous/Gamma-Rapho via Getty Images **72** Eamonn McCabe/Popperfoto via Getty Images **73** Pictorial Press Ltd/Alamy Stock Photo **78** Brian Rasic/Getty Images **80** Tim Roney/Getty Images **82** Mark Baker/Photoshot/Getty Images **83** Frans Schellekens/Redferns **84** Philip Bagenal **85** Zeus Be Held **86–87** Philip Bagenal **89** (top) Gie Knaeps/Getty Images **89** (bottom) Martyn Goodacre/Getty Images **90** Philip Bagenal **93** Depeche Mode, London 1996/© Anton Corbijn **94** Eric Catarina/Gamma-Rapho via Getty Image **95** Philip Bagenal **96** Echoes/Redferns **97** Echoes/Redferns **98** Philip Bagenal **100** Philip Bagenal **103** Martyn Goodacre/Getty Images **104** Hiroyuki Ito/Getty Images **105–109** Philip Bagenal **110** Martyn Goodacre/Getty Images **113** Philip Bagenal **114** (top left) Philip Bagenal **114** (top right) David Tonge/Getty Images **115** John Bentley/Alamy Stock Photo **117** Martyn Goodacre/Getty Images **120** Tabatha Fireman/Redferns **121** Debbie Bragg/Alamy **122–125** Philip Bagenal **127** Philip Bagenal **128–129** Tia Terefe **130** Robin Little/Redferns **132** Andy Willsher/Redferns/Getty Images **133** Tia Terefe **134–135** Philip Bagenal **136** Andy Willsher/Redferns/Getty Images **137** Philip Bagenal **138–139** Philip Bagenal **141** Philip Bagenal **142** Brigitte Engl/Redferns **142** Philip Bagenal **144** Dave M. Benett/Getty Images **145** Julian Broad/National Portrait Gallery **146–147** Philip Bagenal **148** David Corio/Redferns **149** (right) Philip Bagenal **150–151** Philip Bagenal **153** (top and bottom left) Philip Bagenal (bottom right) C Brandon/Redferns **154–157** Philip Bagenal **156** Nick Baines **157–160** Eliot James, Philip Bagenal **162 163** Philip Bagenal **164** Julian Broad/National Portrait Gallery **165** Gary Clark/FilmMagic **166** Fin Costello/Redfern **167** (left) Noel Vasquez/Getty Images **167** (right) Jim Dyson/Getty Images **168–169** Philip Bagenal **170** Philip Bagenal **171** Pablo Blazquez Dominguez/Getty Images **172–173** Philip Bagenal **174** Julian Broad/National Portrait Gallery **176** (Left top and bottom) Philip Bagenal **176** (right) Christie Goodwin/Redferns **178** Howard Denner/Photoshot/Getty Images **180** Samuel Dietz/Getty Images **181** (top right) Timothy Abbey **182–183** Timothy Abbey **185** Kevin Winter/Getty Images **186** Philip Bagenal **188–189** Philip Bagenal **190** Colin D Miller Photography **191** (top) Philip Bagenal (above and right) Gary Husband **192–193** Philip Bagenal **194** Gary Husband **196** Samir Hussein/Redferns **199** (top) Charlotte Speechley (bottom) Philip Bagenal **200** Tom Pallant **201** Stuart C. Wilson/Getty Images **202–203** Airam Mendoza **205** Philip Bagenal **208** Samir Hussein/Redferns via Getty Images **209** Tristan Bejawn **210–211** Sophie Ellis/Nikolaj Torp **213** Evening Standard/Hulton Archive/Getty images **214** George Murphy **215** (left) Gabe Ginsberg/Getty Images **217** Martin Terefe **219** Gavin Batty **220–221** Dyre Gormsen **221** (top left and middle) Tia Terefe **222–223** Tristan Bejawn **224–225** Tristan Bejawn **226–227** Martin Terefe (middle right) Drugstore Romeos, (bottom left) Courtesy of Philip Bagenal (middle left) Tristan Bejawn **230** Charlie Seaward **232** George Murphy

Philip Bagenal, Martin Terefe and Paul Epworth in The Ridings, Oxford. Summer 2020.

ACKNOWLEDGEMENTS

I would not have been able to finish this book without the help and support of the following people.

Tia, Noah and Hanna. Without your love, patience and encouragement I wouldn't even have got started.

Philip and Esther Bagenal. Thank you for your hospitality and support during the days through the summer and fall when I occupied your kitchen bringing various guests for long conversations about Eastcote.

Charlie Seaward. Thank you for being the spider in the web, making vital connections and helping both me and Philip dust off old memories and putting them in order.

Nick Whitecross. Thank you for gently pointing out the times my Swenglish made the text too confusing, and for taking the time to read and re-read my text until it made sense.

To everyone who has contributed to this book by talking, remembering and digging out old photos from the archives. It's been truly humbling and an amazing journey to hear your stories and listen to so much incredible music. Records you have been part of making and the music that is the core and lifeblood of Eastcote.

A big thank you to everyone at Eastcote Studios and Locomotion for all your help and support. George, Jonas, Annie, Tommas, Dyre, Cathrine, Clem, Eliot, Nikolaj, Alex, Insa, Declan and Max. To Julie, for helping to connect me with so many of the remarkable producers and artists who have come through the doors over the years. And to Simmi Bagri for transcribing interviews, following threads, listening to endless Zoom conversations and for helping me to keep things on track.

Chaz Jankel and Zeus B Held. Thank you for all your help with this book. But most of all for being part of building the deeply musical and rebellious house that is Eastcote Studios.

It's still standing.

Paul Stolper and Magne Furuholmen. Thank you for sharing your expertise and connecting me with the professionals... who are: Mark Fletcher and Damian Jaques. What can I say? It's been an honour to work with you and you should both be given some kind of medal for your patience and creative brilliance. In the meanwhile, please accept my sincere gratitude. I can't believe what we've made together!

And Henry Russell. Thank you for signing up for the task of proofreading the entire thing.

To Eastcote Studios in North Kensington. There is magic in these walls.

Martin Terefe and Philip Bagenal. 2020.

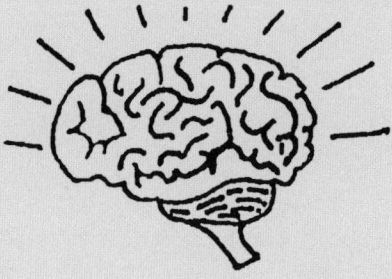

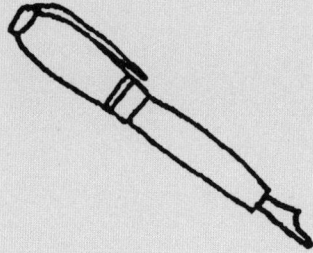

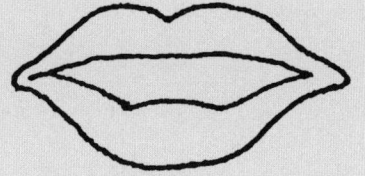

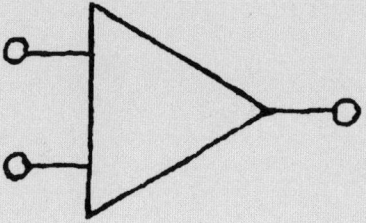

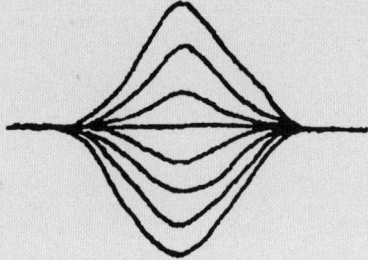

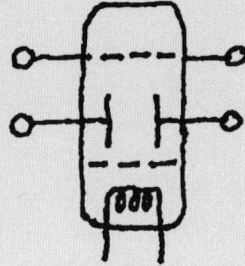

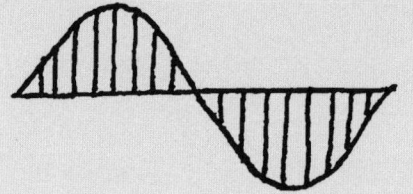

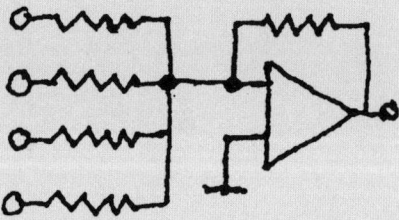

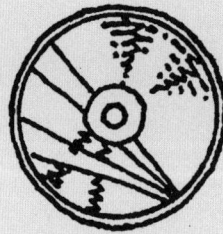

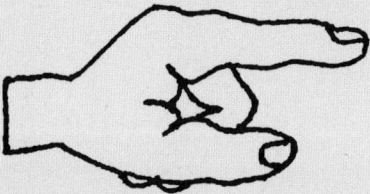

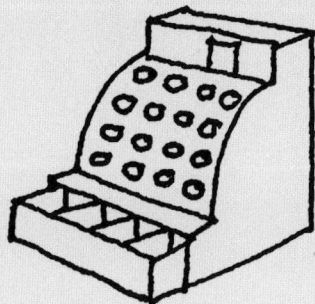